UNDER  **ᴦ 6**

UNDERSTANDING ECMASCRIPT 6

The Definitive Guide for JavaScript Developers

by Nicholas C. Zakas

no starch press

San Francisco

Printed in USA

First printing

20 19 18 17 16   1 2 3 4 5 6 7 8 9

ISBN-10: 1-59327-757-1
ISBN-13: 978-1-59327-757-4

Publisher: William Pollock
Production Editor: Alison Law
Cover Illustration: Garry Booth
Interior Design: Octopod Studios
Developmental Editor: Jennifer Griffith-Delgado
Technical Reviewer: Juriy Zaytsev
Copyeditor: Anne Marie Walker
Proofreader: James Fraleigh
Indexer: BIM Creatives, LLC

For information on distribution, translations, or bulk sales, please contact No Starch Press, Inc. directly:

No Starch Press, Inc.
245 8th Street, San Francisco, CA 94103
phone: 415.863.9900; info@nostarch.com
www.nostarch.com

Library of Congress Cataloging-in-Publication Data
A catalog record of this book is available from the Library of Congress.

About the Author

Nicholas C. Zakas has been working on web applications since 2000, focusing on frontend development, and is known for writing and speaking about frontend best practices. He honed his experience during his five years at Yahoo!, where he was principal frontend engineer for the Yahoo! home page. He is the author of several books, including *The Principles of Object-Oriented JavaScript* (No Starch Press, 2014) and *Professional JavaScript for Web Developers* (Wrox, 2012).

About the Technical Reviewer

Juriy Zaytsev (known online as *kangax*) is a frontend web developer based in New York. He's been exploring and writing about the quirky nature of JavaScript since 2007. Juriy has contributed to several open source projects, including Prototype.js and other popular projects like his own Fabric.js. He co-founded an on-demand custom print service called printio.ru and currently works at Facebook.

BRIEF CONTENTS

CONTENTS IN DETAIL

3
FUNCTIONS   35

4
EXPANDED OBJECT FUNCTIONALITY   67

13
ENCAPSULATING CODE WITH MODULES

A
MINOR CHANGES IN ECMASCRIPT 6

B
UNDERSTANDING ECMASCRIPT 7 (2016)

INDEX

FOREWORD

ECMAScript 6 has taken the world by storm. It came long after people stopped waiting for it, and then it spread faster than most people could learn it. Everybody has a different story about it. Here is mine.

In 2013, I worked at a startup that pivoted from iOS to the web. It was before I co-created Redux or participated in the JavaScript open source community. At the time, I was struggling to learn web development, and I was terrified. My team had to build a web version of our product from scratch in just a few months. In JavaScript.

At first I scoffed at the idea of writing something large in JavaScript. But a new team member persuaded me that JavaScript was not a toy language. I agreed to give it a try. I set my prejudices aside, opened MDN and StackOverflow, and learned JavaScript in depth for the first time. The simplicity I discovered enchanted me. My colleague also taught me how to use tools such as a linter and a bundler. In a few weeks, I woke up and realized that I enjoyed writing JavaScript.

But no language is perfect. I missed the frequent updates that I'd come to expect after working with other languages. The only substantial update to JavaScript in a decade, ECMAScript 5, was a mere cleanup that nevertheless took years for browsers to fully support. At the time, the upcoming ECMAScript 6 (ES6) specification, codenamed *Harmony,* was far from finished and seemed like a distant future. "Maybe in 10 years I'll get to write some ES6 code," I thought.

There were some experimental "transpilers" like Google Traceur that translated code from ES6 into ES5. Most of them were very limited or hard to plug into an existing JavaScript build pipeline. But then a new transpiler called *6to5* came along and changed everything. It was easy to install, integrated well with the existing tools, and produced readable code. It spread like wildfire. Now called *Babel,* 6to5 brought ES6 features to a mainstream audience even before the specification was finalized. In a matter of months, ES6 was everywhere.

ES6 has divided the community for a number of reasons. As this book goes to press, it is still not fully implemented in many major browsers. Having a build step can be intimidating when you're just learning the language. Some libraries have documentation and examples in ES6, and you might wonder if it is possible to use those libraries in ES5 at all. This contributes to the confusion. Many people didn't expect any new features in the language because it had almost never changed before. Others anxiously awaited the new features' arrival and used all of them together—in some cases beyond what was necessary.

Just as I was becoming proficient with JavaScript, I felt that somebody pulled the rug from under my feet, and now I had to learn a new language. I felt bad about this for a few months. Finally, on Christmas Eve, I started reading a draft of this book. I couldn't put it down. Next thing I knew, it was 3 AM, everybody at the party was asleep, and I understood ES6!

Nicholas is an incredibly gifted teacher. He conveys deep details in a straightforward way so they don't go over your head. Apart from this book, he is also known for creating ESLint, a JavaScript code analyzer that has been downloaded millions of times.

Nicholas knows JavaScript like very few people do. Don't miss the chance to soak up some of his knowledge. Read this book, and you, too, will become confident in your understanding of ES6.

Dan Abramov
React core team member and creator of Redux

ACKNOWLEDGMENTS

Thanks to Jennifer Griffith-Delgado, Alison Law, and everyone at No Starch Press for their support and help with this book. Their understanding and patience as my productivity slowed to a crawl during my extended illness is something I will never forget.

I'm grateful for the watchful eye of Juriy Zaytsev as technical editor and to Dr. Axel Rauschmayer for his feedback and several conversations that helped to clarify some of the concepts discussed in this book.

Thanks to everyone who submitted fixes to the version of this book that is hosted on GitHub: 404, alexyans, Ahmad Ali, Raj Anand, Arjunkumar, Pahlevi Fikri Auliya, Mohsen Azimi, Peter Bakondy, Sarbbottam Bandyopadhyay, blacktail, Philip Borisov, Nick Bottomley, Ethan Brown, Jeremy Caney, Jake Champion, David Chang, Carlo Costantini, Aaron Dandy, Niels Dequeker, Aleksandar Djindjic, Joe Eames, Lewis Ellis, Ronen Elster, Jamund Ferguson, Steven Foote, Ross Gerbasi, Shaun Hickson, Darren Huskie, jakub-g, kavun, Navaneeth Kesavan, Dan Kielp, Roy Ling, Roman Lo, Lonniebiz, Kevin Lozandier, Josh Lubaway, Mallory, Jakub Narębski, Robin Pokorný, Kyle Pollock, Francesco Pongiluppi, Nikolas Poniros, AbdulFattah Popoola, Ben Regenspan, Adam Richeimer, robertd, Marián Rusnák, Paul Salaets, Shidhin, ShMcK, Kyle Simpson, Igor Skuhar, Yang Su, Erik Sundahl, Dmitri Suvorov, Kevin Sweeney, Prayag Verma, Rick Waldron, Kale Worsley, Juriy Zaytsev, and Eugene Zubarev.

Also, thanks to Casey Visco, who supported this book on Patreon.

INTRODUCTION

The JavaScript core language features are defined in the ECMA-262 standard. The language defined in this standard is called ECMAScript. What you know as JavaScript in browsers and in Node.js is actually a superset of ECMAScript. Browsers and Node.js add more functionality through additional objects and methods, but the core of JavaScript remains as defined in ECMAScript. The ongoing development of ECMA-262 is vital to the success of JavaScript as a whole, and this book covers the changes brought about by the most recent major update to the language: ECMAScript 6.

The Road to ECMAScript 6

In 2007, JavaScript was at a crossroads. The popularity of Ajax was ushering in a new age of dynamic web applications, whereas JavaScript hadn't changed since the third edition of ECMA-262 was published in 1999.

TC-39, the committee responsible for driving the ECMAScript development process, put together a large draft specification for ECMAScript 4. ECMAScript 4 was massive in scope, introducing both small and large changes to the language. Updated features included new syntax, modules, classes, classical inheritance, private object members, optional type annotations, and more.

The scope of the ECMAScript 4 changes caused a rift to form in TC-39: some members felt that the fourth edition was trying to accomplish too much. A group of leaders from Yahoo!, Google, and Microsoft created an alternate proposal for the next version of ECMAScript that the group initially called ECMAScript 3.1. The "3.1" designation was intended to show that this version was an incremental change to the existing standard.

ECMAScript 3.1 introduced very few syntax changes; instead, it focused on property attributes, native JSON support, and adding methods to already existing objects. Although an early attempt was made to reconcile ECMAScript 3.1 and ECMAScript 4, the effort ultimately failed because the two camps had difficulty resolving the very different perspectives on how the language should grow.

In 2008, Brendan Eich, the creator of JavaScript, announced that TC-39 would focus its efforts on standardizing ECMAScript 3.1. It would table the major syntax and feature changes of ECMAScript 4 until after the next version of ECMAScript was standardized, and all members of the committee would work to bring the best pieces of ECMAScript 3.1 and 4 together after that point into an effort initially nicknamed ECMAScript Harmony.

ECMAScript 3.1 was eventually standardized as the fifth edition of ECMA-262, also described as ECMAScript 5. The committee never released an ECMAScript 4 standard to avoid confusion with the now-defunct effort of the same name. Work then began on ECMAScript Harmony, with ECMAScript 6 being the first standard released in this new "harmonious" spirit.

ECMAScript 6 reached feature complete status in 2015 and was formally dubbed "ECMAScript 2015." (But this text still refers to it as ECMAScript 6, the name most familiar to developers.) The features vary widely from completely new objects and patterns to syntax changes and new methods on existing objects. The exciting aspect of ECMAScript 6 is that all of its changes are geared toward solving problems that developers actually face.

About This Book

A good understanding of ECMAScript 6 features is critical for all JavaScript developers going forward. The language features introduced in ECMAScript 6 represent the foundation upon which JavaScript applications will be built for the foreseeable future. That's where this book comes in. My hope is that you'll read this book to learn about ECMAScript 6 features so you'll be ready to start using them as soon as you need to.

Browser and Node.js Compatibility

Many JavaScript environments, such as web browsers and Node.js, are actively working on implementing ECMAScript 6. This book doesn't attempt to address the inconsistencies between implementations; instead, it focuses on what the specification defines as the correct behavior. As such, it's possible that your JavaScript environment may not conform to the behavior described in this book.

Who This Book Is For

This book is intended as a guide for those who are already familiar with JavaScript and ECMAScript 5. Although a deep understanding of the language isn't necessary to use this book, it will help you understand the differences between ECMAScript 5 and 6. In particular, this book is aimed at intermediate-to-advanced JavaScript developers programming for a browser or Node.js environment who want to learn about the latest developments in the language.

This book is not for beginners who have never written JavaScript. You'll need to have a good basic understanding of the language to use this book.

Overview

Each chapter and appendix in this book covers a different aspect of ECMAScript 6. Many chapters start by discussing problems that ECMAScript 6 changes were made to solve to give you a broader context for those changes. All chapters include code examples to help you learn new syntax and concepts.

- **Chapter 1: Block Bindings** talks about let and const, the block-level replacement for var.

- **Chapter 2: Strings and Regular Expressions** covers additional functionality for string manipulation and inspection as well as the introduction of template strings.

- **Chapter 3: Functions** discusses the various changes to functions, including the arrow function form, default parameters, rest parameters, and a few other features.

- **Chapter 4: Expanded Object Functionality** explains the changes to how objects are created, modified, and used. Topics include changes to object literal syntax and new reflection methods.

- **Chapter 5: Destructuring for Easier Data Access** introduces object and array destructuring, which allow you to decompose objects and arrays using a concise syntax.

- **Chapter 6: Symbols and Symbol Properties** introduces the concept of symbols, a new way to define properties. Symbols are a new primitive type that you can use to obscure (but not hide) object properties and methods.

- **Chapter 7: Sets and Maps** details the new collection types of `Set`, `WeakSet`, `Map`, and `WeakMap`. These types expand on the usefulness of arrays by adding semantics, de-duping, and memory management designed specifically for JavaScript.

- **Chapter 8: Iterators and Generators** discusses the addition of iterators and generators to the language. These features allow you to work with collections of data in powerful ways that were not possible in previous versions of JavaScript.

- **Chapter 9: Introducing JavaScript Classes** introduces the first formal concept of classes in JavaScript. Often a point of confusion for those coming from other languages, the addition of class syntax in JavaScript makes the language more approachable to others and more concise for enthusiasts.

- **Chapter 10: Improved Array Capabilities** details the changes to native arrays and the useful new ways you can use them in JavaScript.

- **Chapter 11: Promises and Asynchronous Programming** introduces promises as a new part of the language. Promises were a grassroots effort that eventually took off and gained popularity due to extensive library support. ECMAScript 6 formalizes promises and makes them available by default.

- **Chapter 12: Proxies and the Reflection API** introduces the formalized reflection API for JavaScript and the new proxy object that allows you to intercept every operation performed on an object. Proxies give developers unprecedented control over objects and, as such, unlimited possibilities for defining new interaction patterns.

- **Chapter 13: Encapsulating Code with Modules** details the official module format for JavaScript. The intent is that these modules can replace the numerous ad hoc module definition formats that have appeared over the years.

- **Appendix A: Minor Changes in ECMAScript 6** covers other changes implemented in ECMAScript 6 that you'll use less frequently or that didn't quite fit into the broader major topics covered in each chapter.

- **Appendix B: Understanding ECMAScript 7 (2016)** describes the three additions to the standard that were implemented in ECMAScript 7, which didn't impact JavaScript nearly as much as ECMAScript 6.

Conventions Used

The following typographical conventions are used in this book:

- *Italics* are used for new terms and filenames.
- `Constant width` indicates a code term within the text.

Additionally, longer code examples are contained in constant width code blocks, such as the following:

```
function doSomething() {
    // empty
}
```

Within a code block, comments to the right of a `console.log()` statement indicate the output you'll see in the browser or Node.js console when the code is executed; for example:

```
console.log("Hi");      // "Hi"
```

If a line of code in a code block throws an error, it is also indicated to the right of the code:

```
doSomething();          // throws an error
```

Help and Support

If you have questions as you read this book, please send a message to my mailing list at *http://groups.google.com/group/zakasbooks*.

1

BLOCK BINDINGS

Traditionally, the way variable declarations work has been one tricky part of programming in JavaScript. In most C-based languages, variables (more formally known as *bindings*, as a name is bound to a value inside a scope) are created at the spot where the declaration occurs. In JavaScript, however, this is not the case. Where your variables are actually created depends on how you declare them, and ECMAScript 6 offers options to make controlling scope easier. This chapter demonstrates why classic var declarations can be confusing, introduces block-level bindings in ECMAScript 6, and then offers some best practices for using them.

var Declarations and Hoisting

Variable declarations using var are treated as if they're at the top of the function (or in the global scope, if declared outside of a function) regardless of where the actual declaration occurs; this is called *hoisting*. For a demonstration of what hoisting does, consider the following function definition:

```
function getValue(condition) {

    if (condition) {
        var value = "blue";

        // other code

        return value;
    } else {

        // value exists here with a value of undefined

        return null;
    }

    // value exists here with a value of undefined
}
```

If you are unfamiliar with JavaScript, you might expect the variable value to be created only if condition evaluates to true. In fact, the variable value is created regardless. Behind the scenes, the JavaScript engine changes the getValue function to look like this:

```
function getValue(condition) {

    var value;

    if (condition) {
        value = "blue";

        // other code

        return value;
    } else {

        return null;
    }
}
```

The declaration of value is hoisted to the top, and the initialization remains in the same spot. That means the variable value is still accessible from within the else clause. If accessed from the else clause, the variable would just have a value of undefined because it hasn't been initialized in the else block.

It often takes new JavaScript developers some time to get used to declaration hoisting, and misunderstanding this unique behavior can end up causing bugs. For this reason, ECMAScript 6 introduces block-level scoping options to give developers more control over a variable's life cycle.

Block-Level Declarations

Block-level declarations declare bindings that are inaccessible outside a given block scope. *Block scopes*, also called *lexical scopes*, are created in the following places:

- Inside a function
- Inside a block (indicated by the { and } characters)

Block scoping is how many C-based languages work, and the introduction of block-level declarations in ECMAScript 6 is intended to provide that same flexibility (and uniformity) to JavaScript.

let Declarations

The let declaration syntax is the same as the syntax for var. You can basically replace var with let to declare a variable but limit the variable's scope to only the current code block (there are a few other subtle differences, which are discussed in "The Temporal Dead Zone" on page 6). Because let declarations are not hoisted to the top of the enclosing block, it's best to place let declarations first in the block so they're available to the entire block. Here's an example:

```
function getValue(condition) {

    if (condition) {
        let value = "blue";

        // other code

        return value;
    } else {

        // value doesn't exist here

        return null;
    }

    // value doesn't exist here
}
```

This version of the getValue function behaves more similarly to how you'd expect it to in other C-based languages. Because the variable value is declared using let instead of var, the declaration isn't hoisted to the top of the function definition, and the variable `value` is no longer accessible once execution flows out of the `if` block. If `condition` evaluates to `false`, then `value` is never declared or initialized.

No Redeclaration

If an identifier has already been defined in a scope, using the identifier in a `let` declaration inside that scope causes an error to be thrown. For example:

```
var count = 30;

// throws an error
let count = 40;
```

In this example, `count` is declared twice: once with `var` and once with `let`. Because `let` will not redefine an identifier that already exists in the same scope, the `let` declaration will throw an error. Conversely, no error is thrown if a `let` declaration creates a new variable with the same name as a variable in its containing scope, as demonstrated in the following code:

```
var count = 30;

if (condition) {

    // doesn't throw an error
    let count = 40;

    // more code
}
```

This `let` declaration doesn't throw an error because it creates a new variable called `count` within the `if` statement instead of creating `count` in the surrounding block. Inside the `if` block, this new variable shadows the global `count`, preventing access to it until execution exits the block.

const Declarations

You can also define bindings in ECMAScript 6 with the `const` declaration syntax. Bindings declared using `const` are considered *constants*, meaning their values cannot be changed once set. For this reason, every `const` binding must be initialized on declaration, as shown in this example:

```
// valid constant
const maxItems = 30;

// syntax error: missing initialization
const name;
```

The maxItems binding is initialized, so its const declaration will work without a problem. However, the name binding would cause a syntax error if you tried to run the program containing this code because name is not initialized.

Constants vs. let Declarations

Constants, like let declarations, are block-level declarations. That means constants are no longer accessible once execution flows out of the block in which they were declared, and declarations are not hoisted, as demonstrated in this example:

```
if (condition) {
    const maxItems = 5;

    // more code
}

// maxItems isn't accessible here
```

In this code, the constant maxItems is declared within an if statement. After the statement finishes executing, maxItems is not accessible outside that block.

In another similarity to let, a const declaration throws an error when made with an identifier for an already defined variable in the same scope. It doesn't matter whether that variable was declared using var (for global or function scope) or let (for block scope). For example, consider this code:

```
var message = "Hello!";
let age = 25;

// each of these throws an error
const message = "Goodbye!";
const age = 30;
```

The two const declarations would be valid alone, but given the previous var and let declarations in this case, they are syntax errors.

Despite those similarities, there is one significant difference between let and const. Attempting to assign a const to a previously defined constant will throw an error in both strict and non-strict modes:

```
const maxItems = 5;

// throws an error
maxItems = 6;
```

Much like constants in other languages, the maxItems variable can't be assigned a new value later on. However, unlike constants in other languages, the value a constant holds can be modified if it is an object.

Object Declarations with const

A const declaration prevents modification of the binding, not of the value. That means const declarations for objects don't prevent modification of those objects. For example:

```
const person = {
    name: "Nicholas"
};

// works
person.name = "Greg";

// throws an error
person = {
    name: "Greg"
};
```

Here, the binding person is created with an initial value of an object with one property. It's possible to change person.name without causing an error because this changes what person contains but doesn't change the value that person is bound to. When this code attempts to assign a value to person (thus attempting to change the binding), an error will be thrown. This subtlety in how const works with objects is easy to misunderstand. Just keep in mind that const prevents modification of the binding, not modification of the bound value.

The Temporal Dead Zone

A variable declared with either let or const cannot be accessed until after the declaration. Attempting to do so results in a reference error, even when using normally safe operations, such as the typeof operation in this if statement:

```
if (condition) {
    console.log(typeof value);  // throws an error
    let value = "blue";
}
```

Here, the variable value is defined and initialized using let, but that statement is never executed because the previous line throws an error. The issue is that value exists in what the JavaScript community has dubbed the *temporal dead zone (TDZ)*. The TDZ is never named explicitly in the ECMAScript specification, but the term is often used to describe why let and const bindings are not accessible before their declaration. This section covers some subtleties of declaration placement that the TDZ causes, and although the examples shown use let, note that the same information applies to const.

When a JavaScript engine looks through an upcoming block and finds a variable declaration, it either hoists the declaration to the top of the function or global scope (for var) or places the declaration in the TDZ (for let and const). Any attempt to access a variable in the TDZ results in a runtime error. That variable is only removed from the TDZ, and therefore is safe to use, once execution flows to the variable declaration.

This is true anytime you attempt to use a variable declared with let or const before it's been defined. As the previous example demonstrated, this even applies to the normally safe typeof operator. However, you can use typeof on a variable outside the block where that variable is declared without throwing an error, although it may not produce the results you're after. Consider this code:

```
console.log(typeof value);      // "undefined"

if (condition) {
    let value = "blue";
}
```

The variable value isn't in the TDZ when the typeof operation executes because it occurs outside the block in which value is declared. That means there is no value binding, and typeof simply returns "undefined".

The TDZ is just one unique aspect of block bindings. Another unique aspect has to do with their use inside loops.

Block Bindings in Loops

Perhaps one area where developers most want block-level scoping of variables is within for loops, where the throwaway counter variable is meant to be used only inside the loop. For instance, it's not uncommon to see code like this in JavaScript:

```
for (var i = 0; i < 10; i++) {
    process(items[i]);
}

// i is still accessible here
console.log(i);                      // 10
```

In other languages where block-level scoping is the default, this example should work as intended—only the for loop should have access to the i variable. However, in JavaScript, the variable i is still accessible after the loop is completed because the var declaration is hoisted. Using let instead, as in the following code, should produce the intended behavior:

```
for (let i = 0; i < 10; i++) {
    process(items[i]);
}

// i is not accessible here - throws an error
console.log(i);
```

In this example, the variable i exists only within the for loop. When the loop is complete, the variable is no longer accessible elsewhere.

Functions in Loops

The characteristics of var have long made creating functions inside loops problematic, because the loop variables are accessible from outside the scope of the loop. Consider the following code:

```
var funcs = [];

for (var i = 0; i < 10; i++) {
    funcs.push(function() {
        console.log(i);
    });
}

funcs.forEach(function(func) {
    func();      // outputs the number "10" ten times
});
```

You might ordinarily expect this code to print the numbers 0 to 9, but it outputs the number 10 ten times in a row. The reason is that i is shared across each iteration of the loop, meaning the functions created inside the loop all hold a reference to the same variable. The variable i has a value of 10 when the loop completes, so when console.log(i) is called, that value prints each time.

To fix this problem, developers use *immediately invoked function expressions (IIFEs)* inside loops to force a new copy of the variable they want to iterate over to be created, as in this example:

```
var funcs = [];

for (var i = 0; i < 10; i++) {
    funcs.push((function(value) {
        return function() {
            console.log(value);
        }
    }(i)));
}

funcs.forEach(function(func) {
    func();      // outputs 0, then 1, then 2, up to 9
});
```

This version uses an IIFE inside the loop. The i variable is passed to the IIFE, which creates its own copy and stores it as value. This is the value used by the function for that iteration, so calling each function returns the expected value as the loop counts up from 0 to 9. Fortunately, block-level binding with let and const in ECMAScript 6 can simplify this loop for you.

let Declarations in Loops

A let declaration simplifies loops by effectively mimicking what the IIFE does in the previous example. On each iteration, the loop creates a new variable and initializes it to the value of the variable with the same name from the previous iteration. That means you can omit the IIFE altogether and get the results you expect, like this:

```
var funcs = [];

for (let i = 0; i < 10; i++) {
    funcs.push(function() {
        console.log(i);
    });
}

funcs.forEach(function(func) {
    func();      // outputs 0, then 1, then 2, up to 9
})
```

This loop works exactly like the loop that used var and an IIFE but is arguably cleaner. The let declaration creates a new variable i each time through the loop, so each function created inside the loop gets its own copy of i. Each copy of i has the value it was assigned at the beginning of the loop iteration in which it was created. The same is true for for-in and for-of loops, as shown here:

```
var funcs = [],
    object = {
        a: true,
        b: true,
        c: true
    };

for (let key in object) {
    funcs.push(function() {
        console.log(key);
    });
}

funcs.forEach(function(func) {
    func();      // outputs "a", then "b", then "c"
});
```

In this example, the for-in loop shows the same behavior as the for loop. Each time through the loop, a new key binding is created, so each function has its own copy of the key variable. The result is that each function outputs a different value. If var were used to declare key, all functions would output "c".

It's important to understand that the behavior of let declarations in loops is a specially defined behavior in the specification and is not necessarily related to the non-hoisting characteristics of let. In fact, early implementations of let did not exhibit this behavior, because it was added later in the process.

const Declarations in Loops

The ECMAScript 6 specification doesn't explicitly disallow const declarations in loops; however, const behaves differently based on the type of loop you're using. For a normal for loop, you can use const in the initializer, but the loop will throw a warning if you attempt to change the value. For example:

```
var funcs = [];

// throws an error after one iteration
for (const i = 0; i < 10; i++) {
    funcs.push(function() {
        console.log(i);
    });
}
```

In this code, the i variable is declared as a constant. The first iteration of the loop, where i is 0, executes successfully. An error is thrown when i++ executes because it's attempting to modify a constant. As such, you can only use const to declare a variable in the loop initializer if you're not modifying that variable.

On the other hand, when used in a for-in or for-of loop, a const variable behaves similarly to a let variable. Therefore, the following should not cause an error:

```
var funcs = [],
    object = {
        a: true,
        b: true,
        c: true
    };

// doesn't cause an error
for (const key in object) {
    funcs.push(function() {
        console.log(key);
    });
}

funcs.forEach(function(func) {
    func();      // outputs "a", then "b", then "c"
});
```

This code functions almost the same as the second example in "let Declarations in Loops" on page 9. The only difference is that the value of key cannot be changed inside the loop. The for-in and for-of loops work with const because the loop initializer creates a new binding on each iteration through the loop rather than attempting to modify the value of an existing binding (as was the case in the for loop example).

Global Block Bindings

Another way in which let and const are different from var is in their global scope behavior. When var is used in the global scope, it creates a new global variable, which is a property on the global object (window in browsers). That means you can accidentally overwrite an existing global using var, as this code does:

```
// in a browser
var RegExp = "Hello!";
console.log(window.RegExp);      // "Hello!"

var ncz = "Hi!";
console.log(window.ncz);         // "Hi!"
```

Even though the RegExp global is defined on the window object, it is not safe from being overwritten by a var declaration. This example declares a new global variable RegExp that overwrites the original. Similarly, ncz is defined as a global variable and then defined as a property on window immediately afterward, which is the way JavaScript has always worked.

If you instead use let or const in the global scope, a new binding is created in the global scope but no property is added to the global object. That also means you cannot overwrite a global variable using let or const declarations; you can only shadow it. Here's an example:

```
// in a browser
let RegExp = "Hello!";
console.log(RegExp);                     // "Hello!"
console.log(window.RegExp === RegExp);   // false

const ncz = "Hi!";
console.log(ncz);                        // "Hi!"
console.log("ncz" in window);            // false
```

A new let declaration for RegExp creates a binding that shadows the global RegExp. Because window.RegExp and RegExp are not the same, there is no disruption to the global scope. Also, the const declaration for ncz creates a binding but does not create a property on the global object. This lack of global object modification makes let and const much safer to use in the global scope when you don't want to create properties on the global object.

NOTE   *You might still want to use var in the global scope if you have code that should be available from the global object. This is most common in a browser when you want to access code across frames or windows.*

Emerging Best Practices for Block Bindings

While ECMAScript 6 was in development, there was widespread belief you should use let by default instead of var for variable declarations. For many JavaScript developers, let behaves exactly the way they thought var should have behaved, so the direct replacement made logical sense. In this case, you would use const for variables that needed modification protection.

However, as more developers migrated to ECMAScript 6, an alternate approach gained popularity: use const by default, and only use let when you know a variable's value needs to change. The rationale is that most variables should not change their value after initialization because unexpected value changes are a source of bugs. This idea has a significant amount of traction and is worth exploring in your code as you adopt ECMAScript 6.

Summary

The let and const block bindings introduce lexical scoping to JavaScript. These declarations are not hoisted and only exist within the block in which they're declared. Block bindings offer behavior that is more like other languages and less likely to cause unintentional errors, because variables can now be declared exactly where they're needed. As a side effect, you cannot access variables before they're declared, even with safe operators, such as typeof. Attempting to access a block binding before its declaration results in an error due to the binding's presence in the TDZ.

In many cases, let and const behave in a manner similar to var; however, this is not true in loops. Inside for-in and for-of loops, both let and const create a new binding with each iteration through the loop. As a result, functions created inside the loop body can access the loop bindings' current values rather than their values after the loop's final iteration (the behavior with var). The same is true for let declarations in for loops, whereas attempting to use a const declaration in a for loop may result in an error.

The current best practice for block bindings is to use const by default and only use let when you know a variable's value needs to change. Doing so ensures a basic level of immutability in code that can help prevent certain types of errors.

2

STRINGS AND REGULAR
EXPRESSIONS

Strings are arguably one of the most
important data types in programming.
They're in nearly every higher-level programming language, and being able to work
with them effectively is fundamental for developers to
create useful programs. By extension, regular expressions are important because of the extra power they
give developers to wield on strings. With these facts in mind, the creators
of ECMAScript 6 improved strings and regular expressions by adding new
capabilities and long-missing functionality. This chapter provides a tour of
both types of changes.

Better Unicode Support

Before ECMAScript 6, JavaScript strings assumed each 16-bit sequence,
called a *code unit*, represented a single character. All string properties and
methods, like the length property and the charAt() method, were based on

these 16-bit code units. Of course, 16 bits used to be enough to contain any character. That's no longer true thanks to the expanded character set introduced by Unicode.

UTF-16 Code Points

Limiting character length to 16 bits wasn't possible for Unicode's stated goal of providing a globally unique identifier to every character in the world. These globally unique identifiers, called *code points*, are simply numbers starting at 0. Code points are what you may think of as character codes, where a number represents a character. A character encoding must encode code points into code units that are internally consistent. For UTF-16, code points can consist of many code units.

The first 2^{16} code points in UTF-16 are represented as single 16-bit code units. This range is called the *Basic Multilingual Plane (BMP)*. Everything beyond this range is considered to be in one of the *supplementary planes*, where the code points can no longer be represented in just 16 bits. UTF-16 solves this problem by introducing *surrogate pairs* in which a single code point is represented by two 16-bit code units. That means any single character in a string can be either one code unit for BMP characters, for a total of 16 bits, or two units for supplementary plane characters, for a total of 32 bits.

In ECMAScript 5, all string operations work on 16-bit code units, meaning that you can get unexpected results from UTF-16 encoded strings containing surrogate pairs, as in this example:

```
let text = "𠮷";

console.log(text.length);           // 2
console.log(/^.$/.test(text));      // false
console.log(text.charAt(0));        // ""
console.log(text.charAt(1));        // ""
console.log(text.charCodeAt(0));    // 55362
console.log(text.charCodeAt(1));    // 57271
```

The single Unicode character "𠮷" is represented using surrogate pairs, and as such, the JavaScript string operations in this example treat the string as having two 16-bit characters. That means:

- The length of text is 2 when it should be 1.
- A regular expression trying to match a single character fails because it thinks there are two characters.
- The charAt() method is unable to return a valid character string because neither set of 16 bits corresponds to a printable character.
- The charCodeAt() method also can't identify the character properly. It returns the appropriate 16-bit number for each code unit, but that is the closest you could get to the real value of text in ECMAScript 5.

But ECMAScript 6 enforces UTF-16 string encoding to address problems like these. Standardizing string operations based on this character encoding means that JavaScript can support functionality designed to work specifically with surrogate pairs. The rest of this section discusses a few key examples of that functionality.

The codePointAt() Method

One method ECMAScript 6 added to fully support UTF-16 is the `codePointAt()` method, which retrieves the Unicode code point that maps to a given position in a string. This method accepts the code unit position rather than the character position and returns an integer value. Compare its results with those of `charCodeAt()`:

```
let text = "𠮷a";

console.log(text.charCodeAt(0));    // 55362
console.log(text.charCodeAt(1));    // 57271
console.log(text.charCodeAt(2));    // 97

console.log(text.codePointAt(0));   // 134071
console.log(text.codePointAt(1));   // 57271
console.log(text.codePointAt(2));   // 97
```

The `codePointAt()` method returns the same value as the `charCodeAt()` method unless it operates on non-BMP characters. The first character in text is non-BMP and is therefore composed of two code units, meaning the `length` property is 3 rather than 2. The `charCodeAt()` method returns only the first code unit for position 0, but `codePointAt()` returns the full code point, even though the code point spans multiple code units. Both methods return the same value for positions 1 (the second code unit of the first character) and 2 (the "a" character).

Calling the `codePointAt()` method on a character is the easiest way to determine whether that character is represented by one or two code points. Here's a function you could write to check:

```
function is32Bit(c) {
    return c.codePointAt(0) > 0xFFFF;
}

console.log(is32Bit("𠮷"));    // true
console.log(is32Bit("a"));     // false
```

The upper bound of 16-bit characters is represented in hexadecimal as FFFF, so any code point greater than that number must be represented by two code units, for a total of 32 bits.

The String.fromCodePoint() Method

When JavaScript provides a way to do something, it also provides a way
to do the reverse. You can use `codePointAt()` to retrieve the code point for
a character in a string, whereas `String.fromCodePoint()` produces a single-
character string from a given code point. For example:

```
console.log(String.fromCodePoint(134071));  // "𠮷"
```

Think of `String.fromCodePoint()` as a more complete version of the
`String.fromCharCode()` method. Both give the same result for all characters
in the BMP. Only when you pass code points for characters outside of the
BMP is there a difference.

The normalize() Method

Another interesting aspect of Unicode is that different characters can be
considered equivalent for sorting or other comparison-based operations.
There are two ways to define these relationships. The first relationship,
canonical equivalence, means that two sequences of code points are considered interchangeable in all respects. For example, a combination of two
characters can be canonically equivalent to one character. The second relationship is *compatibility*. Two compatible sequences of code points look different but can be used interchangeably in certain situations.

Due to these relationships, two strings representing fundamentally the
same text can contain different code point sequences. For example, the
character "æ" and the two-character string "ae" can be used interchangeably but are strictly not equivalent unless normalized in some way.

ECMAScript 6 supports Unicode normalization forms by giving strings
a `normalize()` method. This method optionally accepts a single string parameter that indicates that one of the following Unicode normalization forms
should be applied:

- Normalization Form Canonical Composition (`"NFC"`), the default
- Normalization Form Canonical Decomposition (`"NFD"`)
- Normalization Form Compatibility Composition (`"NFKC"`)
- Normalization Form Compatibility Decomposition (`"NFKD"`)

It's beyond the scope of this book to explain the differences between
these four forms. Just keep in mind that when you're comparing strings,
both strings must be normalized to the same form. For example:

```
let normalized = values.map(function(text) {
    return text.normalize();
});

normalized.sort(function(first, second) {
    if (first < second) {
        return -1;
```

```
    } else if (first === second) {
        return 0;
    } else {
        return 1;
    }
});
```

This code converts the strings in the values array into a normalized form so the array can be sorted appropriately. You can also sort the original array by calling normalize() as part of the comparator, as follows:

```
values.sort(function(first, second) {
    let firstNormalized = first.normalize(),
        secondNormalized = second.normalize();

    if (firstNormalized < secondNormalized) {
        return -1;
    } else if (firstNormalized === secondNormalized) {
        return 0;
    } else {
        return 1;
    }
});
```

Once again, the most important aspect to note about this code is that both first and second are normalized in the same way. These examples used the default, NFC, but you can easily specify one of the others, like this:

```
values.sort(function(first, second) {
    let firstNormalized = first.normalize("NFD"),
        secondNormalized = second.normalize("NFD");

    if (firstNormalized < secondNormalized) {
        return -1;
    } else if (firstNormalized === secondNormalized) {
        return 0;
    } else {
        return 1;
    }
});
```

If you've never worried about Unicode normalization before, you probably won't have much use for this method now. But if you ever work on an internationalized application, you'll definitely find the normalize() method helpful.

New methods aren't the only improvements that ECMAScript 6 provides for working with Unicode strings. ECMAScript 6 also introduces the regular expression u flag and other changes to strings and regular expressions.

The Regular Expression u Flag

You can accomplish many common string operations through regular expressions. But remember that regular expressions assume 16-bit code units, where each represents a single character. To address this problem, ECMAScript 6 defines a u flag (which stands for *Unicode*) for use in regular expressions.

The u Flag in Action

When a regular expression has the u flag set, it switches modes to work on characters, not code units. That means the regular expression should no longer treat surrogate pairs as separate characters in strings and should behave as expected. For example, consider this code:

```
let text = "𠮷";

console.log(text.length);          // 2
console.log(/^.$/.test(text));     // false
console.log(/^.$/u.test(text));    // true
```

The regular expression /^.$/ matches any input string with a single character. When it's used without the u flag, this regular expression matches on code units, so the Japanese character (which is represented by two code units) doesn't match the regular expression. When it's used with the u flag, the regular expression compares characters instead of code units, so the Japanese character matches.

Counting Code Points

Unfortunately, ECMAScript 6 doesn't add a method to determine how many code points a string has (the length property still returns the number of code units in the string), but with the u flag, you can use regular expressions to figure it out, as follows:

```
function codePointLength(text) {
    let result = text.match(/[\s\S]/gu);
    return result ? result.length : 0;
}

console.log(codePointLength("abc"));     // 3
console.log(codePointLength("𠮷bc"));    // 3
```

This example calls match() to check text for both whitespace and non-whitespace characters (using [\s\S] to ensure the pattern matches newlines) using a regular expression that is applied globally with Unicode enabled. The result contains an array of matches when there's at least one match, so the array length is the number of code points in the string. In Unicode, the strings "abc" and "𠮷bc" have three characters, so the array length is three.

NOTE *Although this approach works, it's not very fast, especially when applied to long strings. You can use a string iterator (discussed in Chapter 8) as well. In general, try to minimize counting code points whenever possible.*

Determining Support for the u Flag

Because the u flag is a syntax change, attempting to use it in JavaScript engines that aren't compatible with ECMAScript 6 throws a syntax error. The safest way to determine if the u flag is supported is with a function, like this one:

```
function hasRegExpU() {
    try {
        var pattern = new RegExp(".", "u");
        return true;
    } catch (ex) {
        return false;
    }
}
```

This function uses the RegExp constructor to pass in the u flag as an argument. This syntax is valid even in earlier JavaScript engines, but the constructor will throw an error if u isn't supported.

NOTE *If your code still needs to work in earlier JavaScript engines, always use the RegExp constructor when you're using the u flag. This will prevent syntax errors and allow you to optionally detect and use the u flag without aborting execution.*

Other String Changes

JavaScript's string manipulation abilities and utilities have always lagged behind similar features in other languages. It was only in ECMAScript 5 that a trim() method was added for strings, for example, and ECMAScript 6 continues extending JavaScript's capacity to parse strings using new functionality.

Methods for Identifying Substrings

Developers have used the indexOf() method to identify strings inside other strings since JavaScript was first introduced, and they've long asked for easier ways to identify substrings. ECMAScript 6 includes the following three methods, which are designed to do just that:

- The includes() method returns true if the given text is found anywhere within the string. It returns false if not.
- The startsWith() method returns true if the given text is found at the beginning of the string. It returns false if not.
- The endsWith() method returns true if the given text is found at the end of the string. It returns false if not.

Each method accepts two arguments: the text to search for and an optional index from which to start the search. When the second argument is provided, `includes()` and `startsWith()` start the match from that index, and `endsWith()` starts the match from the length of the string minus the second argument; when the second argument is omitted, `includes()` and `startsWith()` search from the beginning of the string, and `endsWith()` starts from the end. In effect, the second argument minimizes the amount of the string being searched. Here are some examples showing these three methods in action:

```
let msg = "Hello world!";

console.log(msg.startsWith("Hello"));      // true
console.log(msg.endsWith("!"));            // true
console.log(msg.includes("o"));            // true

console.log(msg.startsWith("o"));          // false
console.log(msg.endsWith("world!"));       // true
console.log(msg.includes("x"));            // false

console.log(msg.startsWith("o", 4));       // true
console.log(msg.endsWith("o", 8));         // true
console.log(msg.includes("o", 8));         // false
```

The first three calls don't include a second parameter, so they'll search the entire string if needed. The last three calls check only part of the string. The call to `msg.startsWith("o", 4)` starts the match by looking at index 4 of the msg string, which is the *o* in *Hello*. The call to `msg.endsWith("o", 8)` starts the match at index 4 as well, because the 8 argument is subtracted from the string length (12). The call to `msg.includes("o", 8)` starts the match from index 8, which is the *r* in *world*.

Although these three methods make identifying the existence of substrings easier, each returns only a Boolean value. If you need to find the actual position of one string within another, use the `indexOf()` or `lastIndexOf()` methods.

NOTE *The `startsWith()`, `endsWith()`, and `includes()` methods will throw an error if you pass a regular expression instead of a string. In contrast, `indexOf()` and `lastIndexOf()` convert a regular expression argument into a string and then search for that string.*

The repeat() Method

ECMAScript 6 also adds a `repeat()` method to strings, which accepts the number of times to repeat the string as an argument. It returns a new string containing the original string repeated the specified number of times. For example:

```
console.log("x".repeat(3));        // "xxx"
console.log("hello".repeat(2));    // "hellohello"
console.log("abc".repeat(4));      // "abcabcabcabc"
```

This method is primarily a convenience function, and it can be especially useful when manipulating text. It's particularly useful in code formatting utilities that need to create indentation levels, such as the following:

```
// indent using a specified number of spaces
let indent = " ".repeat(4),
    indentLevel = 0;

// whenever you increase the indent
let newIndent = indent.repeat(++indentLevel);
```

The first `repeat()` call creates a string of four spaces, and the `indentLevel` variable keeps track of the indent level. Then, you can just call `repeat()` with an incremented `indentLevel` to change the number of spaces.

ECMAScript 6 also makes some useful changes to regular expression functionality that don't fit into a particular category. The next section highlights a few of these changes.

Other Regular Expression Changes

Regular expressions are an important part of working with strings in JavaScript, and like many parts of the language, they haven't changed much in recent versions. However, ECMAScript 6 makes several improvements to regular expressions to complement the updates to strings.

The Regular Expression y Flag

ECMAScript 6 standardized the y flag after it was implemented in Firefox as a proprietary extension to regular expressions. The y flag affects a regular expression search's sticky property, and it tells the search to start matching characters in a string at the position specified by the regular expression's lastIndex property. If there is no match at that location, the regular expression stops matching. The following code shows how this works:

```
let text = "hello1 hello2 hello3",
    pattern = /hello\d\s?/,
    result = pattern.exec(text),
    globalPattern = /hello\d\s?/g,
    globalResult = globalPattern.exec(text),
    stickyPattern = /hello\d\s?/y,
    stickyResult = stickyPattern.exec(text);

console.log(result[0]);        // "hello1 "
console.log(globalResult[0]);  // "hello1 "
console.log(stickyResult[0]);  // "hello1 "

pattern.lastIndex = 1;
globalPattern.lastIndex = 1;
stickyPattern.lastIndex = 1;
```

```
result = pattern.exec(text);
globalResult = globalPattern.exec(text);
stickyResult = stickyPattern.exec(text);

console.log(result[0]);          // "hello1 "
console.log(globalResult[0]);    // "hello2 "
console.log(stickyResult[0]);    // throws an error!
```

This example has three regular expressions. The expression in
pattern has no flags, the one in globalPattern uses the g flag, and the one
in stickyPattern uses the y flag. In the first trio of console.log() calls, all
three regular expressions should return "hello1 " with a space at the end.

Then, the lastIndex property is changed to 1 on all three patterns,
meaning that the regular expression should start matching from the second character on all of them. The regular expression with no flags completely ignores the change to lastIndex and still matches "hello1 " without
incident. The regular expression with the g flag goes on to match "hello2 "
because it's searching forward from the second character of the string
("e"). The sticky regular expression doesn't match anything beginning at
the second character, so stickyResult is null.

The y flag saves the index of the next character after the last match in
lastIndex whenever an operation is performed. If an operation results in no
match, lastIndex is set back to 0. The global flag behaves the same way, as
demonstrated here:

```
let text = "hello1 hello2 hello3",
    pattern = /hello\d\s?/,
    result = pattern.exec(text),
    globalPattern = /hello\d\s?/g,
    globalResult = globalPattern.exec(text),
    stickyPattern = /hello\d\s?/y,
    stickyResult = stickyPattern.exec(text);

console.log(result[0]);          // "hello1 "
console.log(globalResult[0]);    // "hello1 "
console.log(stickyResult[0]);    // "hello1 "

console.log(pattern.lastIndex);          // 0
console.log(globalPattern.lastIndex);    // 7
console.log(stickyPattern.lastIndex);    // 7

result = pattern.exec(text);
globalResult = globalPattern.exec(text);
stickyResult = stickyPattern.exec(text);

console.log(result[0]);          // "hello1 "
console.log(globalResult[0]);    // "hello2 "
console.log(stickyResult[0]);    // "hello2 "

console.log(pattern.lastIndex);          // 0
console.log(globalPattern.lastIndex);    // 14
console.log(stickyPattern.lastIndex);    // 14
```

For both the `stickyPattern` and `globalPattern` variables, the value of `lastIndex` changes to 7 after the first call to exec() and changes to 14 after the second call.

You need to keep two more subtle details about the y flag in mind. Firstly, the `lastIndex` property is honored only when you're calling methods that exist on the regular expression object, like the exec() and test() methods. Passing the y flag to a string method, such as match(), will not result in the sticky behavior.

Secondly, when sticky regular expressions use the ^ character to match the start of a string, they only match from the start of the string (or the start of the line in multiline mode). Although `lastIndex` is 0, the ^ makes a sticky regular expression the same as a non-sticky one. If `lastIndex` doesn't correspond to the beginning of the string in single-line mode or the beginning of a line in multiline mode, the sticky regular expression will never match.

As with other regular expression flags, you can detect the presence of y by using a property. In this case, you'd check the sticky property, as follows:

```
let pattern = /hello\d/y;

console.log(pattern.sticky);    // true
```

The sticky property is set to true if the y flag is present and false if not. The property is read-only based on the presence of the flag and cannot be changed in code.

Similar to the u flag, the y flag is a syntax change, so it will cause a syntax error in earlier JavaScript engines. You can use the following approach to detect support:

```
function hasRegExpY() {
    try {
        var pattern = new RegExp(".", "y");
        return true;
    } catch (ex) {
        return false;
    }
}
```

Just like the u check, this code returns false if it's unable to create a regular expression with the y flag. Also similar to u, if you need to use y in code that runs in earlier JavaScript engines, be sure to use the RegExp constructor when defining those regular expressions to avoid a syntax error.

Duplicating Regular Expressions

In ECMAScript 5, you can duplicate regular expressions by passing them into the RegExp constructor, like this:

```
var re1 = /ab/i,
    re2 = new RegExp(re1);
```

The re2 variable is just a copy of the re1 variable. But if you provide the second argument to the RegExp constructor, which specifies the flags for the regular expression, your code won't work, as in this example:

```
var re1 = /ab/i,

    // throws an error in ES5, okay in ES6
    re2 = new RegExp(re1, "g");
```

If you execute this code in an ECMAScript 5 environment, you'll get an error stating that the second argument cannot be used when the first argument is a regular expression. ECMAScript 6 changed this behavior, allowing the second argument, which overrides any flags present on the first argument. For example:

```
let re1 = /ab/i,

    // throws an error in ES5, okay in ES6
    re2 = new RegExp(re1, "g");


console.log(re1.toString());          // "/ab/i"
console.log(re2.toString());          // "/ab/g"

console.log(re1.test("ab"));          // true
console.log(re2.test("ab"));          // true

console.log(re1.test("AB"));          // true
console.log(re2.test("AB"));          // false
```

In this code, re1 has the i (case-insensitive) flag, whereas re2 has only the g (global) flag. The RegExp constructor duplicated the pattern from re1 and substituted the g flag for the i flag. Without the second argument, re2 would have the same flags as re1.

The flags Property

In addition to adding a new flag and changing how you can work with flags, ECMAScript 6 added a property associated with them. In ECMAScript 5, you could get the text of a regular expression by using the source property, but to get the flag string, you'd have to parse the output of the toString() method, as shown here:

```
function getFlags(re) {
    var text = re.toString();
    return text.substring(text.lastIndexOf("/") + 1, text.length);
}

// toString() is "/ab/g"
var re = /ab/g;

console.log(getFlags(re));            // "g"
```

This code converts a regular expression into a string and then returns the characters found after the last /. Those characters are the flags.

ECMAScript 6 makes fetching flags easier by adding a `flags` property to pair with the `source` property. Both properties are prototype accessor properties with only a getter assigned, making them read-only. The `flags` property makes inspecting regular expressions easier for debugging and inheritance purposes.

A late addition to ECMAScript 6, the `flags` property returns the string representation of any flags applied to a regular expression. For example:

```
let re = /ab/g;

console.log(re.source);    // "ab"
console.log(re.flags);     // "g"
```

This code fetches all flags on `re` and prints them to the console with far fewer lines of code than the `toString()` technique can. Using `source` and `flags` together allows you to extract the pieces of the regular expression that you need without parsing the regular expression string directly.

The changes to strings and regular expressions discussed in this chapter so far definitely allow you to do more with them, but ECMAScript 6 improves your power over strings in a more significant way. It introduces a type of literal that makes strings more flexible.

Template Literals

To allow developers to solve more complex problems, ECMAScript 6's *template literals* provide syntax for creating domain-specific languages (DSLs) for working with content in a safer way than the solutions available in ECMAScript 5 and earlier versions. A DSL is a programming language designed for a specific, narrow purpose, as opposed to general-purpose languages like JavaScript. The ECMAScript wiki (*http://wiki.ecmascript.org/doku.php?id=harmony:quasis/*) offers the following description on the template literal strawman:

> This scheme extends ECMAScript syntax with syntactic sugar to allow libraries to provide DSLs that easily produce, query, and manipulate content from other languages that are immune or resistant to injection attacks such as XSS, SQL Injection, etc.

But in reality, template literals are ECMAScript 6's answer to the following features that JavaScript lacked in ECMAScript 5 and in earlier versions:

Multiline strings   A formal concept of multiline strings

Basic string formatting   The ability to substitute parts of the string for values contained in variables

HTML escaping   The ability to transform a string so it is safe to insert into HTML

Rather than trying to add more functionality to JavaScript's already existing strings, template literals represent an entirely new approach to solving these problems.

Basic Syntax

At their simplest, template literals act like regular strings delimited by backticks (`) instead of double or single quotes. For example, consider the following:

```
let message = `Hello world!`;

console.log(message);              // "Hello world!"
console.log(typeof message);       // "string"
console.log(message.length);       // 12
```

This code demonstrates that the variable message contains a normal JavaScript string. The template literal syntax is used to create the string value, which is then assigned to the message variable.

If you want to use a backtick in a string, just escape it with a backslash (\), as in this version of the message variable:

```
let message = `\`Hello\` world!`;

console.log(message);              // "`Hello` world!"
console.log(typeof message);       // "string"
console.log(message.length);       // 14
```

There's no need to escape either double or single quotes inside template literals.

Multiline Strings

JavaScript developers have wanted a way to create multiline strings since the first version of the language. But when you're using double or single quotes, strings must be completely contained on a single line.

Pre-ECMAScript 6 Workarounds

Thanks to a long-standing syntax bug, JavaScript does have a workaround for creating multiline strings. You can create multiline strings by using a backslash (\) before a newline. Here's an example:

```
var message = "Multiline \
string";

console.log(message);         // "Multiline string"
```

The message string has no newlines present when printed to the console because the backslash is treated as a continuation rather than a newline.

To show a newline in output, you'd need to manually include it:

```
var message = "Multiline \n\
string";

console.log(message);      // "Multiline
                           //  string"
```

This code should print the contents of message on two separate lines in all major JavaScript engines; however, the behavior is defined as a bug, and many developers recommend avoiding it.

Other pre-ECMAScript 6 attempts to create multiline strings usually relied on arrays or string concatenation, such as the following:

```
var message = [
    "Multiline ",
    "string"
].join("\n");

let message = "Multiline \n" +
    "string";
```

All the ways developers worked around JavaScript's lack of multiline strings weren't very practical or convenient.

Multiline Strings the Easy Way

ECMAScript 6's template literals make multiline strings easy because there's no special syntax. Just include a newline where you want, and it appears in the result, like so:

```
let message = `Multiline
string`;

console.log(message);           // "Multiline
                                //  string"
console.log(message.length);    // 16
```

All whitespace inside the backticks is part of the string, so be careful with indentation. For example:

```
let message = `Multiline
              string`;

console.log(message);           // "Multiline
                                //               string"
console.log(message.length);    // 31
```

In this code, all whitespace before the second line of the template literal is considered part of the string.

If making the text align with proper indentation is important to you, consider leaving the first line of a multiline template literal empty and then indenting after that, as follows:

```
let html = `
<div>
    <h1>Title</h1>
</div>`.trim();
```

This code begins the template literal on the first line but doesn't have any text until the second line. The HTML tags are indented to look correct and then the trim() method is called to remove the initial empty line.

If you prefer, you can also use \n in a template literal to indicate where a newline should be inserted:

```
let message = `Multiline\nstring`;

console.log(message);           // "Multiline
                                //  string"
console.log(message.length);    // 16
```

Making Substitutions

At this point, template literals may look like fancier versions of normal JavaScript strings. The real difference between the two is in template literal *substitutions*. Substitutions allow you to embed any valid JavaScript expression inside a template literal and output the result as part of the string.

Substitutions are delimited by an opening ${ and a closing } that can have any JavaScript expression inside. The simplest substitutions let you embed local variables directly into a resulting string, like this:

```
let name = "Nicholas",
    message = `Hello, ${name}.`;

console.log(message);        // "Hello, Nicholas."
```

The substitution ${name} accesses the local variable name and inserts it into the message string. The message variable then holds the result of the substitution immediately.

NOTE   *A template literal can access any variable accessible in the scope in which it is defined. Attempting to use an undeclared variable in a template literal throws an error in strict and non-strict modes.*

Because all substitutions are JavaScript expressions, you can substitute more than just simple variable names. You can easily embed calculations, function calls, and more. For example:

```
let count = 10,
    price = 0.25,
    message = `${count} items cost $$${(count * price).toFixed(2)}.`;

console.log(message);        // "10 items cost $2.50."
```

This code performs a calculation as part of the template literal. The variables count and price are multiplied together to produce a result and then are formatted to two decimal places using .toFixed(). The dollar sign before the second substitution is output as is because it's not followed by an opening curly brace.

Template literals are also JavaScript expressions, which means you can place a template literal inside another template literal, as in this example:

```
let name = "Nicholas",
    message = `Hello, ${
        `my name is ${ name }`
    }.`;

console.log(message);        // "Hello, my name is Nicholas."
```

This code nests a second template literal inside the first. After the first ${ delimiter, another template literal begins. The second ${ indicates the beginning of an embedded expression inside the inner template literal. That expression is the variable name, which is inserted into the result.

Tagged Templates

You've seen how template literals can create multiline strings and insert values into strings without concatenation. But the real power of template literals comes from tagged templates. A *template tag* performs a transformation on the template literal and returns the final string value. This tag is specified at the start of the template, just before the first ` character, as shown here:

```
let message = tag`Hello world`;
```

In this example, tag is the template tag to apply to the `Hello world` template literal.

Defining Tags

A *tag* is simply a function that is called with the processed template literal data. The tag receives data about the template literal as individual pieces and must combine the pieces to create the result. The first argument is an array containing the literal strings as interpreted by JavaScript. Each subsequent argument is the interpreted value of each substitution.

Tag functions are typically defined using rest arguments to make handling the data easier than using individual named arguments, as follows:

```
function tag(literals, ...substitutions) {
    // return a string
}
```

To better understand what gets passed to tags, consider the following:

```
let count = 10,
    price = 0.25,
    message = passthru`${count} items cost $$${(count * price).toFixed(2)}.`;
```

If you had a function called passthru(), that function would receive three arguments when used as a template literal tag. The first argument would be a literals array, containing the following elements:

- The empty string before the first substitution ("")
- The string after the first substitution and before the second (" items cost $")
- The string after the second substitution (".")

The next argument would be 10, which is the interpreted value for the count variable. This value becomes the first element in a substitutions array. The third argument would be "2.50", which is the interpreted value for (count * price).toFixed(2) and the second element in the substitutions array.

Note that the first item in literals is an empty string. This ensures that literals[0] is always the start of the string, just like literals[literals.length - 1] is always the end of the string. The number of items in the substitutions array is always one fewer than the number of items in the literals array, which means the expression substitutions.length === literals.length - 1 is always true.

Using this pattern, the literals and substitutions arrays can be interwoven to create a resulting string. The first item in literals comes first, the first item in substitutions is next, and so on until the string is complete. As an example, you can mimic the default behavior of a template literal by alternating values from these two arrays, as in the following code.

```
function passthru(literals, ...substitutions) {
    let result = "";

    // run the loop only for the substitution count
    for (let i = 0; i < substitutions.length; i++) {
        result += literals[i];
        result += substitutions[i];
    }

    // add the last literal
    result += literals[literals.length - 1];

    return result;
}

let count = 10,
    price = 0.25,
    message = passthru`${count} items cost $$${(count * price).toFixed(2)}.`;

console.log(message);        // "10 items cost $2.50."
```

This example defines a passthru tag that performs the same transformation as the default template literal behavior. The only trick is to use substitutions.length for the loop rather than literals.length to avoid accidentally going past the end of the substitutions array. This trick works because the relationship between literals and substitutions is well-defined in ECMAScript 6.

NOTE *The values contained in substitutions are not necessarily strings. If an expression evaluates to a number, as in the previous example, the numeric value is passed in. Determining how such values should output in the result is part of the tag's job.*

Using Raw Values in Template Literals

Template tags also have access to raw string information, which primarily means access to character escapes before they're transformed into their character equivalents. The simplest way to work with raw string values is to use the built-in String.raw() tag. For example:

```
let message1 = `Multiline\nstring`,
    message2 = String.raw`Multiline\nstring`;

console.log(message1);       // "Multiline
                             //  string"
console.log(message2);       // "Multiline\\nstring"
```

In this code, the \n in message1 is interpreted as a newline, and the \n in message2 is returned in its raw form of "\\n" (the slash and n characters). Retrieving the raw string information like this allows for more complex processing when necessary.

The raw string information is also passed into template tags. The first argument in a tag function is an array with an extra property called raw. The raw property is an array containing the raw equivalent of each literal value. For example, the value in literals[0] always has an equivalent literals.raw[0] that contains the raw string information. Knowing that, you can mimic String.raw() using the following code:

```
function raw(literals, ...substitutions) {
    let result = "";

    // run the loop only for the substitution count
    for (let i = 0; i < substitutions.length; i++) {
        // use raw values instead
        result += literals.raw[i];
        result += substitutions[i];
    }

    // add the last literal
    result += literals.raw[literals.length - 1];

    return result;
}

let message = raw`Multiline\nstring`;

console.log(message);           // "Multiline\\nstring"
console.log(message.length);    // 17
```

This code uses literals.raw instead of literals to output the string result. That means any character escapes, including Unicode code point escapes, will be returned in their raw form. Raw strings are helpful when you want to output a string containing code that includes character escape sequences. For instance, if you want to generate documentation about some code, you might want to output the actual code as it appears.

Summary

Full Unicode support in ECMAScript 6 allows JavaScript to handle UTF-16 characters in logical ways. The ability to transfer between code point and character via codePointAt() and String.fromCodePoint() is an important step for string manipulation. The addition of the regular expression u flag makes it possible to operate on code points instead of 16-bit characters, and the normalize() method allows for more appropriate string comparisons.

ECMAScript 6 also added new methods for working with strings, allowing you to more easily identify a substring regardless of its position in the parent string. More functionality was added to regular expressions as well.

Template literals are an important addition to ECMAScript 6 that allows you to create domain-specific languages (DSLs) to make creating strings easier. The ability to embed variables directly into template literals means that developers have a safer tool than string concatenation for composing long strings with variables.

Built-in support for multiline strings also makes template literals a useful upgrade over normal JavaScript strings, which have never had this ability. Although newlines are allowed directly inside the template literal, you can still use \n and other character escape sequences.

Template tags are the most important part of the template literal feature for creating DSLs. Tags are functions that receive the pieces of the template literal as arguments. You can then use that data to return an appropriate string value. The data provided includes literals, their raw equivalents, and any substitution values. These pieces of information can help you determine the correct output for the tag.

3

FUNCTIONS

Functions are an important part of any programming language, and prior to ECMAScript 6, JavaScript functions hadn't changed much since the language was created. This left a backlog of problems and nuanced behavior that made making mistakes easy and often required more code just to produce very basic behaviors.

ECMAScript 6 functions make a big leap forward, taking into account years of complaints and requests from JavaScript developers. The result is a number of incremental improvements that enhance ECMAScript 5 functions and make programming in JavaScript less error prone and more flexible.

Functions with Default Parameter Values

Functions in JavaScript are unique in that they allow any number of parameters to be passed regardless of the number of parameters declared in the function definition. This allows you to define functions that can handle different numbers of parameters, often by just filling in default values when parameters aren't provided. This section covers how default parameters work in and prior to ECMAScript 6, along with some important information on the arguments object, using expressions as parameters, and another TDZ.

Simulating Default Parameter Values in ECMAScript 5

In ECMAScript 5 and earlier, you would likely use the following pattern to create a function with default parameter values:

```
function makeRequest(url, timeout, callback) {

    timeout = timeout || 2000;
    callback = callback || function() {};

    // the rest of the function

}
```

In this example, `timeout` and `callback` are actually optional because they are given a default value if a parameter isn't provided. The logical OR operator (`||`) always returns the second operand when the first is falsy. Because named function parameters that are not explicitly provided are set to `undefined`, the logical OR operator is frequently used to provide default values for missing parameters. However, a flaw exists with this approach in that a valid value for `timeout` might actually be 0, but this would replace it with 2000 because 0 is falsy.

In that case, a safer alternative is to check the type of the argument using `typeof`, as in this example:

```
function makeRequest(url, timeout, callback) {

    timeout = (typeof timeout !== "undefined") ? timeout : 2000;
    callback = (typeof callback !== "undefined") ? callback : function() {};

    // the rest of the function

}
```

Although this approach is safer, it still requires a lot of extra code to execute a very basic operation. This approach represents a common pattern, and popular JavaScript libraries are filled with similar patterns.

Default Parameter Values in ECMAScript 6

ECMAScript 6 makes it easier to provide default values for parameters by supplying initializations that are used when the parameter isn't formally passed. For example:

```
function makeRequest(url, timeout = 2000, callback = function() {}) {

    // the rest of the function

}
```

This function expects only the first parameter to always be passed. The other two parameters have default values, which makes the body of the function much smaller because you don't need to add any code to check for a missing value.

When makeRequest() is called with all three parameters, the defaults are not used. For example:

```
// uses default timeout and callback
makeRequest("/foo");

// uses default callback
makeRequest("/foo", 500);

// doesn't use defaults
makeRequest("/foo", 500, function(body) {
    doSomething(body);
});
```

ECMAScript 6 considers url to be required, which is why "/foo" is passed in all three calls to makeRequest(). The two parameters with a default value are considered optional.

It's possible to specify default values for any arguments, including those that appear before arguments without default values in the function declaration. For example, this is fine:

```
function makeRequest(url, timeout = 2000, callback) {

    // the rest of the function

}
```

In this case, the default value for timeout will be used only if there is no second argument passed in or if the second argument is explicitly passed in as undefined, as in this example:

```
// uses default timeout
makeRequest("/foo", undefined, function(body) {
    doSomething(body);
});
```

```
// uses default timeout
makeRequest("/foo");

// doesn't use default timeout
makeRequest("/foo", null, function(body) {
    doSomething(body);
});
```

In the case of default parameter values, a value of null is considered valid, meaning that in the third call to makeRequest(), the default value for timeout will not be used.

How Default Parameter Values Affect the arguments Object

Keep in mind that the arguments object's behavior is different when default parameter values are present. In ECMAScript 5 non-strict mode, the arguments object reflects changes in the named parameters of a function. Here's some code that illustrates how this works:

```
function mixArgs(first, second) {
    console.log(first === arguments[0]);
    console.log(second === arguments[1]);
    first = "c";
    second = "d";
    console.log(first === arguments[0]);
    console.log(second === arguments[1]);
}

mixArgs("a", "b");
```

This code outputs the following:

```
true
true
true
true
```

The arguments object is always updated in non-strict mode to reflect changes in the named parameters. Thus, when first and second are assigned new values, arguments[0] and arguments[1] are updated accordingly, making all of the === comparisons resolve to true.

However, ECMAScript 5's strict mode eliminates this confusing aspect of the arguments object. In strict mode, the arguments object does not reflect changes to the named parameters. Here's the mixArgs() function again, but in strict mode:

```
function mixArgs(first, second) {
    "use strict";

    console.log(first === arguments[0]);
    console.log(second === arguments[1]);
    first = "c";
```

```
        second = "d"
        console.log(first === arguments[0]);
        console.log(second === arguments[1]);
}

mixArgs("a", "b");
```

The call to `mixArgs()` outputs the following:

```
true
true
false
false
```

This time, changing `first` and `second` doesn't affect `arguments`, so the output behaves as you'd normally expect it to.

The `arguments` object in a function using ECMAScript 6 default parameter values will always behave in the same manner as ECMAScript 5 strict mode regardless of whether the function is explicitly running in strict mode. The presence of default parameter values triggers the `arguments` object to remain detached from the named parameters. This is a subtle but important detail because of how you can use the `arguments` object. Consider the following:

```
// not in strict mode
function mixArgs(first, second = "b") {
    console.log(arguments.length);
    console.log(first === arguments[0]);
    console.log(second === arguments[1]);
    first = "c";
    second = "d"
    console.log(first === arguments[0]);
    console.log(second === arguments[1]);
}

mixArgs("a");
```

This code outputs the following:

```
1
true
false
false
false
```

In this example, `arguments.length` is 1 because only one argument was passed to `mixArgs()`. That also means `arguments[1]` is undefined, which is the expected behavior when only one argument is passed to a function. That means `first` is equal to `arguments[0]` as well. Changing `first` and `second` has no effect on `arguments`. This behavior occurs in non-strict and strict modes, so you can rely on `arguments` to always reflect the initial call state.

Default Parameter Expressions

Perhaps the most interesting feature of default parameter values is that the default value need not be a primitive value. You can, for example, execute a function to retrieve the default parameter value, like this:

```
function getValue() {
    return 5;
}

function add(first, second = getValue()) {
    return first + second;
}

console.log(add(1, 1));    // 2
console.log(add(1));       // 6
```

Here, if the last argument isn't provided, the function getValue() is called to retrieve the correct default value. Keep in mind that getValue() is called only when add() is called without a second parameter, not when the function declaration is first parsed. That means if getValue() were written differently, it could potentially return a different value. For instance:

```
let value = 5;

function getValue() {
    return value++;
}

function add(first, second = getValue()) {
    return first + second;
}

console.log(add(1, 1));    // 2
console.log(add(1));       // 6
console.log(add(1));       // 7
```

In this example, value begins as 5 and increments each time getValue() is called. The first call to add(1) returns 6, and the second call to add(1) returns 7 because value was incremented. Because the default value for second is evaluated only when the function is called, changes to that value can be made at any time.

WARNING *Be careful when using function calls as default parameter values. If you forget the parentheses, such as second = getValue in this example, you are passing a reference to the function rather than the result of the function call.*

This behavior introduces another useful capability. You can use a previous parameter as the default for a later parameter. Here's an example:

```
function add(first, second = first) {
    return first + second;
}

console.log(add(1, 1));          // 2
console.log(add(1));             // 2
```

In this code, the parameter second is given a default value of first, meaning that passing in just one argument leaves both arguments with the same value. So add(1, 1) returns 2 just as add(1) returns 2. Taking this approach a step further, you can pass first into a function to get the value for second as follows:

```
function getValue(value) {
    return value + 5;
}

function add(first, second = getValue(first)) {
    return first + second;
}

console.log(add(1, 1));          // 2
console.log(add(1));             // 7
```

This example sets second equal to the value returned by getValue(first), so although add(1, 1) still returns 2, add(1) returns 7 (1 + 6).

The ability to reference parameters from default parameter assignments works only for previous arguments, so earlier arguments don't have access to later arguments. For example:

```
function add(first = second, second) {
    return first + second;
}

console.log(add(1, 1));          // 2
console.log(add(undefined, 1));  // throws an error
```

The call to add(undefined, 1) throws an error because second is defined after first and is therefore unavailable as a default value. To understand why that happens, it's important to revisit TDZs.

Default Parameter TDZ

Chapter 1 introduced the TDZ as it relates to let and const, and default parameter values also have a TDZ where parameters cannot be accessed. Similar to a let declaration, each parameter creates a new identifier binding that can't be referenced before initialization without throwing an error. Parameter initialization happens when the function is called, either by passing a value for the parameter or by using the default parameter value.

To explore the default parameter value TDZ, reconsider this example from page 41:

```
function getValue(value) {
    return value + 5;
}

function add(first, second = getValue(first)) {
    return first + second;
}

console.log(add(1, 1));     // 2
console.log(add(1));        // 7
```

The calls to add(1, 1) and add(1) effectively execute the following code to create the first and second parameter values:

```
// JavaScript representation of call to add(1, 1)
let first = 1;
let second = 1;

// JavaScript representation of call to add(1)
let first = 1;
let second = getValue(first);
```

When the function add() is first executed, the bindings first and second are added to a parameter-specific TDZ (similar to how let behaves). So although second can be initialized with the value of first because first is always initialized at that time, the reverse is not true. Now, consider this rewritten add() function:

```
function add(first = second, second) {
    return first + second;
}

console.log(add(1, 1));         // 2
console.log(add(undefined, 1)); // throws an error
```

The calls to add(1, 1) and add(undefined, 1) in this example now map to the following code behind the scenes:

```
// JavaScript representation of call to add(1, 1)
let first = 1;
let second = 1;

// JavaScript representation of call to add(undefined, 1)
let first = second;
let second = 1;
```

In this example, the call to add(undefined, 1) throws an error because second hasn't yet been initialized when first is initialized. At that point, second is in the TDZ and therefore any references to second throw an error. This example mirrors the behavior of let bindings discussed in Chapter 1.

NOTE *Function parameters have their own scope and their own TDZ that is separate from the function body scope. That means the default value of a parameter cannot access any variables declared inside the function body.*

Working with Unnamed Parameters

So far, the examples in this chapter have only covered parameters that have been named in the function definition. However, JavaScript functions don't limit the number of parameters that can be passed to the number of named parameters defined. You can always pass fewer or more parameters than formally specified. Default parameter values make it clear when a function can accept fewer parameters, and ECMAScript 6 makes the problem of passing more parameters than defined better as well.

Unnamed Parameters in ECMAScript 5

Early on, JavaScript provided the arguments object as a way to inspect all function parameters that are passed without necessarily defining each parameter. Although inspecting arguments works fine in most cases, this object can be a bit cumbersome to work with. For example, examine this code, which inspects the arguments object:

```
function pick(object) {
    let result = Object.create(null);

    // start at the second parameter
    for (let i = 1, len = arguments.length; i < len; i++) {
        result[arguments[i]] = object[arguments[i]];
    }

    return result;
}

let book = {
    title: "Understanding ECMAScript 6",
    author: "Nicholas C. Zakas",
    year: 2016
};

let bookData = pick(book, "author", "year");

console.log(bookData.author);   // "Nicholas C. Zakas"
console.log(bookData.year);     // 2016
```

This function mimics the pick() method from the *Underscore.js* library, which returns a copy of a given object with some specified subset of the original object's properties. This example defines only one argument and expects the first argument to be the object from which to copy properties. Every other argument passed is the name of a property that should be copied on the result.

You should note a couple of things about this pick() function. First, it's not at all obvious that the function can handle more than one parameter. You could define several more parameters, but you would always fall short of indicating that this function can take any number of parameters. Second, because the first parameter is named and used directly, when you look for the properties to copy, you have to start in the arguments object at index 1 instead of index 0. Remembering to use the appropriate indices with arguments isn't necessarily difficult, but it's one more detail to keep track of.

ECMAScript 6 introduces rest parameters to help with these issues.

Rest Parameters

A *rest* parameter is indicated by three dots (...) preceding a named parameter. That named parameter becomes an Array containing the rest of the parameters passed to the function, which is where the name *rest* parameters originates. For example, pick() can be rewritten using rest parameters, like this:

```
function pick(object, ...keys) {
    let result = Object.create(null);

    for (let i = 0, len = keys.length; i < len; i++) {
        result[keys[i]] = object[keys[i]];
    }

    return result;
}
```

In this version of the function, keys is a rest parameter that contains all parameters passed after object (unlike arguments, which contains all parameters including the first one). That means you can iterate over keys from beginning to end without worry. As a bonus, you can tell by looking at the function that it's capable of handling any number of parameters.

NOTE   *Rest parameters don't affect a function's length property, which indicates the number of named parameters for the function. The value of length for pick() in this example is 1 because only object counts toward this value.*

Rest Parameter Restrictions

Rest parameters have two restrictions. The first restriction is that there can be only one rest parameter, and the rest parameter must be last. For example, this code won't work:

```
// Syntax error: Can't have a named parameter after rest parameters
function pick(object, ...keys, last) {
    let result = Object.create(null);

    for (let i = 0, len = keys.length; i < len; i++) {
        result[keys[i]] = object[keys[i]];
    }

    return result;
}
```

Here, the parameter last follows the rest parameter keys, which would cause a syntax error.

The second restriction is that rest parameters cannot be used in an object literal setter. That means this code would also cause a syntax error:

```
let object = {

    // Syntax error: Can't use rest param in setter
    set name(...value) {
        // do something
    }
};
```

This restriction exists because object literal setters are restricted to a single argument. Rest parameters are, by definition, an infinite number of arguments, so they're not allowed in this context.

How Rest Parameters Affect the arguments Object

Rest parameters were designed to replace arguments in JavaScript. Originally, ECMAScript 4 eliminated arguments and added rest parameters to allow an unlimited number of arguments to be passed to functions. ECMAScript 4 was never standardized, but this idea was retained and reintroduced in ECMAScript 6, despite arguments not being removed from the language.

The arguments object works together with rest parameters by reflecting the arguments that were passed to the function when called, as illustrated in the following example.

```
function checkArgs(...args) {
    console.log(args.length);
    console.log(arguments.length);
    console.log(args[0], arguments[0]);
    console.log(args[1], arguments[1]);
}

checkArgs("a", "b");
```

The call to checkArgs() outputs the following:

```
2
2
a a
b b
```

The arguments object always correctly reflects the parameters that were passed into a function regardless of rest parameter usage.

Increased Capabilities of the Function Constructor

The Function constructor is an infrequently used part of JavaScript that allows you to dynamically create a new function. The arguments to the constructor are the parameters for the function and the function body, all as strings. Here's an example:

```
var add = new Function("first", "second", "return first + second");

console.log(add(1, 1));     // 2
```

ECMAScript 6 augments the capabilities of the Function constructor to allow default parameters and rest parameters. You need only add an equal sign and a value to the parameter names, as follows:

```
var add = new Function("first", "second = first",
    "return first + second");

console.log(add(1, 1));     // 2
console.log(add(1));        // 2
```

In this example, the parameter second is assigned the value of first when only one parameter is passed. The syntax is the same as for function declarations that don't use Function.

For rest parameters, just add the ... before the last parameter, like this:

```
var pickFirst = new Function("...args", "return args[0]");

console.log(pickFirst(1, 2));     // 1
```

This code creates a function that uses only a single rest parameter and returns the first argument that was passed in. The addition of default and rest parameters ensures that Function has the same capabilities as the declarative form of creating functions.

The Spread Operator

Closely related to rest parameters is the spread operator. Whereas rest parameters allow you to specify that multiple independent arguments should be combined into an array, the spread operator allows you to specify an array that should be split and passed in as separate arguments to a function. Consider the built-in Math.max() method, which accepts any number of arguments and returns the one with the highest value. Here's a simple use case for this method:

```
let value1 = 25,
    value2 = 50;

console.log(Math.max(value1, value2));      // 50
```

When you're working with just two values, as in this example, Math.max() is very easy to use. The two values are passed in, and the higher value is returned. But what if you've been tracking values in an array, and now you want to find the highest value? The Math.max() method doesn't allow you to pass in an array, so in ECMAScript 5 and earlier, you'd be stuck either searching the array manually or using apply() as follows:

```
let values = [25, 50, 75, 100]

console.log(Math.max.apply(Math, values)); // 100
```

This solution works, but using apply() in this manner is a bit confusing. It actually seems to obfuscate the true meaning of the code with additional syntax.

The ECMAScript 6 spread operator makes this case very simple. Instead of calling apply(), you can pass the array to Math.max() directly and prefix it with the same ... pattern you use with rest parameters. The JavaScript engine then splits the array into individual arguments and passes them in, like this:

```
let values = [25, 50, 75, 100]

// equivalent to
// console.log(Math.max(25, 50, 75, 100));
console.log(Math.max(...values));          // 100
```

Now the call to Math.max() looks a bit more conventional and avoids the complexity of specifying a this binding (the first argument to Math.max.apply() in the previous example) for a simple mathematical operation.

You can mix and match the spread operator with other arguments as well. Suppose you want the smallest number returned from `Math.max()` to be 0 (just in case negative numbers sneak into the array). You can pass that argument separately and still use the spread operator for the other arguments, as follows:

```
let values = [-25, -50, -75, -100]

console.log(Math.max(...values, 0));        // 0
```

In this example, the last argument passed to `Math.max()` is 0, which comes after the other arguments are passed in using the spread operator.

The spread operator for argument passing makes using arrays for function arguments much easier. You'll likely find it to be a suitable replacement for the `apply()` method in most circumstances.

In addition to the uses you've seen for default and rest parameters so far, in ECMAScript 6, you can also apply both parameter types to JavaScript's `Function` constructor.

The name Property

Identifying functions can be challenging in JavaScript given the various ways you can define a function. Additionally, the prevalence of anonymous function expressions makes debugging a bit more difficult, often resulting in stack traces that are hard to read and decipher. For these reasons, ECMAScript 6 adds the `name` property to all functions.

Choosing Appropriate Names

All functions in an ECMAScript 6 program will have an appropriate value for their `name` property. To see this in action, look at the following example, which shows a function and function expression, and prints the `name` properties for both:

```
function doSomething() {
    // empty
}

var doAnotherThing = function() {
    // empty
};

console.log(doSomething.name);          // "doSomething"
console.log(doAnotherThing.name);       // "doAnotherThing"
```

In this code, `doSomething()` has a `name` property equal to `"doSomething"` because it's a function declaration. The anonymous function expression `doAnotherThing()` has a `name` of `"doAnotherThing"` because that's the name of the variable to which it is assigned.

Special Cases of the name Property

Although appropriate names for function declarations and function expressions are easy to find, ECMAScript 6 goes further to ensure that *all* functions have appropriate names. To illustrate this, consider the following program:

```
var doSomething = function doSomethingElse() {
    // empty
};

var person = {
    get firstName() {
        return "Nicholas"
    },
    sayName: function() {
        console.log(this.name);
    }
}

console.log(doSomething.name);       // "doSomethingElse"
console.log(person.sayName.name);    // "sayName"
console.log(person.firstName.name);  // "get firstName"
```

In this example, doSomething.name is "doSomethingElse" because the function expression has a name, and that name takes priority over the variable to which the function was assigned. The name property of person.sayName() is "sayName" because the value was interpreted from the object literal. Similarly, person.firstName is actually a getter function, so its name is "get firstName" to indicate this difference. Setter functions are prefixed with "set" as well.

There are a couple of other special cases for function names, too. Functions created using bind() will prefix their names with "bound" and a space, and functions created using the Function constructor use the name "anonymous", as in this example:

```
var doSomething = function() {
    // empty
};

console.log(doSomething.bind().name);    // "bound doSomething"

console.log((new Function()).name);      // "anonymous"
```

The name of a bound function will always be the name of the function being bound prefixed with the string "bound " so the bound version of doSomething() is "bound doSomething".

Keep in mind that the value of name for any function does not necessarily refer to a variable of the same name. The name property is meant to be informative, to help with debugging, so there's no way to use the value of name to get a reference to the function.

Clarifying the Dual Purpose of Functions

In ECMAScript 5 and earlier, functions serve the dual purpose of being callable with or without new. When used with new, the this value inside a function is a new object and that new object is returned, as illustrated in this example:

```
function Person(name) {
    this.name = name;
}

var person = new Person("Nicholas");
var notAPerson = Person("Nicholas");

console.log(person);        // "[Object object]"
console.log(notAPerson);    // "undefined"
```

When creating notAPerson, calling Person() without new results in undefined (and sets a name property on the global object in non-strict mode). The capitalization of Person is the only real indicator that the function is meant to be called using new, as is common in JavaScript programs. This confusion over the dual roles of functions led to some changes in ECMAScript 6.

JavaScript has two different internal-only methods for functions: [[Call]] and [[Construct]]. When a function is called without new, the [[Call]] method is executed, which executes the body of the function as it appears in the code. When a function is called with new, that's when the [[Construct]] method is called. The [[Construct]] method is responsible for creating a new object, called the instance, and then executing the function body with this set to the instance. Functions that have a [[Construct]] method are called *constructors*.

Keep in mind that not all functions have [[Construct]], and therefore not all functions can be called with new. Arrow functions, discussed in "Arrow Functions" on page 54, do not have a [[Construct]] method.

Determining How a Function Was Called in ECMAScript 5

The most popular way to determine whether a function was called with new (and hence, as a constructor) in ECMAScript 5 is to use instanceof, for example:

```
function Person(name) {
    if (this instanceof Person) {
        this.name = name;    // using new
    } else {
        throw new Error("You must use new with Person.")
    }
}

var person = new Person("Nicholas");
var notAPerson = Person("Nicholas");    // throws an error
```

Here, the this value is checked to see whether it's an instance of the constructor, and if it is, execution continues as normal. If this isn't an instance of Person, an error is thrown. This approach works because the [[Construct]] method creates a new instance of Person and assigns it to this. Unfortunately, this approach is not completely reliable because this can be an instance of Person without using new, as in this example:

```
function Person(name) {
    if (this instanceof Person) {
        this.name = name;
    } else {
        throw new Error("You must use new with Person.")
    }
}

var person = new Person("Nicholas");
var notAPerson = Person.call(person, "Michael");    // works!
```

The call to Person.call() passes the person variable as the first argument, which means this is set to person inside the Person function. To the function, there's no way to distinguish being called with Person.call() (or Person.apply()) with a Person instance from being called with new.

The new.target Metaproperty

To solve the problem of identifying function calls using new, ECMAScript 6 introduces the new.target metaproperty. A *metaproperty* is a property of a nonobject that provides additional information related to its target (such as new). When a function's [[Construct]] method is called, new.target is filled with the target of the new operator. That target is typically the constructor of the newly created object instance that will become this inside the function body. If [[Call]] is executed, new.target is undefined.

This new metaproperty allows you to safely detect if a function is called with new by checking whether new.target is defined as follows:

```
function Person(name) {
    if (typeof new.target !== "undefined") {
        this.name = name;
    } else {
        throw new Error("You must use new with Person.")
    }
}

var person = new Person("Nicholas");
var notAPerson = Person.call(person, "Michael");    // error!
```

By using new.target instead of this instanceof Person, the Person constructor is now correctly throwing an error when used without new.

You can also check that new.target was called with a specific constructor. For instance, look at this example:

```
function Person(name) {
    if (typeof new.target === Person) {
        this.name = name;
    } else {
        throw new Error("You must use new with Person.")
    }
}

function AnotherPerson(name) {
    Person.call(this, name);
}

var person = new Person("Nicholas");
var anotherPerson = new AnotherPerson("Nicholas");  // error!
```

In this code, new.target must be Person in order to work correctly. When new AnotherPerson("Nicholas") is called, the subsequent call to Person.call(this, name) will throw an error because new.target is undefined inside of the Person constructor (it was called without new).

WARNING *Using new.target outside a function is a syntax error.*

By adding new.target, ECMAScript 6 helped to clarify some ambiguity concerning function calls. Following along this theme, ECMAScript 6 also addresses another previously ambiguous part of the language: declaring functions inside blocks.

Block-Level Functions

In ECMAScript 3 and earlier, a function declaration occurring inside a block (a *block-level function*) was technically a syntax error, but all browsers still supported it. Unfortunately, each browser that allowed the syntax behaved in a slightly different way, so it's considered a best practice to avoid function declarations inside blocks (the best alternative is to use a function expression).

In an attempt to rein in this incompatible behavior, ECMAScript 5 strict mode introduced an error whenever a function declaration was used inside a block in this way:

```
"use strict";

if (true) {

    // throws a syntax error in ES5, not so in ES6
    function doSomething() {
        // empty
    }
}
```

In ECMAScript 5, this code throws a syntax error. In ECMAScript 6, the doSomething() function is considered a block-level declaration and can be accessed and called within the same block in which it was defined. For example:

```
"use strict";

if (true) {

    console.log(typeof doSomething);        // "function"

    function doSomething() {
        // empty
    }

    doSomething();
}

console.log(typeof doSomething);            // "undefined"
```

Block-level functions are hoisted to the top of the block in which they are defined, so typeof doSomething returns "function", even though it appears before the function declaration in the code. Once the if block is finished executing, doSomething() no longer exists.

Deciding When to Use Block-Level Functions

Block-level functions are similar to let function expressions in that the function definition is removed once execution flows out of the block in which it's defined. The key difference is that block-level functions are hoisted to the top of the containing block. Function expressions that use let are not hoisted, as this example illustrates:

```
"use strict";

if (true) {

    console.log(typeof doSomething);        // throws an error

    let doSomething = function () {
        // empty
    }

    doSomething();
}

console.log(typeof doSomething);
```

Here, code execution stops when typeof doSomething is executed, because the let statement hasn't been executed yet, leaving doSomething() in the TDZ. Knowing this difference, you can choose whether to use block-level functions or let expressions based on whether or not you want the hoisting behavior.

Block-Level Functions in Non-Strict Mode

ECMAScript 6 also allows block-level functions in non-strict mode, but the behavior is slightly different. Instead of hoisting these declarations to the top of the block, they are hoisted all the way to the containing function or global environment. For example:

```
// ECMAScript 6 behavior
if (true) {

    console.log(typeof doSomething);        // "function"

    function doSomething() {
        // empty
    }

    doSomething();
}

console.log(typeof doSomething);            // "function"
```

In this example, doSomething() is hoisted into the global scope so it still exists outside the if block. ECMAScript 6 standardized this behavior to remove the incompatible browser behaviors that previously existed, so all ECMAScript 6 runtimes should behave in the same way.

Allowing block-level functions improves your ability to declare functions in JavaScript, but ECMAScript 6 also introduced a completely new way to declare functions.

Arrow Functions

One of the most interesting new parts of ECMAScript 6 is the *arrow function*. Arrow functions are, as the name suggests, functions defined with a new syntax that uses an arrow (=>). But arrow functions behave differently than traditional JavaScript functions in a number of important ways:

No this, super, arguments, and new.target bindings   The values of this, super, arguments, and new.target inside the function are defined by the closest containing non-arrow function. (super is covered in Chapter 4.)

Cannot be called with new   Arrow functions do not have a [[Construct]] method and therefore cannot be used as constructors. Arrow functions throw an error when used with new.

No prototype   Because you can't use new on an arrow function, there's no need for a prototype. The prototype property of an arrow function doesn't exist.

Can't change this The value of this inside the function can't be changed. It remains the same throughout the entire life cycle of the function.

No arguments object Because arrow functions have no arguments binding, you must rely on named and rest parameters to access function arguments.

No duplicate named parameters Arrow functions cannot have duplicate named parameters in strict or non-strict mode, as opposed to non-arrow functions, which cannot have duplicate named parameters only in strict mode.

There are a few reasons for these differences. First and foremost, this binding is a common source of error in JavaScript. It's very easy to lose track of the this value inside a function, which can result in unintended program behavior, and arrow functions eliminate this confusion. Second, by limiting arrow functions to simply executing code with a single this value, JavaScript engines can more easily optimize these operations, unlike regular functions, which might be used as a constructor or otherwise modified.

The remaining differences also focus on reducing errors and ambiguities inside arrow functions. By doing so, JavaScript engines are better able to optimize arrow function execution.

NOTE *Arrow functions also have a name property that follows the same rule as other functions.*

Arrow Function Syntax

The syntax for arrow functions comes in many flavors depending on what you're trying to accomplish. All variations begin with function arguments, followed by the arrow, followed by the body of the function. The arguments and the body can take different forms depending on usage. For example, the following arrow function takes a single argument and simply returns it:

```
let reflect = value => value;

// effectively equivalent to:

let reflect = function(value) {
    return value;
};
```

When there is only one argument for an arrow function, that one argument can be used directly without any further syntax. The arrow comes next, and the expression to the right of the arrow is evaluated and returned. Even though there is no explicit return statement, this arrow function will return the first argument that is passed in.

If you are passing in more than one argument, you must include parentheses around those arguments, like this:

```
let sum = (num1, num2) => num1 + num2;

// effectively equivalent to:

let sum = function(num1, num2) {
    return num1 + num2;
};
```

The sum() function simply adds two arguments together and returns the result. The only difference between this arrow function and the reflect() function is that the arguments are enclosed in parentheses with a comma separating them (like traditional functions).

If there are no arguments to the function, you must include an empty set of parentheses in the declaration, as follows:

```
let getName = () => "Nicholas";

// effectively equivalent to:

let getName = function() {
    return "Nicholas";
};
```

When you want to provide a more traditional function body, perhaps consisting of more than one expression, you need to wrap the function body in curly braces and explicitly define a return value, as in this version of sum():

```
let sum = (num1, num2) => {
    return num1 + num2;
};

// effectively equivalent to:

let sum = function(num1, num2) {
    return num1 + num2;
};
```

You can more or less treat the inside of the curly braces the same as you would in a traditional function except arguments is not available.

If you want to create a function that does nothing, you need to include curly braces, like this:

```
let doNothing = () => {};

// effectively equivalent to:

let doNothing = function() {};
```

Curly braces denote the function's body, which works just fine in the cases you've seen so far. But an arrow function that wants to return an object literal outside a function body must wrap the literal in parentheses. For example:

```
let getTempItem = id => ({ id: id, name: "Temp" });

// effectively equivalent to:

let getTempItem = function(id) {

    return {
        id: id,
        name: "Temp"
    };
};
```

Wrapping the object literal in parentheses signals that the curly braces are an object literal instead of the function body.

Creating Immediately Invoked Function Expressions

One popular use of functions in JavaScript is creating immediately invoked function expressions (IIFEs). IIFEs allow you to define an anonymous function and call it immediately without saving a reference. This pattern comes in handy when you want to create a scope that is shielded from the rest of a program. For example:

```
let person = function(name) {

    return {
        getName: function() {
            return name;
        }
    };

}("Nicholas");

console.log(person.getName());      // "Nicholas"
```

In this code, the IIFE creates an object with a getName() method. The method uses the name argument as the return value, effectively making name a private member of the returned object.

You can accomplish the same thing using arrow functions, as long as you wrap the arrow function in parentheses:

```
let person = ((name) => {

    return {
        getName: function() {
            return name;
        }
```

```
    };

})("Nicholas");

console.log(person.getName());        // "Nicholas"
```

Note that the parentheses are only around the arrow function definition, not around ("Nicholas"). This is different from a formal function
where the parentheses can be placed outside the passed-in parameters as
well as just around the function definition.

No this Binding

One of the most common areas of error in JavaScript is the binding of this
inside functions. Because the value of this can change inside a single function depending on the context in which the function is called, it's possible
to mistakenly affect one object when you meant to affect another. Consider
the following example:

```
let PageHandler = {

    id: "123456",

    init: function() {
        document.addEventListener("click", function(event) {
            this.doSomething(event.type);        // error
        }, false);
    },

    doSomething: function(type) {
        console.log("Handling " + type  + " for " + this.id);
    }
};
```

In this code, the object PageHandler is designed to handle interactions
on the page. The init() method is called to set up the interactions, and that
method in turn assigns an event handler to call this.doSomething(). However,
this code doesn't work exactly as intended.

The call to this.doSomething() is broken because this is a reference to
the object that was the target of the event (in this case document) instead of
being bound to PageHandler. If you tried to run this code, you'd get an error
when the event handler fires because this.doSomething() doesn't exist on the
target document object.

You could fix this by binding the value of this to PageHandler explicitly
using the bind() method on the function instead, like this:

```
let PageHandler = {

    id: "123456",

    init: function() {
```

```
        document.addEventListener("click", (function(event) {
            this.doSomething(event.type);      // no error
        }).bind(this), false);
    },

    doSomething: function(type) {
        console.log("Handling " + type  + " for " + this.id);
    }
};
```

Now the code works as expected, but it might look a bit strange. By calling bind(this), you're actually creating a new function whose this is bound to the current this, which is PageHandler. To avoid creating an extra function, a better way to fix this code is to use an arrow function.

Arrow functions have no this binding, which means the value of this inside an arrow function can only be determined by looking up the scope chain. If the arrow function is contained within a non-arrow function, this will be the same as the containing function; otherwise, this is undefined. Here's one way you could write this code using an arrow function:

```
let PageHandler = {

    id: "123456",

    init: function() {
        document.addEventListener("click",
                event => this.doSomething(event.type), false);
    },

    doSomething: function(type) {
        console.log("Handling " + type  + " for " + this.id);
    }
};
```

The event handler in this example is an arrow function that calls this. doSomething(). The value of this is the same as it is within init(), so this version of the code works similarly to the one using bind(this). Even though the doSomething() method doesn't return a value, it's still the only statement executed in the function body, so there is no need to include curly braces.

Arrow functions are designed to be "throwaway" functions, and so cannot be used to define new types; this is evident from the missing prototype property, which regular functions have. If you try to use the new operator with an arrow function, you'll get an error, as in this example:

```
var MyType = () => {},
    object = new MyType();  // error - you can't use arrow functions with 'new'
```

In this code, the call to new MyType() fails because MyType is an arrow function and therefore has no [[Construct]] behavior. Knowing that arrow functions cannot be used with new allows JavaScript engines to further optimize their behavior.

Also, because the this value is determined by the containing function in which the arrow function is defined, you cannot change the value of this using call(), apply(), or bind().

Arrow Functions and Arrays

The concise syntax for arrow functions makes them ideal for use with array processing, too. For example, if you want to sort an array using a custom comparator, you'd typically write something like this:

```
var result = values.sort(function(a, b) {
    return a - b;
});
```

That's a lot of syntax for a very simple procedure. Compare that to the terser arrow function version:

```
var result = values.sort((a, b) => a - b);
```

The array methods that accept callback functions, such as sort(), map(), and reduce(), can all benefit from simpler arrow function syntax, which changes seemingly complex processes into simpler code.

No arguments Binding

Even though arrow functions don't have their own arguments object, it's possible for them to access the arguments object from a containing function. That arguments object is then available no matter where the arrow function is executed later on. For example:

```
function createArrowFunctionReturningFirstArg() {
    return () => arguments[0];
}

var arrowFunction = createArrowFunctionReturningFirstArg(5);

console.log(arrowFunction());       // 5
```

Inside createArrowFunctionReturningFirstArg(), the arguments[0] element is referenced by the created arrow function. That reference contains the first argument passed to the createArrowFunctionReturningFirstArg() function. When the arrow function is later executed, it returns 5, which was the first argument passed to createArrowFunctionReturningFirstArg(). Even though the arrow function is no longer in the scope of the function that created it, arguments remains accessible due to scope chain resolution of the arguments identifier.

Identifying Arrow Functions

Despite their different syntax, arrow functions are still functions and are identified as such. Consider the following code:

```
var comparator = (a, b) => a - b;

console.log(typeof comparator);              // "function"
console.log(comparator instanceof Function); // true
```

The console.log() output reveals that both typeof and instanceof behave the same with arrow functions as they do with other functions.

Also like other functions, you can still use call(), apply(), and bind() on arrow functions, although the this binding of the function will not be affected. Here are some examples:

```
var sum = (num1, num2) => num1 + num2;

console.log(sum.call(null, 1, 2));    // 3
console.log(sum.apply(null, [1, 2])); // 3

var boundSum = sum.bind(null, 1, 2);

console.log(boundSum());              // 3
```

The sum() function is called using call() and apply() to pass arguments, as you'd do with any function. The bind() method creates boundSum(), which has its two arguments bound to 1 and 2 so they don't need to be passed directly.

Arrow functions are appropriate to use anywhere you're currently using an anonymous function expression, such as with callbacks. The next section covers another major ECMAScript 6 development, but this one is all internal and has no new syntax.

Tail Call Optimization

Perhaps the most interesting change to functions in ECMAScript 6 is an engine optimization that changes the tail call system. A *tail call* is when a function is called as the last statement in another function, like this:

```
function doSomething() {
    return doSomethingElse();   // tail call
}
```

Tail calls as implemented in ECMAScript 5 engines are handled just like any other function call: a new stack frame is created and pushed onto the call stack to represent the function call. That means every previous stack frame is kept in memory, which is problematic when the call stack gets too large.

How Tail Calls Are Different in ECMAScript 6

ECMAScript 6 reduces the size of the call stack for certain tail calls in strict mode (non-strict mode tail calls are left untouched). With this optimization, instead of creating a new stack frame for a tail call, the current stack frame is cleared and reused as long as the following conditions are met:

- The tail call does not require access to variables in the current stack frame (meaning the function is not a closure).
- The function making the tail call has no further work to do after the tail call returns.
- The result of the tail call is returned as the function value.

As an example, this code can easily be optimized because it fits all three criteria:

```
"use strict";

function doSomething() {
    // optimized
    return doSomethingElse();
}
```

This function makes a tail call to doSomethingElse(), returns the result immediately, and doesn't access any variables in the local scope. One small change, not returning the result, results in an unoptimized function:

```
"use strict";

function doSomething() {
    // not optimized - no return
    doSomethingElse();
}
```

Similarly, if you have a function that performs an operation after returning from the tail call, the function can't be optimized:

```
"use strict";

function doSomething() {
    // not optimized - must add after returning
    return 1 + doSomethingElse();
}
```

This example adds the result of doSomethingElse() with 1 before returning the value, and that's enough to turn off optimization.

Another common way to inadvertently turn off optimization is to store the result of a function call in a variable and then return the result, such as:

```
"use strict";

function doSomething() {
    // not optimized - call isn't in tail position
    var result = doSomethingElse();
    return result;
}
```

This example cannot be optimized because the value of doSomethingElse() isn't immediately returned.

Perhaps the hardest situation to avoid is in using closures. Because a closure has access to variables in the containing scope, tail call optimization may be turned off. For example:

```
"use strict";

function doSomething() {
    var num = 1,
        func = () => num;

    // not optimized - function is a closure
    return func();
}
```

The closure func() has access to the local variable num in this example. Even though the call to func() immediately returns the result, optimization can't occur due to referencing the variable num.

How to Harness Tail Call Optimization

In practice, tail call optimization happens behind the scenes, so you don't need to think about it unless you're trying to optimize a function. The primary use case for tail call optimization is in recursive functions, because that is where the optimization has the greatest effect. Consider this function, which computes factorials:

```
function factorial(n) {

    if (n <= 1) {
        return 1;
    } else {

        // not optimized - must multiply after returning
        return n * factorial(n - 1);
    }
}
```

This version of the function cannot be optimized, because multiplication must happen after the recursive call to factorial(). If n is a very large number, the call stack size will grow and could potentially cause a stack overflow.

To optimize the function, you need to ensure that the multiplication doesn't happen after the last function call. To do this, you can use a default parameter to move the multiplication operation outside the return statement. The resulting function carries along the temporary result into the next iteration, creating a function that behaves the same but *can* be optimized by an ECMAScript 6 engine. Here's the new code:

```
function factorial(n, p = 1) {

    if (n <= 1) {
        return 1 * p;
    } else {
        let result = n * p;

        // optimized
        return factorial(n - 1, result);
    }
}
```

In this rewritten version of factorial(), a second argument p is added as a parameter with a default value of 1. The p parameter holds the previous multiplication result so the next result can be computed without another function call. When n is greater than 1, the multiplication is done first and then passed in as the second argument to factorial(). This allows the ECMAScript 6 engine to optimize the recursive call.

Think about tail call optimization whenever you're writing a recursive function, because it can provide a significant performance improvement, especially when applied in a computationally expensive function.

WARNING *At the time of this writing, ECMAScript 6 tail call optimization is undergoing review for changes. It's possible that tail call optimization will eventually require special syntax for increased clarity. The ongoing discussion may result in changes in ECMAScript 8 (ECMAScript 2017).*

Summary

Functions haven't undergone a huge change in ECMAScript 6 but rather a series of incremental changes that make them easier to work with.

Default function parameters allow you to easily specify what value to use when a particular argument isn't passed. Prior to ECMAScript 6, this would require some extra code inside the function to check for the presence of arguments *and* assign a different value.

Rest parameters allow you to specify an array into which all remaining parameters should be placed. Using a real array and letting you indicate which parameters to include makes rest parameters a much more flexible solution than arguments.

The spread operator is a companion to rest parameters, allowing you to deconstruct an array into separate parameters when calling a function. Prior to ECMAScript 6, there were only two ways to pass individual parameters contained in an array: by manually specifying each parameter or using apply(). With the spread operator, you can easily pass an array to any function without worrying about the this binding of the function.

The addition of the name property should help you more easily identify functions for debugging and evaluation purposes. ECMAScript 6 also formally defines the behavior of block-level functions so they are no longer a syntax error in strict mode.

In ECMAScript 6, the behavior of a function is defined by [[Call]], normal function execution, and [[Construct]] when a function is called with new. The new.target metaproperty also allows you to determine if a function was called using new or not.

The biggest change to functions in ECMAScript 6 was the addition of arrow functions. Arrow functions are designed to be used in place of anonymous function expressions. Arrow functions have a more concise syntax, lexical this binding, and no arguments object. Additionally, arrow functions can't change their this binding and therefore can't be used as constructors.

Tail call optimization allows some function calls to be optimized to maintain a smaller call stack, use less memory, and prevent stack overflow errors. This optimization is applied by the engine automatically when it is safe to do so; however, you might decide to rewrite recursive functions to take advantage of this optimization.

4

EXPANDED OBJECT FUNCTIONALITY

ECMAScript 6 focuses heavily on making objects more useful, which makes sense because nearly every value in JavaScript is some type of object. The number of objects developers use in an average JavaScript program continues to increase as the complexity of JavaScript applications increases. With more objects in a program, it has become necessary to use them more effectively.

ECMAScript 6 improves the use of objects in a number of ways, from simple syntax extensions to options for manipulating and interacting with them, and this chapter covers those improvements in detail.

Object Categories

JavaScript uses different terminology to describe objects in the standard as opposed to those added by execution environments, such as the browser. The ECMAScript 6 specification has clear definitions for each object category. It's essential to understand this terminology to grasp the language as a whole. The object categories are:

Ordinary objects   Have all the default internal behaviors for objects in JavaScript.

Exotic objects   Have internal behavior that differs from the default in some way.

Standard objects   Defined by ECMAScript 6, such as Array, Date, and so on. Standard objects can be ordinary or exotic.

Built-in objects   Present in a JavaScript execution environment when a script begins to execute. All standard objects are built-in objects.

I'll use these terms throughout the book to explain the various objects that ECMAScript 6 defines.

Object Literal Syntax Extensions

The object literal is one of the most popular patterns in JavaScript. JSON is built on its syntax, and it's in nearly every JavaScript file on the Internet. The object literal's popularity is due to its succinct syntax for creating objects that would otherwise take several lines of code to create. Fortunately for developers, ECMAScript 6 makes object literals more powerful and even more succinct by extending the syntax in several ways.

Property Initializer Shorthand

In ECMAScript 5 and earlier, object literals were simply collections of name-value pairs, meaning that some duplication could occur when property values are initialized. For example:

```
function createPerson(name, age) {
    return {
        name: name,
        age: age
    };
}
```

The createPerson() function creates an object whose property names are the same as the function parameter names. The result appears to be the duplication of name and age, even though one is the name of an object property and the other provides the value of that property. The key name in the returned object is assigned the value contained in the variable name, and the key age in the returned object is assigned the value contained in the variable age.

In ECMAScript 6, you can eliminate the duplication that exists around property names and local variables by using the *property initializer* shorthand syntax. When an object property name is the same as the local variable name, you can simply include the name without a colon and value. For example, createPerson() can be rewritten for ECMAScript 6 as follows:

```
function createPerson(name, age) {
    return {
        name,
        age
    };
}
```

When a property in an object literal only has a name, the JavaScript engine looks in the surrounding scope for a variable of the same name. If it finds one, that variable's value is assigned to the same name on the object literal. In this example, the object literal property name is assigned the value of the local variable name.

Shorthand property syntax makes object literal initialization even more succinct and helps to eliminate naming errors. Assigning a property with the same name as a local variable is a very common pattern in JavaScript, making this extension a welcome addition.

Concise Methods

ECMAScript 6 also improves the syntax for assigning methods to object literals. In ECMAScript 5 and earlier, you must specify a name and then the full function definition to add a method to an object, as follows:

```
var person = {
    name: "Nicholas",
    sayName: function() {
        console.log(this.name);
    }
};
```

In ECMAScript 6, the syntax is made more concise by eliminating the colon and the function keyword. That means you can rewrite the example like this:

```
var person = {
    name: "Nicholas",
    sayName() {
        console.log(this.name);
    }
};
```

This shorthand syntax, also called *concise method* syntax, creates a method on the person object just as the previous example did. The sayName() property is assigned an anonymous function expression and has all the same characteristics as the ECMAScript 5 sayName() function. The one difference is that concise methods can use super (discussed in "Easy Prototype Access with Super References" on page 77), whereas the non-concise methods cannot.

The name property of a method created using concise method shorthand is the name used before the parentheses. In this example, the name property for person.sayName() is "sayName".

Computed Property Names

ECMAScript 5 and earlier could compute property names on object instances when those properties were set with square brackets instead of dot notation. The square brackets allow you to specify property names using variables and string literals that might contain characters that would cause a syntax error if they were used in an identifier. Here's an example:

```
var person = {},
    lastName = "last name";

person["first name"] = "Nicholas";
person[lastName] = "Zakas";

console.log(person["first name"]);    // "Nicholas"
console.log(person[lastName]);        // "Zakas"
```

Because lastName is assigned a value of "last name", both property names in this example use a space, making it impossible to reference them using dot notation. However, bracket notation allows any string value to be used as a property name, so assigning "first name" to "Nicholas" and "last name" to "Zakas" works.

Additionally, you can use string literals directly as property names in object literals, like this:

```
var person = {
    "first name": "Nicholas"
};

console.log(person["first name"]);    // "Nicholas"
```

This pattern works for property names that are known ahead of time and can be represented with a string literal. However, if the property name "first name" were contained in a variable (as in the previous example) or had to be calculated, there would be no way to define that property using an object literal in ECMAScript 5.

In ECMAScript 6, computed property names are part of the object literal syntax, and they use the same square bracket notation that has been used to reference computed property names in object instances. For example:

```
let lastName = "last name";

let person = {
    "first name": "Nicholas",
    [lastName]: "Zakas"
};

console.log(person["first name"]);     // "Nicholas"
console.log(person[lastName]);         // "Zakas"
```

The square brackets inside the object literal indicate that the property name is computed, so its contents are evaluated as a string. That means you can also include expressions, such as the following:

```
var suffix = " name";

var person = {
    ["first" + suffix]: "Nicholas",
    ["last" + suffix]: "Zakas"
};

console.log(person["first name"]);     // "Nicholas"
console.log(person["last name"]);      // "Zakas"
```

These properties evaluate to "first name" and "last name", and you can use those strings to reference the properties later. Anything you would put inside square brackets while using bracket notation on object instances will also work for computed property names inside object literals.

New Methods

One of the design goals of ECMAScript, beginning with ECMAScript 5, was to avoid both creating new global functions and creating methods on Object.prototype. Instead, when the developers want to add new methods to the standard, they make those methods available on an appropriate existing object. As a result, the Object global has received an increasing number of methods when no other objects are more appropriate. ECMAScript 6 introduces a couple of new methods on the Object global that are designed to make certain tasks easier.

The Object.is() Method

When you want to compare two values in JavaScript, you're probably used to using either the equals operator (==) or the identically equals operator (===). Many developers prefer the latter to avoid type coercion during comparison. But even the identically equals operator isn't entirely accurate. For example, the values +0 and –0 are considered equal by ===, even though they're represented differently in the JavaScript engine. Also, NaN === NaN returns false, which necessitates using isNaN() to detect NaN properly.

ECMAScript 6 introduces the Object.is() method to remedy the remaining inaccuracies of the identically equals operator. This method accepts two arguments and returns true if the values are equivalent. Two values are considered equivalent when they're the same type and have the same value. Here are some examples:

```
console.log(+0 == -0);              // true
console.log(+0 === -0);             // true
console.log(Object.is(+0, -0));     // false

console.log(NaN == NaN);            // false
console.log(NaN === NaN);           // false
console.log(Object.is(NaN, NaN));   // true

console.log(5 == 5);                // true
console.log(5 == "5");              // true
console.log(5 === 5);               // true
console.log(5 === "5");             // false
console.log(Object.is(5, 5));       // true
console.log(Object.is(5, "5"));     // false
```

In many cases, Object.is() works the same as the === operator. The only differences are that +0 and –0 are considered not equivalent, and NaN is considered equivalent to NaN. But there's no need to stop using equality operators. Choose whether to use Object.is() instead of == or === based on how those special cases affect your code.

The Object.assign() Method

Mixins are among the most popular patterns for object composition in JavaScript. In a mixin, one object receives properties and methods from another object. Many JavaScript libraries have a mixin method similar to this:

```
function mixin(receiver, supplier) {
    Object.keys(supplier).forEach(function(key) {
        receiver[key] = supplier[key];
    });

    return receiver;
}
```

The `mixin()` function iterates over the own properties of supplier and copies them onto receiver (a shallow copy, where object references are shared when property values are objects). This allows the receiver to gain new properties without inheritance, as in this code:

```
function EventTarget() { /*...*/ }
EventTarget.prototype = {
    constructor: EventTarget,
    emit: function() { /*...*/ },
    on: function() { /*...*/ }
};

var myObject = {};
mixin(myObject, EventTarget.prototype);

myObject.emit("somethingChanged");
```

Here, `myObject` receives behavior from the `EventTarget.prototype` object. This gives `myObject` the ability to publish events and subscribe to them using the `emit()` and `on()` methods, respectively.

This mixin pattern became popular enough that ECMAScript 6 added the `Object.assign()` method, which behaves the same way, accepting a receiver and any number of suppliers and then returning the receiver. The name change from `mixin()` to `assign()` reflects the actual operation that occurs. Because the `mixin()` function uses the assignment operator (=), it cannot copy accessor properties to the receiver as accessor properties. The name `Object.assign()` was chosen to reflect this distinction.

NOTE *Similar methods in various libraries might have other names for the same basic functionality; popular alternates include the `extend()` and `mix()` methods. In addition to the `Object.assign()` method, an `Object.mixin()` method was briefly added in ECMAScript 6. The primary difference was that `Object.mixin()` also copied over accessor properties, but the method was removed due to concerns over the use of `super` (discussed in "Easy Prototype Access with Super References" on page 77).*

You can use `Object.assign()` anywhere you would have used the `mixin()` function. Here's an example:

```
function EventTarget() { /*...*/ }
EventTarget.prototype = {
    constructor: EventTarget,
    emit: function() { /*...*/ },
    on: function() { /*...*/ }
}

var myObject = {}
Object.assign(myObject, EventTarget.prototype);

myObject.emit("somethingChanged");
```

The `Object.assign()` method accepts any number of suppliers, and the receiver receives the properties in the order in which the suppliers are specified. That means the second supplier might overwrite a value from the first supplier on the receiver, which is what happens in this code snippet:

```
var receiver = {};

Object.assign(receiver,
    {
        type: "js",
        name: "file.js"
    },
    {
        type: "css"
    }
);

console.log(receiver.type);     // "css"
console.log(receiver.name);     // "file.js"
```

The value of `receiver.type` is `"css"` because the second supplier overwrote the value of the first.

The `Object.assign()` method isn't a significant addition to ECMAScript 6, but it does formalize a common function found in many JavaScript libraries.

WORKING WITH ACCESSOR PROPERTIES

Keep in mind that `Object.assign()` doesn't create accessor properties on the receiver when a supplier has accessor properties. Because `Object.assign()` uses the assignment operator, an accessor property on a supplier will become a data property on the receiver. For example:

```
var receiver = {},
    supplier = {
        get name() {
            return "file.js"
        }
    };

Object.assign(receiver, supplier);

var descriptor = Object.getOwnPropertyDescriptor(receiver, "name");

console.log(descriptor.value);      // "file.js"
console.log(descriptor.get);        // undefined
```

In this code, the supplier has an accessor property called name. After using the `Object.assign()` method, `receiver.name` exists as a data property with a value of `"file.js"` because `supplier.name` returned `"file.js"` when `Object.assign()` was called.

Duplicate Object Literal Properties

ECMAScript 5 strict mode introduced a check for duplicate object literal properties that would throw an error if a duplicate was found. For example, this code was problematic:

```
"use strict";

var person = {
    name: "Nicholas",
    name: "Greg"        // syntax error in ES5 strict mode
};
```

When running in ECMAScript 5 strict mode, the second `name` property causes a syntax error. But in ECMAScript 6, the duplicate property check was removed. Strict and non-strict mode code no longer check for duplicate properties. Instead, the last property of the given name becomes the property's actual value, as shown here:

```
"use strict";

var person = {
    name: "Nicholas",
    name: "Greg"        // no error in ES6 strict mode
};

console.log(person.name);        // "Greg"
```

In this example, the value of `person.name` is `"Greg"` because that's the last value assigned to the property.

Own Property Enumeration Order

ECMAScript 5 didn't define the enumeration order of object properties; the JavaScript engine vendors did. However, ECMAScript 6 strictly defines the order in which own properties must be returned when they're enumerated. This affects how properties are returned using `Object.getOwnPropertyNames()` and `Reflect.ownKeys` (covered in Chapter 12). It also affects the order in which properties are processed by `Object.assign()`.

The basic order for own property enumeration is:

1. All numeric keys in ascending order
2. All string keys in the order in which they were added to the object
3. All symbol keys (covered in Chapter 6) in the order in which they were added to the object

Here's an example:

```
var obj = {
    a: 1,
```

```
    0: 1,
    c: 1,
    2: 1,
    b: 1,
    1: 1
};

obj.d = 1;

console.log(Object.getOwnPropertyNames(obj).join(""));    // "012acbd"
```

The Object.getOwnPropertyNames() method returns the properties in obj in the order 0, 1, 2, a, c, b, d. Note that the numeric keys are grouped together and sorted, even though they appear out of order in the object literal. The string keys come after the numeric keys and appear in the order in which they were added to obj. The keys in the object literal come first, followed by any dynamic keys that were added later (in this case, d).

NOTE   *The for-in loop still has an unspecified enumeration order because not all JavaScript engines implement it the same way. The Object.keys() method and JSON.stringify() are both specified to use the same (unspecified) enumeration order as for-in.*

Although enumeration order is a subtle change to how JavaScript works, it's not uncommon to find programs that rely on a specific enumeration order to work correctly. ECMAScript 6, by defining the enumeration order, ensures that JavaScript code relying on enumeration will work correctly regardless of where it is executed.

Enhancements for Prototypes

Prototypes are the foundation of inheritance in JavaScript, and ECMAScript 6 continues to make prototypes more useful. Early versions of JavaScript severely limited what you could do with prototypes. However, as the language matured and developers became more familiar with how prototypes work, it became clear that developers wanted more control over prototypes and easier ways to work with them. As a result, ECMAScript 6 introduced some improvements to prototypes.

Changing an Object's Prototype

Normally, an object's prototype is specified when the object is created, via either a constructor or the Object.create() method. The idea that an object's prototype remains unchanged after instantiation was one of the predominant assumptions in JavaScript programming through ECMAScript 5. ECMAScript 5 did add the Object.getPrototypeOf() method for retrieving the prototype of any given object, but it still lacked a standard way to change an object's prototype after instantiation.

ECMAScript 6 changes that assumption with the addition of the Object.setPrototypeOf() method, which allows you to change the prototype of any given object. The `Object.setPrototypeOf()` method accepts two arguments: the object whose prototype should change and the object that should become the first argument's prototype. For example:

```
let person = {
    getGreeting() {
        return "Hello";
    }
};

let dog = {
    getGreeting() {
        return "Woof";
    }
};

// prototype is person
let friend = Object.create(person);
console.log(friend.getGreeting());                   // "Hello"
console.log(Object.getPrototypeOf(friend) === person); // true

// set prototype to dog
Object.setPrototypeOf(friend, dog);
console.log(friend.getGreeting());                   // "Woof"
console.log(Object.getPrototypeOf(friend) === dog);  // true
```

This code defines two base objects: person and dog. Both objects have a getGreeting() method that returns a string. The object friend first inherits from the person object, meaning that getGreeting() outputs "Hello". When the prototype becomes the dog object, person.getGreeting() outputs "Woof" because the original relationship to person is broken.

The actual value of an object's prototype is stored in an internal-only property called [[Prototype]]. The Object.getPrototypeOf() method returns the value stored in [[Prototype]] and Object.setPrototypeOf() changes the value stored in [[Prototype]]. However, these aren't the only ways to work with the [[Prototype]] value.

Easy Prototype Access with Super References

As previously mentioned, prototypes are very important in JavaScript, and a lot of work went into making them easier to use in ECMAScript 6. Another improvement is the introduction of super references, which make accessing functionality on an object's prototype easier. For example, to override a method on an object instance so it also calls the prototype method of the same name, you'd do the following in ECMAScript 5:

```
let person = {
    getGreeting() {
        return "Hello";
    }
};
```

```
let dog = {
    getGreeting() {
        return "Woof";
    }
};
```

```
let friend = {
    getGreeting() {
        return Object.getPrototypeOf(this).getGreeting.call(this) + ", hi!";
    }
};
```

```
// set prototype to person
Object.setPrototypeOf(friend, person);
console.log(friend.getGreeting());                  // "Hello, hi!"
console.log(Object.getPrototypeOf(friend) === person);  // true

// set prototype to dog
Object.setPrototypeOf(friend, dog);
console.log(friend.getGreeting());                  // "Woof, hi!"
console.log(Object.getPrototypeOf(friend) === dog);     // true
```

In this example, getGreeting() on friend calls the prototype method of the same name. The Object.getPrototypeOf() method ensures the correct prototype is called, and then an additional string is appended to the output. The additional .call(this) ensures that the this value inside the prototype method is set correctly.

Remembering to use Object.getPrototypeOf() and .call(this) to call a method on the prototype is a bit involved, so ECMAScript 6 introduced super. At its simplest, super is a pointer to the current object's prototype, effectively the Object.getPrototypeOf(this) value. Knowing that, you can simplify the getGreeting() method as follows:

```
let friend = {
    getGreeting() {
        // in the previous example, this is the same as:
        // Object.getPrototypeOf(this).getGreeting.call(this)
        return super.getGreeting() + ", hi!";
    }
};
```

The call to super.getGreeting() is the same as Object.getPrototypeOf(this) .getGreeting.call(this) in this context. Similarly, you can call any method on an object's prototype by using a super reference, as long as it's inside a concise method. Attempting to use super outside of concise methods results in a syntax error, as in this example:

```
let friend = {
    getGreeting: function() {
```

```
        // syntax error
        return super.getGreeting() + ", hi!";
    }
};
```

This example uses a named property with a function, and the call to super.getGreeting() results in a syntax error because super is invalid in this context.

The super reference is really helpful when you have multiple levels of inheritance, because in that case, Object.getPrototypeOf() no longer works in all circumstances. For example:

```
let person = {
    getGreeting() {
        return "Hello";
    }
};

// prototype is person
let friend = {
    getGreeting() {
        return Object.getPrototypeOf(this).getGreeting.call(this) + ", hi!";
    }
};
Object.setPrototypeOf(friend, person);


// prototype is friend
let relative = Object.create(friend);

console.log(person.getGreeting());          // "Hello"
console.log(friend.getGreeting());          // "Hello, hi!"
console.log(relative.getGreeting());        // error!
```

When relative.getGreeting() is called, the call to Object.getPrototypeOf() results in an error. The reason is that this is relative, and the prototype of relative is the friend object. When friend.getGreeting().call() is called with relative as this, the process starts over again and continues to call recursively until a stack overflow error occurs.

This problem is difficult to solve in ECMAScript 5, but with ECMAScript 6 and super, it's easy:

```
let person = {
    getGreeting() {
        return "Hello";
    }
};

// prototype is person
let friend = {
    getGreeting() {
        return super.getGreeting() + ", hi!";
```

```
    }
};
Object.setPrototypeOf(friend, person);

// prototype is friend
let relative = Object.create(friend);

console.log(person.getGreeting());        // "Hello"
console.log(friend.getGreeting());        // "Hello, hi!"
console.log(relative.getGreeting());      // "Hello, hi!"
```

Because super references are not dynamic, they always refer to the correct object. In this case, super.getGreeting() always refers to person.getGreeting() regardless of how many other objects inherit the method.

A Formal Method Definition

Prior to ECMAScript 6, the concept of a "method" wasn't formally defined. Methods were just object properties that contained functions instead of data. ECMAScript 6 formally defines a method as a function that has an internal [[HomeObject]] property containing the object to which the method belongs. Consider the following:

```
let person = {

    // method
    getGreeting() {
        return "Hello";
    }
};

// not a method
function shareGreeting() {
    return "Hi!";
}
```

This code example defines person with a single method called getGreeting(). The [[HomeObject]] for getGreeting() is person by virtue of assigning the function directly to an object. However, the shareGreeting() function has no [[HomeObject]] specified because it wasn't assigned to an object when it was created. In most cases, this difference isn't important, but it becomes very important when using super references.

Any reference to super uses the [[HomeObject]] to determine what to do. The first step in the process is to call Object.getPrototypeOf() on the [[HomeObject]] to retrieve a reference to the prototype. Next, the prototype is searched for a function with the same name. Then, the this binding is set and the method is called. Take a look at the following example.

```
let person = {
    getGreeting() {
        return "Hello";
    }
};

// prototype is person
let friend = {
    getGreeting() {
        return super.getGreeting() + ", hi!";
    }
};
Object.setPrototypeOf(friend, person);

console.log(friend.getGreeting());  // "Hello, hi!"
```

Calling `friend.getGreeting()` returns a string, which combines the value from `person.getGreeting()` with ", hi!". The [[HomeObject]] of `friend.getGreeting()` is friend, and the prototype of friend is person, so `super.getGreeting()` is equivalent to `person.getGreeting.call(this)`.

Summary

Objects are the center of JavaScript programming, and ECMAScript 6 makes some helpful changes to objects that make them easier to work with and more flexible.

ECMAScript 6 makes several changes to object literals. Shorthand property definitions make assigning properties with the same names as in-scope variables simpler. Computed property names allow you to specify non-literal values as property names, which you've been able to do in other areas of the language. Shorthand methods let you type far fewer characters to define methods on object literals by completely omitting the colon and `function` keyword. ECMAScript 6 loosens the strict mode check for duplicate object literal property names as well, meaning two properties with the same name can be in a single object literal without throwing an error.

The `Object.assign()` method makes it easier to change multiple properties on a single object at once and is very useful when you use the mixin pattern. The `Object.is()` method performs strict equality on any value, effectively becoming a safer version of === when you're working with special JavaScript values.

ECMAScript 6 clearly defines enumeration order for own properties. Numeric keys always come first in ascending order followed by string keys in insertion order and symbol keys in insertion order.

It's now possible to modify an object's prototype after it's been created thanks to ECMAScript 6's `Object.setPrototypeOf()` method.

In addition, you can use the `super` keyword to call methods on an object's prototype. The `this` binding inside a method invoked using `super` is set up to automatically work with the current value of this.

5

DESTRUCTURING FOR EASIER DATA ACCESS

Object and array literals are two of the most frequently used notations in JavaScript, and thanks to the popular JSON data format, they have become a particularly important part of the language. It's quite common to define objects and arrays, and then systematically pull out relevant pieces of information from those structures. ECMAScript 6 simplifies this task by adding *destructuring*, which is the process of breaking down a data structure into smaller parts. This chapter shows you how to harness destructuring for objects and arrays.

Why Is Destructuring Useful?

In ECMAScript 5 and earlier, the need to fetch information from objects and arrays could result in a lot of duplicate code to get certain data into local variables.

For example:

```
let options = {
    repeat: true,
    save: false
};

// extract data from the object
let repeat = options.repeat,
    save = options.save;
```

This code extracts the values of repeat and save from the options object, and stores that data in local variables with the same names. Although this code looks simple, imagine if you had a large number of variables to assign: you would have to assign them all one by one. And if you had to traverse a nested data structure to find the information instead, you might have to dig through the entire structure just to find one piece of data.

That's why ECMAScript 6 adds destructuring for objects *and* arrays. When you break down a data structure into smaller parts, getting the information you need from it becomes much easier. Many languages implement destructuring with a minimal amount of syntax to make the process simpler to use. The ECMAScript 6 implementation actually uses syntax you're already familiar with: the syntax for object and array literals.

Object Destructuring

Object destructuring syntax uses an object literal on the left side of an assignment operation. For example:

```
let node = {
    type: "Identifier",
    name: "foo"
};

let { type, name } = node;

console.log(type);      // "Identifier"
console.log(name);      // "foo"
```

In this code, the value of node.type is stored in a variable called type, and the value of node.name is stored in a variable called name. This syntax is the same as the object literal property initializer shorthand introduced in Chapter 4. The identifiers type and name are both declarations of local variables and the properties to read the value from on the node object.

Destructuring Assignment

The object destructuring examples you've seen so far have used variable declarations. However, it's also possible to use destructuring in assignments. For instance, you might decide to change the values of variables after they're defined, as follows:

```
let node = {
    type: "Identifier",
    name: "foo"
},
type = "Literal",
name = 5;

// assign different values using destructuring
({ type, name } = node);

console.log(type);      // "Identifier"
console.log(name);      // "foo"
```

In this example, type and name are initialized with values when declared, and then two variables with the same names are initialized with different values. The next line uses destructuring assignments to change those values by reading from the node object. Note that you must put parentheses around a destructuring assignment statement. The reason is that an opening curly brace is expected to be a block statement, and a block statement cannot appear on the left side of an assignment. The parentheses signal that the next curly brace is not a block statement and should be interpreted as an expression, allowing the assignment to complete.

A destructuring assignment expression evaluates to the right side of the expression (after the =). That means you can use a destructuring assignment expression anywhere a value is expected. For instance, consider this example, which passes a value to a function:

```
let node = {
        type: "Identifier",
        name: "foo"
    },
    type = "Literal",
    name = 5;

function outputInfo(value) {
    console.log(value === node);        // true
}

outputInfo({ type, name } = node);

console.log(type);      // "Identifier"
console.log(name);      // "foo"
```

The outputInfo() function is called with a destructuring assignment expression. The expression evaluates to node because that is the value of the right side of the expression. The assignments to type and name behave normally, and node is passed to the outputInfo() function.

NOTE   *An error is thrown when the right side of the destructuring assignment expression (the expression after =) evaluates to null or undefined. This happens because any attempt to read a property of null or undefined results in a runtime error.*

Default Values

When you use a destructuring assignment statement and you specify a local variable with a property name that doesn't exist on the object, that local variable is assigned a value of undefined. For example:

```
let node = {
    type: "Identifier",
    name: "foo"
};

let { type, name, value } = node;

console.log(type);      // "Identifier"
console.log(name);      // "foo"
console.log(value);     // undefined
```

This code defines an additional local variable called value and attempts to assign it a value. However, no corresponding value property is on the node object, so the variable is assigned the value of undefined as expected.

You can optionally define a default value to use when a specified property doesn't exist. To do so, insert an equal sign (=) after the property name and specify the default value, like this:

```
let node = {
    type: "Identifier",
    name: "foo"
};

let { type, name, value = true } = node;

console.log(type);      // "Identifier"
console.log(name);      // "foo"
console.log(value);     // true
```

In this example, the variable value is given true as a default value. The default value is only used if the property is missing on node or has a value of undefined. Because no node.value property exists, the variable value uses the default value. This works similarly to the default parameter values for functions, as discussed in Chapter 3.

Assigning to Different Local Variable Names

Up to this point, each destructuring assignment example has used the object property name as the local variable name; for example, the value of node.type was stored in a type variable. That works well when you want to use the same name, but what if you don't? ECMAScript 6 has an extended syntax that allows you to assign to a local variable with a different name, and that syntax looks like the object literal non-shorthand property initializer syntax. Here's an example:

```
let node = {
    type: "Identifier",
    name: "foo"
};

let { type: localType, name: localName } = node;

console.log(localType);     // "Identifier"
console.log(localName);     // "foo"
```

This code uses destructuring assignments to declare the localType and localName variables, which contain the values from the node.type and node.name properties, respectively. The syntax type: localType reads the property named type and stores its value in the localType variable. This syntax is effectively the opposite of traditional object literal syntax, where the name is on the left of the colon and the value is on the right. In this case, the name is on the right of the colon and the location of the value to read is on the left.

You can add default values when you're using a different variable name, as well. The equal sign and default value are still placed after the local variable name. For example:

```
let node = {
    type: "Identifier"
};

let { type: localType, name: localName = "bar" } = node;

console.log(localType);     // "Identifier"
console.log(localName);     // "bar"
```

Here, the localName variable has a default value of "bar". The variable is assigned its default value because no node.name property exists.

So far, you've learned how to use object destructuring on an object whose properties are primitive values. You can also use object destructuring to retrieve values in nested object structures.

Nested Object Destructuring

By using syntax similar to that of object literals, you can navigate into a nested object structure to retrieve just the information you want. Here's an example:

```
let node = {
    type: "Identifier",
    name: "foo",
    loc: {
        start: {
            line: 1,
            column: 1
        },
        end: {
            line: 1,
            column: 4
        }
    }
};

let { loc: { start }} = node;

console.log(start.line);        // 1
console.log(start.column);      // 1
```

The destructuring pattern in this example uses curly braces to indicate that the pattern should descend into the property named loc on node and look for the start property. Recall from the previous section that a colon in a destructuring pattern means the identifier before the colon is giving a location to inspect, and the right side assigns a value. A curly brace after the colon indicates that the destination is nested another level into the object.

You can go one step further and use a different name for the local variable as well:

```
let node = {
    type: "Identifier",
    name: "foo",
    loc: {
        start: {
            line: 1,
            column: 1
        },
        end: {
            line: 1,
            column: 4
        }
    }
};

// extract node.loc.start
let { loc: { start: localStart }} = node;

console.log(localStart.line);    // 1
console.log(localStart.column); // 1
```

In this version of the code, `node.loc.start` is stored in a new local variable called `localStart`. Destructuring patterns can be nested to an arbitrary level of depth, and all capabilities will be available at each level.

Object destructuring is very powerful because it provides you with lots of options, but array destructuring offers some unique capabilities that allow you to extract information from arrays.

SYNTAX GOTCHA

Be careful when you're using nested destructuring because you can inadvertently create a statement that has no effect. Empty curly braces are legal in object destructuring; however, they don't do anything. For example:

```
// no variables declared!
let { loc: {} } = node;
```

No bindings are declared in this statement. Due to the curly braces on the right, `loc` is used as a location to inspect rather than a binding to create. In such cases, it's likely that the intent was to use = to define a default value rather than : to define a location. It's possible that this syntax will be made illegal in the future, but for now, this is a gotcha to look out for.

Array Destructuring

Array destructuring syntax is very similar to object destructuring: it just uses array literal syntax instead of object literal syntax. The destructuring operates on positions within an array rather than the named properties that are available in objects. For example:

```
let colors = [ "red", "green", "blue" ];

let [ firstColor, secondColor ] = colors;

console.log(firstColor);        // "red"
console.log(secondColor);       // "green"
```

Here, array destructuring pulls out the values "red" and "green" from the colors array, and stores them in the firstColor and secondColor variables. Those values are chosen because of their position in the array; the actual variable names could be anything. Any items not explicitly mentioned in the destructuring pattern are ignored. Keep in mind that the array isn't changed in any way.

You can also omit items in the destructuring pattern and only provide variable names for the items you're interested in. If, for example, you just want the third value of an array, you don't need to supply variable names for the first and second items. Here's how that works:

```
let colors = [ "red", "green", "blue" ];

let [ , , thirdColor ] = colors;

console.log(thirdColor);        // "blue"
```

This code uses a destructuring assignment to retrieve the third item in colors. The commas preceding thirdColor in the pattern are placeholders for the array items that come before it. By using this approach, you can easily pick out values from any number of slots in the middle of an array without needing to provide variable names for them.

NOTE   *Similar to object destructuring, you must always provide an initializer when using array destructuring with var, let, or const.*

Destructuring Assignment

You can use array destructuring in the context of an assignment, but unlike object destructuring, there is no need to wrap the expression in parentheses. Consider the following example.

```
let colors = [ "red", "green", "blue" ],
    firstColor = "black",
    secondColor = "purple";

[ firstColor, secondColor ] = colors;

console.log(firstColor);      // "red"
console.log(secondColor);     // "green"
```

The destructured assignment in this code works in a similar manner
to the previous array destructuring example. The only difference is that
firstColor and secondColor have already been defined. Most of the time, what
you know now about array destructuring assignment is all you'll need to
know, but there's a bit more to it that you'll probably find useful.

Array destructuring assignment has a very unique use case that makes
it easier to swap the values of two variables. Value swapping is a common
operation in sorting algorithms, and the ECMAScript 5 way of swapping
variables involves a third, temporary variable, as in this example:

```
// swapping variables in ECMAScript 5
let a = 1,
    b = 2,
    tmp;

tmp = a;
a = b;
b = tmp;

console.log(a);     // 2
console.log(b);     // 1
```

The intermediate variable tmp is necessary to swap the values of a and
b. However, using array destructuring assignment, there's no need for that
extra variable. Here's how you can swap variables in ECMAScript 6:

```
// swapping variables in ECMAScript 6
let a = 1,
    b = 2;

[ a, b ] = [ b, a ];

console.log(a);     // 2
console.log(b);     // 1
```

The array destructuring assignment in this example looks like a mirror
image. The left side of the assignment (before the equal sign) is a destructuring pattern just like those in the other array destructuring examples.
The right side is an array literal that is temporarily created for the swap. The

destructuring happens on the temporary array, which has the values of b and a copied into its first and second positions. The effect is that the variables have swapped values.

NOTE   *Like object destructuring assignment, an error is thrown when the right side of an array destructured assignment expression evaluates to null or undefined.*

Default Values

Array destructuring assignment allows you to specify a default value for any position in the array, too. The default value is used when the property at the given position either doesn't exist or has the value undefined. For example:

```
let colors = [ "red" ];

let [ firstColor, secondColor = "green" ] = colors;

console.log(firstColor);        // "red"
console.log(secondColor);       // "green"
```

In this code, the colors array has only one item, so there is nothing for secondColor to match. Because there is a default value, secondColor is set to "green" instead of undefined.

Nested Array Destructuring

You can destructure nested arrays in a manner similar to destructuring nested objects. By inserting another array pattern into the overall pattern, the destructuring will descend into a nested array, like this:

```
let colors = [ "red", [ "green", "lightgreen" ], "blue" ];

// later

let [ firstColor, [ secondColor ] ] = colors;

console.log(firstColor);        // "red"
console.log(secondColor);       // "green"
```

Here, the secondColor variable refers to the "green" value inside the colors array. That item is contained within a second array, so the extra square brackets around secondColor in the destructuring pattern are necessary. As with objects, you can nest arrays arbitrarily deep.

Rest Items

Chapter 3 introduced rest parameters for functions, and array destructuring has a similar concept called *rest items*. Rest items use the ... syntax to assign the remaining items in an array to a particular variable. Take a look at the following example.

```
let colors = [ "red", "green", "blue" ];

let [ firstColor, ...restColors ] = colors;

console.log(firstColor);        // "red"
console.log(restColors.length); // 2
console.log(restColors[0]);     // "green"
console.log(restColors[1]);     // "blue"
```

The first item in colors is assigned to firstColor, and the rest are assigned into a new restColors array. Therefore, the restColors array has two items: "green" and "blue". Rest items are useful for extracting certain items from an array and keeping the rest available, but there's another helpful use.

A glaring omission from JavaScript arrays is the ability to easily create a clone. In ECMAScript 5, developers frequently used the concat() method as an easy way to clone an array. For example:

```
// cloning an array in ECMAScript 5
var colors = [ "red", "green", "blue" ];
var clonedColors = colors.concat();

console.log(clonedColors);      // "[red,green,blue]"
```

Although the concat() method is intended to concatenate two arrays, calling it without an argument returns a clone of the array. In ECMAScript 6, you can use rest items to achieve the same task through syntax intended to function that way. It works like this:

```
// cloning an array in ECMAScript 6
let colors = [ "red", "green", "blue" ];
let [ ...clonedColors ] = colors;

console.log(clonedColors);      // "[red,green,blue]"
```

In this example, rest items are used to copy values from the colors array into the clonedColors array. Although it's a matter of perception as to whether this technique makes the developer's intent clearer than using the concat() method, it's still a useful approach to be aware of.

NOTE *Rest items must be the last entry in the destructured array and cannot be followed by a comma. Including a comma after rest items is a syntax error.*

Mixed Destructuring

You can use object and array destructuring together to create more complex expressions. By doing so, you're able to extract just the pieces of information you want from any mixture of objects and arrays. Consider the following example.

```
let node = {
    type: "Identifier",
    name: "foo",
    loc: {
        start: {
            line: 1,
            column: 1
        },
        end: {
            line: 1,
            column: 4
        }
    },
    range: [0, 3]
};

let {
    loc: { start },
    range: [ startIndex ]
} = node;

console.log(start.line);        // 1
console.log(start.column);      // 1
console.log(startIndex);        // 0
```

This code extracts node.loc.start and node.range[0] into start and startIndex, respectively. Keep in mind that loc: and range: in the destructured pattern are just locations that correspond to properties in the node object. There is no part of node that cannot be extracted using destructuring when you use a mix of object and array destructuring. This approach is particularly useful for pulling values out of JSON configuration structures without navigating the entire structure.

Destructured Parameters

Destructuring has one more particularly helpful use case and that is when passing function arguments. When a JavaScript function takes a large number of optional parameters, one common pattern is to create an options object whose properties specify the additional parameters, like this:

```
// properties on options represent additional parameters
function setCookie(name, value, options) {

    options = options || {};

    let secure = options.secure,
        path = options.path,
        domain = options.domain,
        expires = options.expires;
```

```
    // code to set the cookie
}

// third argument maps to options
setCookie("type", "js", {
    secure: true,
    expires: 60000
});
```

Many JavaScript libraries contain setCookie() functions that look similar to this one. In this function, the name and value arguments are required, but secure, path, domain, and expires are not. And because there is no priority order for the other data, it's efficient to just have an options object with named properties rather than list extra named parameters. This approach works, but now you can't tell what input the function expects just by looking at the function definition: you need to read the function body.

Destructured parameters offer an alternative that makes it clearer what arguments a function expects. A destructured parameter uses an object or array destructuring pattern in place of a named parameter. To see this in action, look at this rewritten version of the setCookie() function from the previous example:

```
function setCookie(name, value, { secure, path, domain, expires }) {

    // code to set the cookie
}

setCookie("type", "js", {
    secure: true,
    expires: 60000
});
```

This function behaves similarly to the previous example, but the third argument now uses destructuring to pull out the necessary data. The parameters outside the destructured parameter are clearly expected, and it's also clear to someone using setCookie() what options are available in terms of extra arguments. And of course, if the third argument is required, the values it should contain are crystal clear. The destructured parameters also act like regular parameters in that they are set to undefined if they're not passed.

NOTE   *Destructured parameters have all the capabilities of destructuring that you've learned so far in this chapter. You can use default values, mix object and array patterns, and use variable names that differ from the properties you're reading from.*

Destructured Parameters Are Required

One quirk of using destructured parameters is that, by default, an error is thrown when they're not provided in a function call. For instance, the following call to the setCookie() function from the previous example throws an error.

```
// error!
setCookie("type", "js");
```

The missing third argument evaluates to undefined as expected, causing an error because destructured parameters are just a shorthand for destructured declaration. When the setCookie() function is called, the JavaScript engine actually does this:

```
function setCookie(name, value, options) {

    let { secure, path, domain, expires } = options;

    // code to set the cookie
}
```

Because destructuring throws an error when the right side expression evaluates to null or undefined, it also throws an error when the third argument isn't passed to the setCookie() function.

If you want the destructured parameter to be required, this behavior isn't all that troubling. But if you want the destructured parameter to be optional, you can work around this behavior by providing a default value for the destructured parameter, like this:

```
function setCookie(name, value, { secure, path, domain, expires } = {}) {

    // empty
}
```

This example provides a new object as the default value for the third parameter. Providing a default value for the destructured parameter means that secure, path, domain, and expires will all be undefined if the third argument to setCookie() isn't provided, and no error will be thrown.

Default Values for Destructured Parameters

You can specify destructured default values for destructured parameters just as you would in destructured assignment. Just add the equal sign after the parameter and specify the default value. For example:

```
function setCookie(name, value,
    {
        secure = false,
        path = "/",
        domain = "example.com",
        expires = new Date(Date.now() + 360000000)
    } = {}
) {

    // empty
}
```

Each property in the destructured parameter has a default value in this code, so you can avoid checking to see if a given property has been included in order to use the correct value. Also, the entire destructured parameter has a default value of an empty object, making the parameter optional. This does make the function declaration look a bit more complicated than usual, but that's a small price to pay for ensuring each argument has a usable value.

Summary

Destructuring makes working with objects and arrays in JavaScript easier. Using the familiar object literal and array literal syntax, you can dissect data structures to get at the information you're interested in. Object patterns allow you to extract data from objects, and array patterns let you extract data from arrays.

Both object and array destructuring can specify default values for any property or item that is undefined, and both throw errors when the right side of an assignment evaluates to null or undefined. You can also navigate deeply nested data structures with object and array destructuring, descending to any arbitrary depth.

Destructuring declarations use var, let, or const to create variables and must always have an initializer. Destructuring assignments are used in place of other assignments and allow you to destructure into object properties and already existing variables.

Destructured parameters use the destructuring syntax to make options objects more transparent when used as function parameters. You can list all the actual data you're interested in along with other named parameters. Destructured parameters can be array patterns, object patterns, or a mixture, and you can use all the features of destructuring.

6

SYMBOLS AND
SYMBOL PROPERTIES

ECMAScript 6 introduces symbols as a primitive type. (The language already had five primitive types: strings, numbers, Booleans, null, and undefined.) Symbols began as a way to create private object members, a feature JavaScript developers wanted for a long time. Before symbols, any property with a string name was easy to access regardless of the obscurity of the name, and the *private names* feature was meant to let developers create non-string property names. That way, normal techniques for detecting these private names wouldn't work.

The private names proposal eventually evolved into ECMAScript 6 symbols, and this chapter teaches you how to use symbols effectively. Although symbols do add non-string values for property names, the goal of privacy was dropped. Instead, symbol properties are categorized separately from other object properties.

Creating Symbols

Symbols are unique among JavaScript primitives in that they don't have a literal form, like true for Booleans or 42 for numbers. You can create a symbol using the global Symbol function, as in this example:

```
let firstName = Symbol();
let person = {};

person[firstName] = "Nicholas";
console.log(person[firstName]);      // "Nicholas"
```

Here, the symbol firstName is created and used to assign a new property on the person object. When you use a symbol to assign a property, you must use that symbol each time you want to access the property. Be sure to name the symbol variable appropriately, so you can easily tell what the symbol represents.

NOTE   *Because symbols are primitive values, calling new Symbol() throws an error. You can create an instance of Symbol via new Object(yourSymbol) as well, but it's unclear when this capability would be useful.*

The Symbol function also accepts a description of the symbol as an optional argument. You cannot use the description to access the property, but I recommend always providing a description to make reading and debugging symbols easier. For example:

```
let firstName = Symbol("first name");
let person = {};

person[firstName] = "Nicholas";

console.log("first name" in person);      // false
console.log(person[firstName]);           // "Nicholas"
console.log(firstName);                    // "Symbol(first name)"
```

A symbol's description is stored internally in the [[Description]] property. This property is read whenever the symbol's toString() method is called either explicitly or implicitly. The firstName symbol's toString() method is called implicitly by console.log() in this example, so the description is printed to the log. It is not otherwise possible to access [[Description]] directly from code.

Using Symbols

You can use symbols anywhere you would use a computed property name. You've already seen bracket notation used with symbols in this chapter, but you can use symbols in computed object literal property names as well as with Object.defineProperty() and Object.defineProperties() calls:

```
let firstName = Symbol("first name");

// use a computed object literal property
let person = {
    [firstName]: "Nicholas"
};

// make the property read only
Object.defineProperty(person, firstName, { writable: false });

let lastName = Symbol("last name");

Object.defineProperties(person, {
    [lastName]: {
        value: "Zakas",
        writable: false
    }
});

console.log(person[firstName]);     // "Nicholas"
console.log(person[lastName]);      // "Zakas"
```

This example first uses a computed object literal property to create the firstName symbol property. The property is created as non-enumerable, which is different from computed properties created using non-symbol names. The following line then sets the property to be read-only. Later, a read-only `lastName` symbol property is created using the `Object.defineProperties()` method. A computed object literal property is used once again, but this time it's part of the second argument to the `Object.defineProperties()` call.

Although you can use symbols in any place that computed property names are allowed, you'll need to have a system for sharing these symbols between different pieces of code to use them effectively.

Sharing Symbols

At times, you might want different parts of your code to share symbols. For example, suppose you have two different object types in your application that should use the same symbol property to represent a unique identifier. Keeping track of symbols across files or large codebases can be difficult and error prone. For these reasons, ECMAScript 6 provides a global symbol registry that you can access at any time.

When you want to create a symbol to be shared, use the `Symbol.for()` method instead of calling the `Symbol()` method. The `Symbol.for()` method accepts a single parameter, which is a string identifier for the symbol you want to create. That parameter is also used as the symbol's description, as shown in this example:

```
let uid = Symbol.for("uid");
let object = {};

object[uid] = "12345";

console.log(object[uid]);       // "12345"
console.log(uid);               // "Symbol(uid)"
```

The `Symbol.for()` method first searches the global symbol registry to see whether a symbol with the key `"uid"` exists. If so, the method returns the existing symbol. If no such symbol exists, a new symbol is created and registered to the global symbol registry using the specified key. The new symbol is then returned.

Subsequent calls to `Symbol.for()` using the same key will return the same symbol, as follows:

```
let uid = Symbol.for("uid");
let object = {
    [uid]: "12345"
};

console.log(object[uid]);       // "12345"
console.log(uid);               // "Symbol(uid)"

let uid2 = Symbol.for("uid");
```

```
console.log(uid === uid2);        // true
console.log(object[uid2]);        // "12345"
console.log(uid2);                // "Symbol(uid)"
```

In this example, `uid` and `uid2` contain the same symbol and can be used interchangeably. The first call to `Symbol.for()` creates the symbol, and the second call retrieves the symbol from the global symbol registry.

Another unique aspect of shared symbols is that you can retrieve the key associated with a symbol in the global symbol registry by calling the `Symbol.keyFor()` method. For example:

```
let uid = Symbol.for("uid");
console.log(Symbol.keyFor(uid));      // "uid"

let uid2 = Symbol.for("uid");
console.log(Symbol.keyFor(uid2));     // "uid"

let uid3 = Symbol("uid");
console.log(Symbol.keyFor(uid3));     // undefined
```

Notice that both `uid` and `uid2` return the "uid" key. The symbol `uid3` doesn't exist in the global symbol registry, so it has no key associated with it and `Symbol.keyFor()` returns `undefined`.

NOTE *The global symbol registry is a shared environment, just like the global scope. That means you can't make assumptions about what is or is not already present in that environment. Use namespacing of symbol keys to reduce the likelihood of naming collisions when you're using third-party components. For example, jQuery code might use "jquery." to prefix all keys for keys like "jquery.element" or similar keys.*

Symbol Coercion

Type coercion is a significant part of JavaScript, and there's a lot of flexibility in the language's capability to coerce one data type into another. However, symbols are quite inflexible when it comes to coercion because other types lack a logical equivalent to a symbol. Specifically, symbols cannot be coerced into strings or numbers to prevent them from being accidentally used as properties that would otherwise be expected to behave as symbols.

The examples in this chapter have used `console.log()` to indicate the output for symbols, which works because `console.log()` calls `String()` on symbols to create useful output. You can use `String()` directly to get the same result. For instance:

```
let uid = Symbol.for("uid"),
    desc = String(uid);

console.log(desc);            // "Symbol(uid)"
```

The `String()` function calls `uid.toString()`, which returns the symbol's string description. However, if you try to concatenate the symbol directly with a string, an error is thrown:

```
var uid = Symbol.for("uid"),
    desc = uid + "";           // error!
```

Concatenating `uid` with an empty string requires that `uid` first be coerced into a string. An error is thrown when the coercion is detected, preventing its use in this manner.

Similarly, you cannot coerce a symbol to a number. All mathematical operators cause an error when they're applied to a symbol. For example:

```
var uid = Symbol.for("uid"),
    sum = uid / 1;            // error!
```

This example attempts to divide the symbol by 1, which causes an error. Errors are thrown regardless of the mathematical operator used (logical operators do not throw an error because all symbols are considered equivalent to true, just like any other non-empty value in JavaScript).

Retrieving Symbol Properties

The `Object.keys()` and `Object.getOwnPropertyNames()` methods can retrieve all property names in an object. The former method returns all enumerable property names, and the latter returns all properties regardless of enumerability. However, neither method returns symbol properties to preserve their ECMAScript 5 functionality. Instead, the `Object.getOwnPropertySymbols()` method was added in ECMAScript 6 to allow you to retrieve property symbols from an object.

The return value of `Object.getOwnPropertySymbols()` is an array of own property symbols, as shown here:

```
let uid = Symbol.for("uid");
let object = {
    [uid]: "12345"
};

let symbols = Object.getOwnPropertySymbols(object);

console.log(symbols.length);          // 1
console.log(symbols[0]);              // "Symbol(uid)"
console.log(object[symbols[0]]);      // "12345"
```

In this code, `object` has a single symbol property called `uid`. The array that `Object.getOwnPropertySymbols()` returns is an array containing just that symbol.

All objects start with zero own symbol properties, but objects can inherit symbol properties from their prototypes. ECMAScript 6 predefines several such properties that are implemented using *well-known symbols*.

Exposing Internal Operations with Well-Known Symbols

A central theme for ECMAScript 5 was exposing and defining some of the "magic" parts of JavaScript, the parts that developers couldn't emulate at the time. ECMAScript 6 carries on that tradition by exposing even more of the previously internal logic of the language, primarily by using symbol prototype properties to define the basic behavior of certain objects.

ECMAScript 6 has predefined symbols called *well-known symbols* that represent common behaviors in JavaScript that were previously considered internal-only operations. Each well-known symbol is represented by a property on the `Symbol` object, such as `Symbol.match`.

The well-known symbols are:

`Symbol.hasInstance`   A method used by `instanceof` to determine an object's inheritance

`Symbol.isConcatSpreadable`   A Boolean value indicating that `Array.prototype.concat()` should flatten the collection's elements if the collection is passed as a parameter to `Array.prototype.concat()`

`Symbol.iterator`   A method that returns an iterator (covered in Chapter 8)

`Symbol.match`   A method used by `String.prototype.match()` to compare strings

`Symbol.replace`   A method used by `String.prototype.replace()` to replace substrings

`Symbol.search`   A method used by `String.prototype.search()` to locate substrings

`Symbol.species`   The constructor for making derived classes (covered in Chapter 9)

`Symbol.split`   A method used by `String.prototype.split()` to split up strings

`Symbol.toPrimitive`   A method that returns a primitive value representation of an object

`Symbol.toStringTag`   A string used by `Object.prototype.toString()` to create an object description

`Symbol.unscopables`   An object whose properties are the names of object properties that should not be included in a `with` statement

Some commonly used well-known symbols are discussed in the following sections; others are discussed throughout the rest of the book to keep them in the correct context.

Overwriting a method defined with a well-known symbol changes an ordinary object to an exotic object because some internal default behavior is changed. There is no practical impact on your code as a result; the way the specification describes the object just changes.

The Symbol.hasInstance Method

Every function has a `Symbol.hasInstance` method that determines whether or not a given object is an instance of that function. The method is defined on `Function.prototype` so all functions inherit the default behavior for the `instanceof` property. The `Symbol.hasInstance` property is defined as nonwritable and nonconfigurable as well as nonenumerable to ensure it doesn't get overwritten by mistake.

The `Symbol.hasInstance` method accepts a single argument: the value to check. It returns `true` if the value passed is an instance of the function. To understand how `Symbol.hasInstance` works, consider the following:

```
obj instanceof Array;
```

This code is equivalent to the following:

```
Array[Symbol.hasInstance](obj);
```

ECMAScript 6 essentially redefined the `instanceof` operator as shorthand syntax for this method call. And now that a method call is involved, you can actually change how `instanceof` works.

For instance, suppose you want to define a function that claims no object as an instance. You can do so by hardcoding the return value of `Symbol.hasInstance` to false, such as:

```
function MyObject() {
    // empty
}

Object.defineProperty(MyObject, Symbol.hasInstance, {
    value: function(v) {
        return false;
    }
});

let obj = new MyObject();

console.log(obj instanceof MyObject);       // false
```

You must use `Object.defineProperty()` to overwrite a nonwritable property, so this example uses that method to overwrite the `Symbol.hasInstance` method with a new function. The new function always returns false, so even though obj is actually an instance of the `MyObject` class, the `instanceof` operator returns false after the `Object.defineProperty()` call.

Of course, you can also inspect the value and decide whether or not it should be considered an instance based on any arbitrary condition. For instance, maybe numbers with values between 1 and 100 should be considered instances of a special number type. To achieve that behavior, you might write code like this:

```
function SpecialNumber() {
    // empty
}

Object.defineProperty(SpecialNumber, Symbol.hasInstance, {
    value: function(v) {
        return (v instanceof Number) && (v >=1 && v <= 100);
    }
});

var two = new Number(2),
    zero = new Number(0);

console.log(two instanceof SpecialNumber);    // true
console.log(zero instanceof SpecialNumber);   // false
```

This code defines a `Symbol.hasInstance` method that returns `true` if the value is an instance of `Number` and also has a value between 1 and 100. Thus, `SpecialNumber` will claim `two` as an instance, even though no directly defined relationship exists between the `SpecialNumber` function and the `two` variable. Note that the left operand to `instanceof` must be an object to trigger the `Symbol.hasInstance` call, because nonobjects cause `instanceof` to simply return `false` all the time.

NOTE *You can also overwrite the default `Symbol.hasInstance` property for all built-in functions, such as the `Date` and `Error` functions. However, this isn't recommended because the effects on your code can be unexpected and confusing. It's best to only overwrite `Symbol.hasInstance` on your own functions and only when necessary.*

The Symbol.isConcatSpreadable Property

JavaScript arrays' `concat()` method is designed to concatenate two arrays together. Here's how to use that method:

```
let colors1 = [ "red", "green" ],
    colors2 = colors1.concat([ "blue", "black" ]);

console.log(colors2.length);    // 4
console.log(colors2);           // ["red","green","blue","black"]
```

This code concatenates a new array to the end of `colors1` and creates `colors2`, a single array with all items from both arrays. However, the `concat()`

method can also accept nonarray arguments; in that case, those arguments are simply added to the end of the array. For example:

```
let colors1 = [ "red", "green" ],
    colors2 = colors1.concat([ "blue", "black" ], "brown");

console.log(colors2.length);    // 5
console.log(colors2);           // ["red","green","blue","black","brown"]
```

Here, the extra argument "brown" is passed to concat() and becomes the fifth item in the colors2 array. Why is an array argument treated differently than a string argument? The JavaScript specification states that arrays are automatically split into their individual items and all other types are not. Prior to ECMAScript 6, there was no way to adjust this behavior.

The Symbol.isConcatSpreadable property is a Boolean value, which indicates that an object has a length property and numeric keys, and that its numeric property values should be added individually to the result of a concat() call. Unlike other well-known symbols, this symbol property doesn't appear on any standard objects by default. Instead, the symbol is available as a way to augment how concat() works on certain types of objects, effectively short-circuiting the default behavior. You can define any type to behave like arrays do in a concat() call, like this:

```
let collection = {
    0: "Hello",
    1: "world",
    length: 2,
    [Symbol.isConcatSpreadable]: true
};

let messages = [ "Hi" ].concat(collection);

console.log(messages.length);    // 3
console.log(messages);           // ["hi","Hello","world"]
```

The collection object in this example is set up to look like an array: it has a length property and two numeric keys. The Symbol.isConcatSpreadable property is set to true to indicate that the property values should be added as individual items to an array. When collection is passed to the concat() method, the resulting array has "Hello" and "world" as separate items after the "hi" element.

NOTE   *You can also set* Symbol.isConcatSpreadable *to false on derived array classes to prevent items from being separated by* concat() *calls. See "Inheritance with Derived Classes" on page 178.*

The Symbol.match, Symbol.replace, Symbol.search, and Symbol.split Properties

Strings and regular expressions have always had a close relationship in JavaScript. In particular, the string type has several methods that accept regular expressions as arguments:

`match(regex)`   Determines whether the given string matches a regular expression

`replace(regex, replacement)`   Replaces regular expression matches with a *replacement*

`search(regex)`   Locates a regular expression match inside the string

`split(regex)`   Splits a string into an array on a regular expression match

The way these methods interacted with regular expressions was hidden from developers prior to ECMAScript 6, leaving no way to mimic regular expressions using developer-defined objects. ECMAScript 6 defines four symbols that correspond to these four methods, effectively outsourcing the native behavior to the `RegExp` built-in object.

The `Symbol.match`, `Symbol.replace`, `Symbol.search`, and `Symbol.split` symbols represent methods on the regular expression argument that should be called on the first argument to the `match()` method, the `replace()` method, the `search()` method, and the `split()` method, respectively. The four symbol properties are defined on `RegExp.prototype` as the default implementation that the string methods should use.

Knowing this, you can create an object to use with the string methods in a way that is similar to regular expressions. To do so, you can use the following symbol functions in code:

`Symbol.match`   Accepts a string argument and returns an array of matches, or `null` if no match is found

`Symbol.replace`   Accepts a string argument and a replacement string, and returns a string

`Symbol.search`   Accepts a string argument and returns the numeric index of the match, or −1 if no match is found

`Symbol.split`   Accepts a string argument and returns an array containing pieces of the string split on the match

The ability to define these properties on an object allows you to create objects that implement pattern matching without regular expressions and use those objects in methods that expect regular expressions. Here's an example that shows these symbols in action:

```
// effectively equivalent to /^.{10}$/
let hasLengthOf10 = {
    [Symbol.match]: function(value) {
        return value.length === 10 ? [value.substring(0, 10)] : null;
    },
```

```
    [Symbol.replace]: function(value, replacement) {
        return value.length === 10 ? replacement + value.substring(10) : value;
    },
    [Symbol.search]: function(value) {
        return value.length === 10 ? 0 : -1;
    },
    [Symbol.split]: function(value) {
        return value.length === 10 ? ["", ""] : [value];
    }
};

let message1 = "Hello world",    // 11 characters
    message2 = "Hello John";     // 10 characters


let match1 = message1.match(hasLengthOf10),
    match2 = message2.match(hasLengthOf10);

console.log(match1);             // null
console.log(match2);             // ["Hello John"]

let replace1 = message1.replace(hasLengthOf10),
    replace2 = message2.replace(hasLengthOf10);

console.log(replace1);          // "Hello world"
console.log(replace2);          // "Hello John"

let search1 = message1.search(hasLengthOf10),
    search2 = message2.search(hasLengthOf10);

console.log(search1);           // -1
console.log(search2);           // 0

let split1 = message1.split(hasLengthOf10),
    split2 = message2.split(hasLengthOf10);

console.log(split1);            // ["Hello world"]
console.log(split2);            // ["", ""]
```

The hasLengthOf10 object is intended to work like a regular expression that matches whenever the string length is exactly 10. Each of the four methods on hasLengthOf10 is implemented using the appropriate symbol, and then the corresponding methods on two strings are called. The first string, message1, has 11 characters and will not match; the second string, message2, has 10 characters and will match. Despite not being a regular expression, hasLengthOf10 is passed to each string method and used correctly due to the additional methods.

Although this is a simple example, the ability to perform more complex matches than are currently possible with regular expressions opens lots of possibilities for custom pattern matchers.

The Symbol.toPrimitive Method

JavaScript frequently attempts to convert objects into primitive values implicitly when you apply certain operations. For instance, when you compare a string to an object using the double equals (==) operator, the object is converted into a primitive value before comparing. Exactly what primitive value should be used was previously an internal operation, but ECMAScript 6 exposes that value (making it changeable) through the Symbol.toPrimitive method.

The Symbol.toPrimitive method is defined on the prototype of each standard type and prescribes what should happen when the object is converted into a primitive. When a primitive conversion is needed, Symbol.toPrimitive is called with a single argument, referred to as hint in the specification. The hint argument is one of three string values. If "number" is passed, Symbol.toPrimitive should return a number. If "string" is passed, a string should be returned, and if "default" is passed, the operation has no preference as to the type.

For most standard objects, number mode has the following behaviors, which are listed in order by priority:

1. Call the valueOf() method, and if the result is a primitive value, return it.
2. Otherwise, call the toString() method, and if the result is a primitive value, return it.
3. Otherwise, throw an error.

Similarly, for most standard objects, the behaviors of string mode have the following priority:

1. Call the toString() method, and if the result is a primitive value, return it.
2. Otherwise, call the valueOf() method, and if the result is a primitive value, return it.
3. Otherwise, throw an error.

In many cases, standard objects treat default mode as equivalent to number mode (except for Date, which treats default mode as equivalent to string mode). By defining a Symbol.toPrimitive method, you can override these default coercion behaviors.

NOTE *Default mode is used only for the == operator, the + operator, and when passing a single argument to the Date constructor. Most operations use string or number mode.*

To override the default conversion behaviors, use Symbol.toPrimitive and assign a function as its value. For example:

```
function Temperature(degrees) {
    this.degrees = degrees;
}
```

```
Temperature.prototype[Symbol.toPrimitive] = function(hint) {

    switch (hint) {
        case "string":
            return this.degrees + "\u00b0"; // degrees symbol

        case "number":
            return this.degrees;

        case "default":
            return this.degrees + " degrees";
    }
};

var freezing = new Temperature(32);

console.log(freezing + "!");          // "32 degrees!"
console.log(freezing / 2);            // 16
console.log(String(freezing));        // "32°"
```

This script defines a `Temperature` constructor and overrides the default `Symbol.toPrimitive` method on the prototype. A different value is returned depending on whether the `hint` argument indicates string, number, or default mode (the `hint` argument is filled in by the JavaScript engine). In string mode, the `Temperature()` function returns the temperature with the Unicode degrees symbol. In number mode, it returns just the numeric value, and in default mode, it appends the word *degrees* after the number.

Each of the log statements triggers a different `hint` argument value. The `+` operator triggers default mode by setting `hint` to `"default"`, the `/` operator triggers number mode by setting `hint` to `"number"`, and the `String()` function triggers string mode by setting `hint` to `"string"`. Returning different values for all three modes is possible, but it's much more common to set the default mode to be the same as string or number mode.

The Symbol.toStringTag Property

One of the most interesting problems in JavaScript has been the existence of multiple global execution environments. This occurs in web browsers when a page includes an iframe, because the page and the iframe each has its own execution environment. In most cases, this isn't a problem, because data can be passed back and forth between the environments with little cause for concern. The problem arises when you're trying to identify what type of object you're dealing with after the object has been passed between different objects.

The canonical example of this issue is passing an array from an iframe into the page containing the iframe or vice versa. In ECMAScript 6 terminology, the iframe and the containing page each represent a different *realm*, which is an execution environment for JavaScript. Each realm has its own global scope with its own copy of global objects. In whichever realm the array is created, it is definitely an array. However, when it's passed to a different realm, an `instanceof Array` call returns `false` because the array was created with a constructor from a different realm and `Array` represents the constructor in the current realm.

A Workaround for the Identification Problem

Faced with the problem of identifying arrays, developers soon found a good way to do so. They discovered that by calling the standard `toString()` method on the object, a predictable string was always returned. Thus, many JavaScript libraries began including a function like this:

```
function isArray(value) {
    return Object.prototype.toString.call(value) === "[object Array]";
}

console.log(isArray([]));    // true
```

Although this solution might look a bit roundabout, it worked quite well for identifying arrays in all browsers. Using the `toString()` method on arrays isn't helpful for identifying an object, because it returns a string representation of the items the object contains. But using the `toString()` method on `Object.prototype` had a quirk: it included an internally defined name called `[[Class]]` in the returned result. Developers could use this method on an object to retrieve what the JavaScript environment thought the object's data type was.

Developers quickly realized that because there was no way to change this behavior, it was possible to use the same approach to distinguish between native objects and those created by developers. The most important case was the ECMAScript 5 `JSON` object.

Prior to ECMAScript 5, many developers used Douglas Crockford's *json2.js*, which creates a global `JSON` object. As browsers started to implement the `JSON` global object, figuring out whether the global `JSON` was provided by the JavaScript environment or through some other library became necessary. Using the same technique I showed with the `isArray()` function, many developers created functions like this:

```
function supportsNativeJSON() {
    return typeof JSON !== "undefined" &&
        Object.prototype.toString.call(JSON) === "[object JSON]";
}
```

The same characteristic of `Object.prototype` that allowed developers to identify arrays across iframe boundaries also provided a way to tell if `JSON` was the native `JSON` object or not. A non-native `JSON` object would return `[object Object]`, whereas the native version returned `[object JSON]` instead. This approach became the de facto standard for identifying native objects.

Defining Object String Tags in ECMAScript 6

ECMAScript 6 redefines the tendency of native objects to reveal their identity using `Object.prototype.toString()` through the `Symbol.toStringTag` symbol. This symbol represents a property on each object that defines what value should be produced when `Object.prototype.toString.call()` is called on it. For an array, the value that function returns is explained by storing "Array" in the `Symbol.toStringTag` property.

Likewise, you can define the `Symbol.toStringTag` value for your own objects:

```
function Person(name) {
    this.name = name;
}

Person.prototype[Symbol.toStringTag] = "Person";

var me = new Person("Nicholas");

console.log(me.toString());                       // "[object Person]"
console.log(Object.prototype.toString.call(me));  // "[object Person]"
```

Here, a `Symbol.toStringTag` property is defined on `Person.prototype` to provide the default behavior for creating a string representation. Because `Person.prototype` inherits the `Object.prototype.toString()` method, the value returned from `Symbol.toStringTag` is also used when calling the `me.toString()` method. However, you can still define your own `toString()` method that provides a different behavior without affecting the use of the `Object.prototype.toString.call()` method. Here's how that might look:

```
function Person(name) {
    this.name = name;
}

Person.prototype[Symbol.toStringTag] = "Person";

Person.prototype.toString = function() {
    return this.name;
};

var me = new Person("Nicholas");

console.log(me.toString());                       // "Nicholas"
console.log(Object.prototype.toString.call(me));  // "[object Person]"
```

This code defines `Person.prototype.toString()` to return the value of the `name` property. Because `Person` instances no longer inherit the `Object.prototype.toString()` method, calling `me.toString()` exhibits a different behavior.

NOTE *All objects inherit* `Symbol.toStringTag` *from* `Object.prototype` *unless otherwise specified. The string* `"Object"` *is the default property value.*

There is no restriction on which values you can use for `Symbol.toStringTag` on developer-defined objects. For example, nothing prevents you from using `"Array"` as the value of the `Symbol.toStringTag` property, such as:

```
function Person(name) {
    this.name = name;
}

Person.prototype[Symbol.toStringTag] = "Array";

Person.prototype.toString = function() {
    return this.name;
};

var me = new Person("Nicholas");

console.log(me.toString());                        // "Nicholas"
console.log(Object.prototype.toString.call(me));   // "[object Array]"
```

The result of calling `Object.prototype.toString()` is `"[object Array]"` in this code, which is the same result you'd get from an actual array. This highlights the fact that `Object.prototype.toString()` is no longer a completely reliable way of identifying an object's type.

Changing the string tag for native objects is also possible. Just assign to `Symbol.toStringTag` on the object's prototype, like this:

```
Array.prototype[Symbol.toStringTag] = "Magic";

var values = [];

console.log(Object.prototype.toString.call(values));   // "[object Magic]"
```

`Symbol.toStringTag` is overwritten for arrays in this example, meaning the call to `Object.prototype.toString()` results in `"[object Magic]"` instead of `"[object Array]"`. Even though I recommended not changing built-in objects in this way, there's nothing in the language that forbids you from doing so.

The Symbol.unscopables Property

The `with` statement is one of the most controversial parts of JavaScript. Originally designed to avoid repetitive typing, the `with` statement was roundly criticized for making code more difficult to understand, for negative performance implications, and for being error prone. As a result, the `with` statement is not allowed in strict mode; that restriction also affects classes and modules, which are strict mode by default and have no opt-out condition.

Although future code will undoubtedly not use the `with` statement, ECMAScript 6 still supports `with` in non-strict mode for backward compatibility and, as such, had to find ways to allow code that does use `with` to continue to work properly.

To understand the complexity of this task, consider the following code:

```
var values = [1, 2, 3],
    colors = ["red", "green", "blue"],
    color = "black";

with(colors) {
    push(color);
    push(...values);
}

console.log(colors);    // ["red", "green", "blue", "black", 1, 2, 3]
```

In this example, the two calls to push() inside the with statement are equivalent to colors.push() because the with statement added push as a local binding. The color reference refers to the variable created outside the with statement, as does the values reference.

But ECMAScript 6 added a values method to arrays. (The values() method is discussed in detail in Chapter 8.) As a result, in an ECMAScript 6 environment, the values reference inside the with statement should refer not to the local variable values, but to the array's values method, which would break the code. This is why the Symbol.unscopables symbol exists.

The Symbol.unscopables symbol is used on Array.prototype to indicate which properties shouldn't create bindings inside a with statement. When present, Symbol.unscopables is an object whose keys are the identifiers to omit from with statement bindings and whose values are true to enforce the block. Here's the default Symbol.unscopables property for arrays:

```
// built into ECMAScript 6 by default
Array.prototype[Symbol.unscopables] = Object.assign(Object.create(null), {
    copyWithin: true,
    entries: true,
    fill: true,
    find: true,
    findIndex: true,
    keys: true,
    values: true
});
```

The Symbol.unscopables object has a null prototype, which is created by the Object.create(null) call, and contains all the new array methods in ECMAScript 6. (These methods are covered in detail in Chapter 8 and Chapter 10.) Bindings for these methods are not created inside a with statement, allowing old code to continue working without any problem.

In general, you shouldn't need to define Symbol.unscopables for your objects unless you use the with statement and are making changes to an existing object in your code base.

Summary

Symbols are a new type of primitive value in JavaScript and are used to create nonenumerable properties that can't be accessed without referencing the symbol. Although not truly private, these properties are harder to accidentally change or overwrite and are therefore suitable for functionality that needs a level of protection from developers.

You can provide descriptions for symbols that allow you to identify symbol values easier. A global symbol registry allows you to use shared symbols in different parts of code by using the same description. Thus, the same symbol can be used for the same reason in multiple places.

Methods like `Object.keys()` or `Object.getOwnPropertyNames()` don't return symbols, so a new method called `Object.getOwnPropertySymbols()` was added in ECMAScript 6 to allow you to retrieve symbol properties. You can still make changes to symbol properties by calling the `Object.defineProperty()` and `Object.defineProperties()` methods.

Well-known symbols define previously internal-only functionality for standard objects and use globally available symbol constants, such as the `Symbol.hasInstance` property. These symbols use the prefix `Symbol.` in the specification and allow developers to modify standard object behavior in a variety of ways.

7

SETS AND MAPS

For most of its history, JavaScript had only one type of collection, which was represented by the Array type. (Although some developers may argue that all nonarray objects are just collections of key-value pairs, their intended use was originally quite different from arrays.) Arrays in JavaScript are used just like arrays in other languages, but before ECMA-Script 6, the lack of other collection options meant arrays were often used as queues and stacks as well. Because arrays use only numeric indexes, developers used nonarray objects whenever a nonnumeric index was necessary. That technique led to custom implementations of sets and maps using nonarray objects.

A *set* is a list of values that cannot contain duplicates. You typically don't access individual items in a set like you would items in an array; instead, it's much more common to just check a set to see if a value is present. A *map* is a collection of keys that correspond to specific values. Each item in a map stores two pieces of data, and values are retrieved by specifying the key to read from. Maps are frequently used as caches for storing data that is quickly retrieved at a later time. Although ECMAScript 5 didn't formally have sets and maps, developers worked around this limitation using non-array objects, too.

ECMAScript 6 added sets and maps to JavaScript, and this chapter discusses everything you need to know about these two collection types. First, I'll discuss the workarounds developers used to implement sets and maps before ECMAScript 6, and why those implementations were problematic. Then I'll cover how sets and maps work in ECMAScript 6.

Sets and Maps in ECMAScript 5

In ECMAScript 5, developers mimicked sets and maps by using object properties, like this:

```
var set = Object.create(null);

set.foo = true;

// checking for existence
if (set.foo) {
    // code to execute
}
```

The set variable in this example is an object with a null prototype, ensuring no inherited properties are on the object. Using object properties as unique values to be checked is a common approach in ECMAScript 5. When a property is added to the set object, it is set to true so conditional statements (such as the if statement in this example) can easily check whether the value is present.

The only real difference between an object used as a set and an object used as a map is the value being stored. For instance, this example uses an object as a map:

```
var map = Object.create(null);
map.foo = "bar";

// retrieving a value
var value = map.foo;

console.log(value);        // "bar"
```

This code stores a string value "bar" under the key foo. Unlike sets, maps are mostly used to retrieve information rather than just to check for the key's existence.

Problems with Workarounds

Using objects as sets and maps works okay in simple situations, but the approach can get more complicated when you run into the limitations of object properties. For example, because all object properties must be strings, you must be certain no two keys evaluate to the same string. Consider the following:

```
var map = Object.create(null);
map[5] = "foo";

console.log(map["5"]);      // "foo"
```

This example assigns the string value `"foo"` to a numeric key of 5. Internally, that numeric value is converted to a string, so `map["5"]` and `map[5]` actually reference the same property. That internal conversion can cause problems when you want to use numbers and strings as keys. Another problem arises when you use objects as keys, like this:

```
var map = Object.create(null),
    key1 = {},
    key2 = {};
map[key1] = "foo";

console.log(map[key2]);      // "foo"
```

Here, `map[key2]` and `map[key1]` reference the same value. The objects `key1` and `key2` are converted to strings because object properties must be strings. Because `"[object Object]"` is the default string representation for objects, both `key1` and `key2` are converted to that string. This can cause errors that may not be obvious because it's logical to assume that different object keys would, in fact, be different.

The conversion to the default string representation makes it difficult to use objects as keys.

Maps with a key whose value is falsy present their own particular problem. A falsy value is automatically converted to `false` when used in situations in which a Boolean value is required, such as in the condition of an `if` statement. This conversion alone isn't a problem, as long as you're careful in how you use values. For instance, look at this code:

```
var map = Object.create(null);

map.count = 1;

// checking for the existence of "count" or for a nonzero value?
if (map.count) {
    // code to execute
}
```

This example has some ambiguity as to how `map.count` should be used. Is the `if` statement intended to check for the existence of `map.count` or whether the value is nonzero? In this case, the code inside the `if` statement will execute because the value 1 is truthy. However, if `map.count` is 0 or if `map.count` doesn't exist, the code inside the `if` statement would not be executed.

These are difficult problems to identify and debug when they occur in large applications, which is a prime reason that ECMAScript 6 adds sets and maps to the language.

NOTE *JavaScript has the `in` operator that returns `true` if a property exists in an object without reading the value of the object. However, the `in` operator also searches the prototype of an object, which makes it safe to use only when an object has a null prototype. Even so, many developers still incorrectly use code like the preceding example rather than using `in`.*

Sets in ECMAScript 6

ECMAScript 6 adds a `Set` type that is an ordered list of values without duplicates. Sets allow fast access to the data they contain, adding a more efficient manner of tracking discrete values.

Creating Sets and Adding Items

Sets are created using `new Set()`, and items are added to a set by calling the `add()` method. You can see how many items are in a set by checking the `size` property:

```
let set = new Set();
set.add(5);
set.add("5");

console.log(set.size);    // 2
```

Sets don't coerce values to determine whether they're the same. That means a set can contain the number 5 and the string "5" as two separate items. (Internally, the comparison uses the `Object.is()` method discussed in Chapter 4 to determine if two values are the same.) You can also add multiple objects to the set, and those objects will remain distinct:

```
let set = new Set(),
    key1 = {},
    key2 = {};

set.add(key1);
set.add(key2);

console.log(set.size);    // 2
```

Because key1 and key2 are not converted to strings, they count as two unique items in the set. If they were converted to strings, they would both be equal to "[object Object]" instead.

If the add() method is called more than once with the same value, all calls after the first one are effectively ignored:

```
let set = new Set();
set.add(5);
set.add("5");
set.add(5);        // duplicate - this is ignored

console.log(set.size);    // 2
```

When console.log() outputs the size of set, it displays 2 because the second 5 wasn't added. You can also initialize a set using an array, and the Set constructor will ensure that only unique values are used. For instance:

```
let set = new Set([1, 2, 3, 4, 5, 5, 5, 5]);
console.log(set.size);    // 5
```

In this example, an array with duplicate values is used to initialize the set. The number 5 only appears once in the set, even though it appears four times in the array. This functionality makes converting existing code or JSON structures to use sets easy.

NOTE   *The Set constructor actually accepts any iterable object as an argument. Arrays work because they are iterable by default, as are sets and maps. The Set constructor uses an iterator to extract values from the argument. Iterables and iterators are discussed in detail in Chapter 8.*

You can test which values are in a set using the has() method, like this:

```
let set = new Set();
set.add(5);
set.add("5");

console.log(set.has(5));    // true
console.log(set.has(6));    // false
```

Here, set.has(6) returns false because the set doesn't have that value.

Removing Items

It's also possible to remove items from a set. You can remove a single item by using the delete() method, or you can remove all items from the set by calling the clear() method. This code shows both in action:

```
let set = new Set();
set.add(5);
set.add("5");
```

```
console.log(set.has(5));      // true

set.delete(5);

console.log(set.has(5));      // false
console.log(set.size);        // 1

set.clear();

console.log(set.has("5"));    // false
console.log(set.size);        // 0
```

After the delete() call, only 5 is gone; after the clear() method executes, set is empty.

Sets are a very easy mechanism for tracking unique ordered values. However, what if you want to add items to a set and then perform an operation on each item? That's where the forEach() method comes in.

The forEach() Method for Sets

If you're used to working with arrays, you may already be familiar with the forEach() method. ECMAScript 5 added forEach() to arrays to simplify working on each item in an array without setting up a for loop. The method proved popular among developers, so the same method is available on sets and works the same way.

The forEach() method is passed a callback function that accepts three arguments:

- The value from the next position in the set
- The same value as the first argument
- The set from which the value is read

The strange difference between the set version of forEach() and the array version is that the first and second arguments to the callback function are the same value in the set version. Although this might look like a mistake, there's a good reason for the behavior.

The other objects that have forEach() methods (arrays and maps) pass three arguments to their callback functions. The first two arguments for arrays and maps are the value and the key (the numeric index for arrays).

Sets don't have keys, however. The people behind the ECMAScript 6 standard could have made the callback function in the set version of forEach() accept two arguments, but that would have made it different from the other two. Instead, they found a way to keep the callback function the same and accept three arguments: each value in a set is considered to be the key and the value. As such, the first and second argument are always the same in forEach() on sets to keep this functionality consistent with the other forEach() methods on arrays and maps.

Other than the difference in arguments, using forEach() is basically the same for a set as it is for an array. The following code shows the method at work:

```
let set = new Set([1, 2]);

set.forEach(function(value, key, ownerSet) {
    console.log(key + " " + value);
    console.log(ownerSet === set);
});
```

This code iterates over each item in the set and outputs the values passed to the forEach() callback function. Each time the callback function executes, key and value are the same, and ownerSet is always equal to set. The output is:

```
1 1
true
2 2
true
```

Also the same as arrays, you can pass a this value as the second argument to forEach() if you need to use this in your callback function:

```
let set = new Set([1, 2]);

let processor = {
    output(value) {
        console.log(value);
    },
    process(dataSet) {
        dataSet.forEach(function(value) {
            this.output(value);
        }, this);
    }
};

processor.process(set);
```

In this example, the processor.process() method calls forEach() on the set and passes this as the this value for the callback. That's necessary so this.output() will correctly resolve to the processor.output() method. The forEach() callback function only uses the first argument, value, so the others are omitted. You can also use an arrow function to get the same effect without passing the second argument:

```
let set = new Set([1, 2]);

let processor = {
    output(value) {
        console.log(value);
    },
```

```
    process(dataSet) {
        dataSet.forEach(value => this.output(value));
    }
};

processor.process(set);
```

The arrow function in this example reads this from the containing process() function, so it will correctly resolve this.output() to a processor.output() call.

Keep in mind that although sets are great for tracking values and forEach() lets you work on each item sequentially, you can't directly access an item by index like you can with an array. If you need to do so, the best option is to convert the set to an array.

Converting a Set to an Array

Converting an array to a set is easy because you can pass the array to the Set constructor; converting a set back to an array is also easy if you use the spread operator (...). Chapter 3 introduced the spread operator as a way to split items in an array into separate function parameters. The spread operator can convert iterable objects, such as sets, to arrays, too. For example:

```
let set = new Set([1, 2, 3, 3, 3, 4, 5]),
    array = [...set];

console.log(array);            // [1,2,3,4,5]
```

Here, a set is initially loaded with an array that contains duplicates. The set removes the duplicates, and then the items are placed into a new array using the spread operator. The set still contains the same items (1, 2, 3, 4, and 5) it received when it was created. They've just been copied to a new array.

This approach is useful when you already have an array and want to create an array without duplicates, as in this example:

```
function eliminateDuplicates(items) {
    return [...new Set(items)];
}

let numbers = [1, 2, 3, 3, 3, 4, 5],
    noDuplicates = eliminateDuplicates(numbers);

console.log(noDuplicates);     // [1,2,3,4,5]
```

In the eliminateDuplicates() function, the set is just a temporary intermediary used to filter out duplicate values before creating a new array that has no duplicates.

Weak Sets

The Set type could be called a *strong set* because of the way it stores object references. Storing an object in an instance of Set is effectively the same as storing that object inside a variable. As long as a reference to that Set instance exists, the object cannot be garbage-collected to free memory. For example:

```
let set = new Set(),
    key = {};

set.add(key);
console.log(set.size);      // 1

// eliminate original reference
key = null;

console.log(set.size);      // 1

// get the original reference back
key = [...set][0];
```

In this example, setting key to null clears one reference of the key object, but another remains inside set. You can still retrieve key by converting the set to an array using the spread operator and accessing the first item. That result works fine for most programs, but sometimes it's best for references in a set to disappear when all other references disappear. For instance, if your JavaScript code is running in a web page and needs to keep track of DOM elements that might be removed by another script, you don't want your code holding onto the last reference to a DOM element. (That situation is called a *memory leak*.)

To address such issues, ECMAScript 6 also includes *weak sets*, which only store weak object references and cannot store primitive values. A *weak reference* to an object doesn't prevent garbage collection if it's the only remaining reference.

Creating Weak Sets

Weak sets are created using the WeakSet constructor and have an add() method, a has() method, and a delete() method. Here's an example that uses all three:

```
let set = new WeakSet(),
    key = {};

// add the object to the set
set.add(key);

console.log(set.has(key));      // true

set.delete(key);

console.log(set.has(key));      // false
```

Using a weak set is a lot like using a regular set. You can add, remove, and check for references in the weak set. You can also seed a weak set with values by passing an iterable to the constructor:

```
let key1 = {},
    key2 = {},
    set = new WeakSet([key1, key2]);

console.log(set.has(key1));     // true
console.log(set.has(key2));     // true
```

In this example, an array is passed to the WeakSet constructor. Because this array contains two objects, those objects are added into the weak set. Keep in mind that an error will be thrown if the array contains any non-object values, because WeakSet can't accept primitive values.

Key Differences Between Set Types

The biggest difference between weak sets and regular sets is that the weak reference is held to the object value. Here's an example that demonstrates this difference:

```
let set = new WeakSet(),
    key = {};

// add the object to the set
set.add(key);

console.log(set.has(key));      // true

// remove the last strong reference to key (also removes from weak set)
key = null;
```

After this code executes, the reference to key in the weak set is no longer accessible. It's not possible to verify its removal because you would need a reference to that object to pass to the has() method. This can make testing weak sets a little confusing, but you can trust that the reference has been properly removed by the JavaScript engine.

The preceding examples show that weak sets share some characteristics with regular sets, but there are some key differences:

- In a WeakSet instance, the add() method, has() method, and delete() method all throw an error when passed a nonobject.
- Weak sets aren't iterables and therefore cannot be used in a for-of loop.
- Weak sets don't expose any iterators (such as the keys() and values() methods), so there is no way to programmatically determine the contents of a weak set.
- Weak sets don't have a forEach() method.
- Weak sets don't have a size property.

The seemingly limited functionality of weak sets is necessary to properly handle memory. In general, if you only need to track object references, you should use a weak set instead of a regular set.

Sets give you a new way to handle lists of values, but they aren't useful when you need to associate additional information with those values. That's why ECMAScript 6 also adds maps.

Maps in ECMAScript 6

The ECMAScript 6 Map type is an ordered list of key-value pairs, where the key and the value can be any type. Key equivalence is determined by calling the Object.is() method, so you can have a key of 5 and a key of "5" because they're different types. This is quite different from using object properties as keys, because object properties always coerce values into strings.

You can add items to maps by calling the set() method and passing it a key and the value to associate with the key. You can later retrieve a value by passing the key to the get() method. For example:

```
let map = new Map();
map.set("title", "Understanding ECMAScript 6");
map.set("year", 2016);

console.log(map.get("title"));    // "Understanding ECMAScript 6"
console.log(map.get("year"));     // 2016
```

In this example, two key-value pairs are stored. The "title" key stores a string, and the "year" key stores a number. The get() method is called later to retrieve the values for both keys. If either key didn't exist in the map, get() would have returned the special value undefined instead of a value.

You can also use objects as keys, which isn't possible when you're using object properties to create a map in the old workaround approach. Here's an example:

```
let map = new Map(),
    key1 = {},
    key2 = {};

map.set(key1, 5);
map.set(key2, 42);

console.log(map.get(key1));    // 5
console.log(map.get(key2));    // 42
```

This code uses the objects key1 and key2 as keys in the map to store two different values. Because these keys are not coerced into another form, each object is considered unique. This allows you to associate additional data with an object without modifying the object.

Map Methods

Maps share several methods with sets, which is intentional and allows you to interact with maps and sets in similar ways. These three methods are available on maps and sets:

has(*key*)   Determines if the given key exists in the map

delete(*key*)   Removes the key and its associated value from the map

clear()   Removes all keys and values from the map

Maps also have a size property that indicates how many key-value pairs it contains. This code uses all three methods and size in different ways:

```
let map = new Map();
map.set("name", "Nicholas");
map.set("age", 25);

console.log(map.size);            // 2

console.log(map.has("name"));     // true
console.log(map.get("name"));     // "Nicholas"

console.log(map.has("age"));      // true
console.log(map.get("age"));      // 25

map.delete("name");
console.log(map.has("name"));     // false
console.log(map.get("name"));     // undefined
console.log(map.size);            // 1

map.clear();
console.log(map.has("name"));     // false
console.log(map.get("name"));     // undefined
console.log(map.has("age"));      // false
console.log(map.get("age"));      // undefined
console.log(map.size);            // 0
```

As with sets, the size property always contains the number of key-value pairs in the map. The Map instance in this example starts with the "name" and "age" keys, so has() returns true when passed either key. After the "name" key is removed by the delete() method, the has() method returns false when passed "name", and the size property indicates one less item. The clear() method then removes the remaining key, as indicated by has() returning false for both keys and size being 0.

The clear() method is a fast way to remove a lot of data from a map, but there's also a way to add a lot of data to a map at one time.

Map Initialization

Also similar to sets, you can initialize a map with data by passing an array to the Map constructor. Each item in the array must itself be an array where the first item is the key and the second is that key's corresponding value. Therefore, the entire map is an array of these two-item arrays, for example:

```
let map = new Map([["name", "Nicholas"], ["age", 25]]);

console.log(map.has("name"));    // true
console.log(map.get("name"));    // "Nicholas"
console.log(map.has("age"));     // true
console.log(map.get("age"));     // 25
console.log(map.size);           // 2
```

The keys "name" and "age" are added into map through initialization in the constructor. Although the array of arrays may look a bit strange, it's necessary to accurately represent keys, because keys can be any data type. Storing the keys in an array is the only way to ensure they aren't coerced into another data type before being stored in the map.

The forEach() Method for Maps

The forEach() method for maps is similar to forEach() for sets and arrays in that it accepts a callback function that receives three arguments:

- The value from the next position in the map
- The key for that value
- The map from which the value is read

These callback arguments more closely match the forEach() behavior in arrays, where the first argument is the value and the second is the key (corresponding to a numeric index in arrays). Here's an example:

```
let map = new Map([["name", "Nicholas"], ["age", 25]]);

map.forEach(function(value, key, ownerMap) {
    console.log(key + " " + value);
    console.log(ownerMap === map);
});
```

The forEach() callback function outputs the information that is passed to it. The value and key are output directly, and ownerMap is compared to map to show that the values are equivalent. The code outputs the following:

```
name Nicholas
true
age 25
true
```

The callback passed to forEach() receives each key-value pair in the order in which the pairs were inserted into the map. This behavior differs slightly from calling forEach() on arrays, where the callback receives each item in order of numeric index.

NOTE *You can also provide a second argument to forEach() to specify the* this *value inside the callback function. A call like that behaves the same as the set version of the forEach() method.*

Weak Maps

Weak maps are to maps what weak sets are to sets: they're a way to store weak object references. In *weak maps*, every key must be an object (an error is thrown if you try to use a nonobject key), and those object references are held weakly so they don't interfere with garbage collection. When there are no references to a weak map key outside a weak map, the key-value pair is removed from the weak map. But only weak map keys, not weak map values, are weak references. An object stored as a weak map value will prevent garbage collection, even if all other references are removed.

The most useful place to employ weak maps is when you're creating an object related to a particular DOM element in a web page. For example, some JavaScript libraries for web pages maintain one custom object for every DOM element referenced in the library, and that mapping is stored in a cache of objects internally.

The difficult part of this approach is determining when a DOM element no longer exists in the web page so the library can remove its associated object. Otherwise, the library would hold onto the DOM element reference past the reference's usefulness and cause a memory leak. Tracking the DOM elements with a weak map would still allow the library to associate a custom object with every DOM element, and it could automatically destroy any object in the map when that object's DOM element no longer exists.

Using Weak Maps

The ECMAScript 6 WeakMap type is an unordered list of key-value pairs, where a key must be a non-null object and a value can be of any type. The interface for WeakMap is very similar to that of Map in that set() and get() are used to add and retrieve data, respectively:

```
let map = new WeakMap(),
    element = document.querySelector(".element");

map.set(element, "Original");

let value = map.get(element);
console.log(value);              // "Original"
```

```
// remove the element
element.parentNode.removeChild(element);
element = null;

// the weak map is empty at this point
```

In this example, one key-value pair is stored. The `element` key is a DOM element used to store a corresponding string value. That value is then retrieved by passing in the DOM element to the `get()` method. When the DOM element is later removed from the document and the variable referencing it is set to `null`, the data is also removed from the weak map.

Similar to weak sets, there is no way to verify that a weak map is empty, because it doesn't have a `size` property. Because there are no remaining references to the key, you can't retrieve the value by calling the `get()` method, either. The weak map has cut off access to the value for that key, and when the garbage collector runs, the memory occupied by the value will be freed.

Weak Map Initialization

To initialize a weak map, pass an array of arrays to the `WeakMap` constructor. Just like initializing a regular map, each array inside the containing array should have two items: the first item is the non-null object key, and the second item is the value (any data type). For example:

```
let key1 = {},
    key2 = {},
    map = new WeakMap([[key1, "Hello"], [key2, 42]]);

console.log(map.has(key1));    // true
console.log(map.get(key1));    // "Hello"
console.log(map.has(key2));    // true
console.log(map.get(key2));    // 42
```

The objects `key1` and `key2` are used as keys in the weak map, and the `get()` and `has()` methods can access them. An error is thrown if the `WeakMap` constructor receives a nonobject key in any of the key-value pairs.

Weak Map Methods

Weak maps have only two additional methods available to interact with key-value pairs. A `has()` method determines if a given key exists in the map, and a `delete()` method removes a specific key-value pair. There is no `clear()` method because that would require enumerating keys, and like weak sets, that isn't possible with weak maps. This example uses the `has()` and `delete()` methods:

```
let map = new WeakMap(),
    element = document.querySelector(".element");

map.set(element, "Original");
```

```
console.log(map.has(element));    // true
console.log(map.get(element));    // "Original"

map.delete(element);
console.log(map.has(element));    // false
console.log(map.get(element));    // undefined
```

Here, a DOM element is once again used as the key in a weak map. The has() method is useful for checking to see if a reference is currently being used as a key in the weak map. Keep in mind that this only works when you have a non-null reference to a key. The key is forcibly removed from the weak map by the delete() method, at which point has() returns false and get() returns undefined.

Private Object Data

Although most developers consider the main use case of weak maps to be associating data with DOM elements, there are many other possible uses (and no doubt some that have yet to be discovered). One practical use of weak maps is to store data that is private to object instances. All object properties are public in ECMAScript 6, so you need to use some creativity to make data accessible to objects but not accessible to everything. Consider the following example:

```
function Person(name) {
    this._name = name;
}

Person.prototype.getName = function() {
    return this._name;
};
```

This code uses the common convention of a leading underscore to indicate that a property is considered private and should not be modified outside the object instance. The intent is to use getName() to read this._name and not allow the _name value to change. However, there is nothing standing in the way of someone writing to the _name property, so it can be overwritten either intentionally or accidentally.

In ECMAScript 5, it's possible to get close to having truly private data by creating an object using a pattern such as this:

```
var Person = (function() {

    var privateData = {},
        privateId = 0;

    function Person(name) {
        Object.defineProperty(this, "_id", { value: privateId++ });

        privateData[this._id] = {
            name: name
```

```
        };
    }

    Person.prototype.getName = function() {
        return privateData[this._id].name;
    };

    return Person;
}());
```

This example wraps the definition of Person in an immediately invoked function expression (IIFE) that contains two private variables, privateData and privateId. The privateData object stores private information for each instance, and privateId generates a unique ID for each instance. When the Person constructor is called, a nonenumerable, nonconfigurable, and non-writable _id property is added.

Then, an entry is made into the privateData object that corresponds to the ID for the object instance; that's where the name is stored. Later, in the getName() function, the name can be retrieved by using this._id as the key into privateData. Because privateData is not accessible outside the IIFE, the actual data is safe, even though this._id is exposed publicly.

The big problem with this approach is that the data in privateData never disappears because there is no way to know when an object instance is destroyed: the privateData object will always contain extra data. This problem can be solved by using a weak map instead, as follows:

```
let Person = (function() {

    let privateData = new WeakMap();

    function Person(name) {
        privateData.set(this, { name: name });
    }

    Person.prototype.getName = function() {
        return privateData.get(this).name;
    };

    return Person;
}());
```

This version of the Person example uses a weak map for the private data instead of an object. Because the Person object instance can be used as a key, there's no need to keep track of a separate ID. When the Person constructor is called, a new entry is made into the weak map with a key of this and a value of an object containing private information. In this case, that value is an object containing only name. The getName() function retrieves that private information by passing this to the privateData.get() method, which fetches the value object and accesses the name property. This technique keeps the private information private and destroys that information whenever an object instance associated with it is destroyed.

Weak Map Uses and Limitations

When you're deciding whether to use a weak map or a regular map, the primary decision to consider is whether you want to use only object keys. Anytime you'll be using only object keys, a weak map is the best choice. A weak map will allow you to optimize memory usage and avoid memory leaks by ensuring that extra data isn't retained after it's no longer accessible.

Keep in mind that weak maps give you very little visibility into their contents, so you can't use the forEach() method, the size property, or the clear() method to manage the items. If you need some inspection capabilities, regular maps are a better choice. Just be sure to keep an eye on memory usage.

Of course, if you only want to use nonobject keys, regular maps are your only choice.

Summary

ECMAScript 6 formally introduces sets and maps into JavaScript. Prior to this addition, developers frequently used objects to mimic sets and maps, often running into problems due to the limitations associated with object properties.

Sets are unordered lists of unique values. Values are considered unique if they're not equivalent according to the Object.is() method. Sets automatically remove duplicate values, so you can use a set to filter an array for duplicates and return the result. Sets aren't subclasses of arrays, so you cannot randomly access a set's values. Instead, you can use the has() method to determine if a value is contained in the set and use the size property to inspect the number of values in the set. The Set type also has a forEach() method to process each set value.

Weak sets are special sets that can contain only objects. The objects are stored with weak references, meaning that an item in a weak set will not block garbage collection if that item is the only remaining reference to an object. Weak set contents can't be inspected due to the complexities of memory management, so it's best to use weak sets only for tracking objects that need to be grouped together.

Maps are unordered key-value pairs where the key can be any data type. Similar to sets, duplicate keys are determined by a call to the Object.is() method, which means you can have a numeric key 5 and a string "5" as two separate keys. A value of any data type can be associated with a key using the set() method, and that value can later be retrieved by using the get() method. Maps also have a size property and a forEach() method to allow for easier item access.

Weak maps are a special type of map that can only have object keys. As with weak sets, an object key reference is weak and doesn't prevent garbage collection when it's the only remaining reference to an object. When a key is garbage-collected, the value associated with the key is also removed from the weak map. This memory management aspect makes weak maps uniquely suited for correlating additional information with objects whose life cycles are managed outside the code accessing them.

8

ITERATORS AND GENERATORS

Many programming languages have shifted from iterating over data with `for` loops, which requires initializing variables to track position in a collection, to using iterator objects that programmatically return the next item in a collection. Iterators make working with collections of data easier, and ECMAScript 6 adds iterators to JavaScript. When coupled with new array methods and new types of collections (such as sets and maps), iterators are essential for efficient data processing and you'll find them in many parts of the language. The new `for-of` loop works with iterators; the spread operator (`...`) uses iterators; and even asynchronous programming can use iterators.

This chapter covers the many uses of iterators, but before discussing those uses, it's important to understand the history behind why iterators were added to JavaScript.

The Loop Problem

If you've ever programmed in JavaScript, you've probably written code that looks like this:

```
var colors = ["red", "green", "blue"];

for (var i = 0, len = colors.length; i < len; i++) {
    console.log(colors[i]);
}
```

This standard for loop tracks the index into the colors array using the i variable. The value of i increments each time the loop executes if i isn't larger than the length of the array (stored in len).

Although this loop is fairly straightforward, loops grow in complexity when you nest them and need to keep track of multiple variables. Additional complexity can lead to errors, and the boilerplate nature of the for loop lends itself to more errors because similar code is written in multiple places. Iterators are meant to eliminate the complexity and error-prone nature of loops.

What Are Iterators?

Iterators are objects with a specific interface designed for iteration. All iterator objects have a next() method that returns a result object. The result object has two properties: value, which is the next value, and done, which is a Boolean that's true when there are no more values to return. The iterator keeps an internal pointer to a location within a collection of values, and with each call to the next() method, it returns the next appropriate value.

If you call next() after the last value has been returned, the method returns done as true and value contains the *return value* for the iterator. That return value is not part of the data set; rather, it's a final piece of related data or undefined if no such data exists. An iterator's return value is similar to a function's return value in that it's a final way to pass information to the caller.

With this information in mind, creating an iterator using ECMAScript 5 is possible, as shown here:

```
function createIterator(items) {

    var i = 0;

    return {
        next: function() {

            var done = (i >= items.length);
            var value = !done ? items[i++] : undefined;
```

```
        return {
            done: done,
            value: value
        };

    }
};
}

var iterator = createIterator([1, 2, 3]);

console.log(iterator.next());        // "{ value: 1, done: false }"
console.log(iterator.next());        // "{ value: 2, done: false }"
console.log(iterator.next());        // "{ value: 3, done: false }"
console.log(iterator.next());        // "{ value: undefined, done: true }"

// for all further calls
console.log(iterator.next());        // "{ value: undefined, done: true }"
```

The createIterator() function returns an object with a next() method. Each time the method is called, the next value in the items array is returned as value. When i is 3, done becomes true and the ternary conditional operator that sets value evaluates to undefined. These two results fulfill the special last case for iterators in ECMAScript 6, where next() is called on an iterator after the last piece of data has been used.

As this example shows, writing iterators that behave according to the rules laid out in ECMAScript 6 is a bit complex. Fortunately, ECMAScript 6 also provides generators, which make creating iterator objects much simpler.

What Are Generators?

A *generator* is a function that returns an iterator. Generator functions are indicated by an asterisk character (*) after the function keyword and use the new yield keyword. It doesn't matter if the asterisk is directly next to function or if some whitespace is between it and the * character, as in this example:

```
// generator
function *createIterator() {
    yield 1;
    yield 2;
    yield 3;
}

// generators are called like regular functions but return an iterator
let iterator = createIterator();

console.log(iterator.next().value);     // 1
console.log(iterator.next().value);     // 2
console.log(iterator.next().value);     // 3
```

The * before createIterator() makes this function a generator. The yield keyword, also new to ECMAScript 6, specifies values the resulting iterator should return when next() is called and the order in which they should be returned. The iterator generated in this example has three different values to return on successive calls to the next() method: first 1, then 2, and finally 3. A generator gets called like any other function, as shown when iterator is created.

Perhaps the most interesting aspect of generator functions is that they stop execution after each yield statement. For instance, after yield 1 executes in this code, the function doesn't execute anything else until the iterator's next() method is called. At that point, yield 2 executes. This ability to stop execution in the middle of a function leads to some interesting uses of generator functions (which I discuss in "Advanced Iterator Functionality" on page 152).

You can use the yield keyword with any value or expression, so you can write generator functions that add items to iterators without just listing the items one by one. For example, here's one way you could use yield inside a for loop:

```
function *createIterator(items) {
    for (let i = 0; i < items.length; i++) {
        yield items[i];
    }
}

let iterator = createIterator([1, 2, 3]);

console.log(iterator.next());      // "{ value: 1, done: false }"
console.log(iterator.next());      // "{ value: 2, done: false }"
console.log(iterator.next());      // "{ value: 3, done: false }"
console.log(iterator.next());      // "{ value: undefined, done: true }"

// for all further calls
console.log(iterator.next());      // "{ value: undefined, done: true }"
```

This example passes an array called items to the createIterator() generator function. Inside the function, a for loop yields the elements from the array into the iterator as the loop progresses. Each time yield is encountered, the loop stops, and each time next() is called on iterator, the loop picks up with the next yield statement.

Generator functions are an important ECMAScript 6 feature, and because they are just functions, you can use them in all the same places. The rest of this section focuses on other useful ways to write generators.

Generator Function Expressions

You can use function expressions to create generators by just including an asterisk (*) between the function keyword and the opening parenthesis. For example:

```
let createIterator = function *(items) {
    for (let i = 0; i < items.length; i++) {
        yield items[i];
    }
};

let iterator = createIterator([1, 2, 3]);

console.log(iterator.next());        // "{ value: 1, done: false }"
console.log(iterator.next());        // "{ value: 2, done: false }"
console.log(iterator.next());        // "{ value: 3, done: false }"
console.log(iterator.next());        // "{ value: undefined, done: true }"

// for all further calls
console.log(iterator.next());        // "{ value: undefined, done: true }"
```

In this code, createIterator() is a generator function expression instead of a function declaration. The asterisk goes between the function keyword and the opening parenthesis because the function expression is anonymous. Otherwise, this example is the same as the previous example, which also used a for loop.

NOTE *Creating an arrow function that is also a generator is not possible.*

Generator Object Methods

Because generators are just functions, you can add them to objects, too. For example, you can make a generator in an ECMAScript 5–style object literal with a function expression, like this:

```
let o = {

    createIterator: function *(items) {
        for (let i = 0; i < items.length; i++) {
            yield items[i];
        }
    }
};

let iterator = o.createIterator([1, 2, 3]);
```

You can also use the ECMAScript 6 method shorthand by prepending the method name with an asterisk (*), as shown here:

```
let o = {

    *createIterator(items) {
        for (let i = 0; i < items.length; i++) {
            yield items[i];
        }
    }
};

let iterator = o.createIterator([1, 2, 3]);
```

These examples are functionally equivalent to the example in the previous section; they just use different syntax. In the shorthand version, because the createIterator() method is defined with no function keyword, the asterisk is placed immediately before the method name, although you can leave whitespace between the asterisk and the method name.

Iterables and for-of Loops

Closely related to iterators, an *iterable* is an object with a Symbol.iterator property. The well-known Symbol.iterator symbol specifies a function that returns an iterator for the given object. All collection objects (arrays, sets, and maps) and strings are iterables in ECMAScript 6, so they have a default iterator specified. Iterables are designed to be used with a new addition to ECMAScript: the for-of loop.

NOTE *All iterators created by generators are also iterables, because generators assign the Symbol.iterator property by default.*

At the beginning of this chapter, I mentioned the problem of tracking an index inside a for loop. Iterators are the first part of the solution to that problem. The for-of loop is the second part: it removes the need to track an index into a collection entirely, freeing you to focus on working with the contents of the collection.

A for-of loop calls next() on an iterable each time the loop executes and stores the value from the result object in a variable. The loop continues this process until the returned object's done property is true. Here's an example:

```
let values = [1, 2, 3];

for (let num of values) {
    console.log(num);
}
```

This code outputs the following:

```
1
2
3
```

This for-of loop first calls the Symbol.iterator method on the values array to retrieve an iterator. (The call to Symbol.iterator happens behind the scenes in the JavaScript engine.) Then iterator.next() is called, and the value property on the iterator's result object is read into num. The num variable is first 1, then 2, and finally 3. When done on the result object is true, the loop exits, so num is never assigned the value of undefined.

If you're simply iterating over values in an array or collection, it's a good idea to use a for-of loop instead of a for loop. The for-of loop is generally less error prone because there are fewer conditions to track. Use the traditional for loop for more complex control conditions.

WARNING *The for-of statement will throw an error when you use it on a non-iterable object, null, or undefined.*

Accessing the Default Iterator

You can use Symbol.iterator to access the default iterator for an object, like this:

```
let values = [1, 2, 3];
let iterator = values[Symbol.iterator]();

console.log(iterator.next());        // "{ value: 1, done: false }"
console.log(iterator.next());        // "{ value: 2, done: false }"
console.log(iterator.next());        // "{ value: 3, done: false }"
console.log(iterator.next());        // "{ value: undefined, done: true }"
```

This code gets the default iterator for values and uses that to iterate over the items in the array. This is the same process that happens behind the scenes when you're using a for-of loop.

Because Symbol.iterator specifies the default iterator, you can use it to detect whether an object is iterable, as follows:

```
function isIterable(object) {
    return typeof object[Symbol.iterator] === "function";
}

console.log(isIterable([1, 2, 3]));         // true
console.log(isIterable("Hello"));           // true
console.log(isIterable(new Map()));         // true
console.log(isIterable(new Set()));         // true
console.log(isIterable(new WeakMap()));     // false
console.log(isIterable(new WeakSet()));     // false
```

The isIterable() function simply checks whether a default iterator exists on the object and is a function. The for-of loop does a similar check before executing.

So far, the examples in this section have shown ways to use Symbol.iterator with built-in iterable types, but you can also use the Symbol.iterator property to create your own iterables.

Creating Iterables

Developer-defined objects are not iterable by default, but you can make them iterable by creating a Symbol.iterator property containing a generator. For example:

```
let collection = {
    items: [],
    *[Symbol.iterator]() {
        for (let item of this.items) {
            yield item;
        }
    }

};

collection.items.push(1);
collection.items.push(2);
collection.items.push(3);

for (let x of collection) {
    console.log(x);
}
```

This code outputs the following:

```
1
2
3
```

First, the example defines a default iterator for an object called `collection`. The default iterator is created by the `Symbol.iterator` method, which is a generator (note that the asterisk still comes before the name). The generator then uses a `for-of` loop to iterate over the values in `this.items` and uses `yield` to return each one. Instead of manually iterating to define values for the default iterator of `collection` to return, the `collection` object relies on the default iterator of `this.items` to do the work.

 "Delegating Generators" on page 156 describes a different approach to using the iterator of another object.

Now you've seen some uses for the default array iterator, but there are many more iterators built in to ECMAScript 6 to make working with collections of data easy.

Built-In Iterators

Iterators are an important part of ECMAScript 6, and as such, you don't need to create your own iterators for many built-in types: the language includes them by default. You only need to create iterators when the built-in iterators don't serve your purpose, which will most frequently be when defining your own objects or classes. Otherwise, you can rely on built-in iterators to do your work. Perhaps the most common iterators you'll use are those that work on collections.

Collection Iterators

ECMAScript 6 has three types of collection objects: arrays, maps, and sets. All three have the following built-in iterators to help you navigate their content:

`entries()` Returns an iterator whose values are key-value pairs

`values()` Returns an iterator whose values are the values of the collection

`keys()` Returns an iterator whose values are the keys contained in the collection

You can retrieve an iterator for a collection by calling one of these methods.

The entries() Iterator

The entries() iterator returns a two-item array each time next() is called. The two-item array represents the key and value for each item in the collection. For arrays, the first item is the numeric index; for sets, the first item is also the value (because values double as keys in sets); for maps, the first item is the key.

Here are some examples that use the entries() iterator:

```
let colors = [ "red", "green", "blue" ];
let tracking = new Set([1234, 5678, 9012]);
let data = new Map();

data.set("title", "Understanding ECMAScript 6");
data.set("format", "ebook");

for (let entry of colors.entries()) {
    console.log(entry);
}

for (let entry of tracking.entries()) {
    console.log(entry);
}

for (let entry of data.entries()) {
    console.log(entry);
}
```

The console.log() calls produce the following output:

```
[0, "red"]
[1, "green"]
[2, "blue"]
[1234, 1234]
[5678, 5678]
[9012, 9012]
["title", "Understanding ECMAScript 6"]
["format", "ebook"]
```

This code uses the entries() method on each type of collection to retrieve an iterator, and it uses for-of loops to iterate the items. The console output shows how the keys and values are returned in pairs for each object.

The values() Iterator

The values() iterator simply returns values as they are stored in the collection. For example:

```
let colors = [ "red", "green", "blue" ];
let tracking = new Set([1234, 5678, 9012]);
let data = new Map();
```

```
data.set("title", "Understanding ECMAScript 6");
data.set("format", "ebook");

for (let value of colors.values()) {
    console.log(value);
}

for (let value of tracking.values()) {
    console.log(value);
}

for (let value of data.values()) {
    console.log(value);
}
```

This code outputs the following:

```
"red"
"green"
"blue"
1234
5678
9012
"Understanding ECMAScript 6"
"ebook"
```

Calling the values() iterator, as in this example, returns the exact data contained in each collection without any information about that data's location in the collection.

The keys() Iterator

The keys() iterator returns each key present in a collection. For arrays, it returns only numeric keys; it never returns other own properties of the array. For sets, the keys are the same as the values, so keys() and values() return the same iterator. For maps, the keys() iterator returns each unique key. Here's an example that demonstrates all three:

```
let colors = [ "red", "green", "blue" ];
let tracking = new Set([1234, 5678, 9012]);
let data = new Map();

data.set("title", "Understanding ECMAScript 6");
data.set("format", "ebook");

for (let key of colors.keys()) {
    console.log(key);
}

for (let key of tracking.keys()) {
    console.log(key);
}
```

```
for (let key of data.keys()) {
    console.log(key);
}
```

This example outputs the following:

```
0
1
2
1234
5678
9012
"title"
"format"
```

The keys() iterator fetches each key in colors, tracking, and data, and those keys are printed from inside the three for-of loops. For the array object, only numeric indexes are printed, which would still happen even if you added named properties to the array. This is different from the way the for-in loop works with arrays, because the for-in loop iterates over properties rather than just the numeric indexes.

Default Iterators for Collection Types

Each collection type also has a default iterator that is used by for-of whenever an iterator isn't explicitly specified. The values() method is the default iterator for arrays and sets, whereas the entries() method is the default iterator for maps. These defaults make using collection objects in for-of loops a little easier. For instance, consider this example:

```
let colors = [ "red", "green", "blue" ];
let tracking = new Set([1234, 5678, 9012]);
let data = new Map();

data.set("title", "Understanding ECMAScript 6");
data.set("format", "print");

// same as using colors.values()
for (let value of colors) {
    console.log(value);
}

// same as using tracking.values()
for (let num of tracking) {
    console.log(num);
}

// same as using data.entries()
for (let entry of data) {
    console.log(entry);
}
```

No iterator is specified, so the default iterator functions will be used. The default iterators for arrays, sets, and maps are designed to reflect how these objects are initialized, so this code outputs the following:

```
"red"
"green"
"blue"
1234
5678
9012
["title", "Understanding ECMAScript 6"]
["format", "print"]
```

Arrays and sets return their values by default, whereas maps return the same array format that can be passed into the Map constructor. On the other hand, weak sets and weak maps do not have built-in iterators. Managing weak references means there's no way to know exactly how many values are in these collections, which also means there's no way to iterate over them.

DESTRUCTURING AND FOR-OF LOOPS

The behavior of the default constructor for maps is also helpful when you use it in for-of loops with destructuring, as in this example:

```
let data = new Map();

data.set("title", "Understanding ECMAScript 6");
data.set("format", "ebook");

// same as using data.entries()
for (let [key, value] of data) {
    console.log(key + "=" + value);
}
```

The for-of loop in this code uses a destructured array to assign key and value for each entry in the map. In this way, you can easily work with keys and values at the same time without needing to access a two-item array or going back to the map to fetch either the key or the value. Using a destructured array for maps makes the for-of loop equally useful for maps as it is for sets and arrays.

String Iterators

JavaScript strings have slowly become more like arrays since ECMAScript 5 was released. For example, ECMAScript 5 formalized bracket notation for accessing characters in strings (that is, using text[0] to get the first character, and so on). But bracket notation works on code units rather than characters, so it cannot be used to access double-byte characters correctly, as this example demonstrates:

```
var message = "A 吉 B";

for (let i=0; i < message.length; i++) {
    console.log(message[i]);
}
```

This code uses bracket notation and the length property to iterate over and print a string containing a Unicode character. The output is a bit unexpected:

```
A
(blank)
(blank)
(blank)
(blank)
B
```

Because the double-byte character is treated as two separate code units, four empty lines are between A and B in the output.

Fortunately, ECMAScript 6 aims to fully support Unicode (see Chapter 2), and the default string iterator is an attempt to solve the string iteration problem. As such, the default iterator for strings works on characters rather than code units. Changing the preceding example to use the default string iterator with a for-of loop results in more appropriate output. Here's the tweaked code:

```
var message = "A 吉 B";

for (let c of message) {
    console.log(c);
}
```

This code outputs the following:

```
A
(blank)
吉
(blank)
B
```

This result is more in line with what you'd expect when you're working with characters: the loop successfully prints the Unicode character as well as all the rest.

NodeList Iterators

The DOM has a NodeList type that represents a collection of elements in a document. For those who write JavaScript to run in web browsers, understanding the difference between NodeList objects and arrays has always been a bit difficult. Both NodeList objects and arrays use the length property to indicate the number of items, and both use bracket notation to access individual items. Internally, however, a NodeList and an array behave quite differently, which has led to a lot of confusion.

With the addition of default iterators in ECMAScript 6, the DOM definition of NodeList (included in the HTML specification rather than ECMAScript 6) includes a default iterator that behaves in the same manner as the array default iterator. That means you can use NodeList in a for-of loop or any other place that uses an object's default iterator. For example:

```
var divs = document.getElementsByTagName("div");

for (let div of divs) {
    console.log(div.id);
}
```

This code calls getElementsByTagName() to retrieve a NodeList that represents all of the <div> elements in the document object. The for-of loop then iterates over each element and outputs the element IDs, effectively making the code the same as it would be for a standard array.

The Spread Operator and Nonarray Iterables

Recall from Chapter 7 that you can use the spread operator (...) to convert a set into an array. For example:

```
let set = new Set([1, 2, 3, 3, 3, 4, 5]),
    array = [...set];

console.log(array);            // [1,2,3,4,5]
```

This code uses the spread operator inside an array literal to fill in that array with the values from set. The spread operator works on all iterables and uses the default iterator to determine which values to include. All values are read from the iterator and inserted into the array in the order in which values where returned from the iterator. This example runs properly because sets are iterables, but the spread operator works equally well on any iterable. Here's another example:

```
let map = new Map([["name", "Nicholas"], ["age", 25]]),
    array = [...map];

console.log(array);            // [["name", "Nicholas"], ["age", 25]]
```

Here, the spread operator converts `map` into an array of arrays. Because the default iterator for maps returns key-value pairs, the resulting array looks like the array that was passed during the `new Map()` call.

You can use the spread operator in an array literal as many times as you want, and you can use it wherever you want to insert multiple items from an iterable. Those items will just appear in order in the new array at the location of the spread operator. For example:

```
let smallNumbers = [1, 2, 3],
    bigNumbers = [100, 101, 102],
    allNumbers = [0, ...smallNumbers, ...bigNumbers];

console.log(allNumbers.length);    // 7
console.log(allNumbers);           // [0, 1, 2, 3, 100, 101, 102]
```

Here, the spread operator is used to create `allNumbers` from the values in `smallNumbers` and `bigNumbers`. The values are placed in `allNumbers` in the same order the arrays are added when `allNumbers` is created: 0 is first, followed by the values from `smallNumbers`, followed by the values from `bigNumbers`. However, the original arrays are unchanged, because their values have just been copied into `allNumbers`.

Because you can use the spread operator on any iterable, using it is the easiest way to convert an iterable into an array. You can convert strings into arrays of characters (not code units) and `NodeList` objects in the browser into arrays of nodes.

Now that you understand the basics of how iterators work, including `for-of` and the spread operator, it's time to look at some more complex uses of iterators.

Advanced Iterator Functionality

You can accomplish a lot with the basic functionality of iterators and the convenience of creating them using generators. However, iterators can be used for tasks other than simply iterating over a collection of values. During the development of ECMAScript 6, many unique ideas and patterns emerged that encouraged the creators to add more functionality to the language. Some of those additions are subtle, but when used together, they can accomplish some interesting interactions, as discussed in the following sections.

Passing Arguments to Iterators

Throughout this chapter, examples have shown iterators passing values out via the `next()` method or by using `yield` in a generator. But you can also pass arguments to the iterator through the `next()` method. When you pass an argument to the `next()` method, that argument becomes the value of the `yield` statement inside a generator. This capability is important for more advanced functionality, such as asynchronous programming. Here's a basic example:

```
function *createIterator() {
    let first = yield 1;
    let second = yield first + 2;      // 4 + 2
    yield second + 3;                   // 5 + 3
}

let iterator = createIterator();

console.log(iterator.next());      // "{ value: 1, done: false }"
console.log(iterator.next(4));     // "{ value: 6, done: false }"
console.log(iterator.next(5));     // "{ value: 8, done: false }"
console.log(iterator.next());      // "{ value: undefined, done: true }"
```

The first call to next() is a special case where any argument passed to it is lost. Because arguments passed to next() become the values returned by yield, an argument from the first call to next() could only replace the first yield statement in the generator function if it could be accessed before that yield statement. That's not possible, so there's no reason to pass an argument the first time next() is called.

On the second call to next(), the value 4 is passed as the argument. The 4 ends up assigned to the variable first inside the generator function. In a yield statement including an assignment, the right side of the expression is evaluated on the first call to next() and the left side is evaluated on the second call to next() before the function continues executing. Because the second call to next() passes in 4, that value is assigned to first and then execution continues.

The second yield uses the result of the first yield and adds two, which means it returns a value of 6. When next() is called a third time, the value 5 is passed as an argument. That value is assigned to the variable second and then used in the third yield statement to return 8.

It's a bit easier to think about what's happening by considering which code is executing each time execution continues inside the generator function. Figure 8-1 uses shades of gray to show the code being executed before yielding.

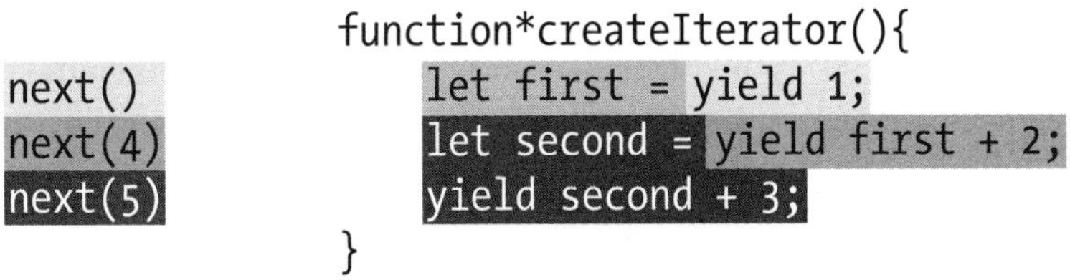

Figure 8-1: Code execution inside a generator

Light gray highlights the first call to next() and all the code executed inside the generator as a result. Medium gray represents the call to next(4) and the code that is executed with that call. Dark gray represents the call to next(5) and the code that is executed as a result. The tricky part is how the code on the right side of each expression executes and stops before the left side is executed. This makes debugging complicated generators a bit more involved than debugging regular functions.

You've seen that yield can act like return when a value is passed to the next() method, but that's not the only execution trick you can do inside a generator. You can also cause iterators to throw an error.

Throwing Errors in Iterators

It's possible to pass not just data into iterators, but also error conditions. Iterators can implement a throw() method that instructs the iterator to throw an error when it resumes. This is an important capability for asynchronous programming but also for flexibility inside generators, where you want to be able to mimic return values and thrown errors (the two ways of exiting a function). You can pass an error object to throw() that should be thrown when the iterator continues processing. For example:

```
function *createIterator() {
    let first = yield 1;
    let second = yield first + 2;      // yield 4 + 2, then throw
    yield second + 3;                  // never is executed
}

let iterator = createIterator();

console.log(iterator.next());                        // "{ value: 1, done: false }"
console.log(iterator.next(4));                       // "{ value: 6, done: false }"
console.log(iterator.throw(new Error("Boom")));      // error thrown from generator
```

In this example, the first two yield expressions are evaluated normally, but when throw() is called, an error is thrown before let second is evaluated. This effectively halts code execution similar to directly throwing an error. The only difference is the location in which the error is thrown. Figure 8-2 shows which code is executed at each step.

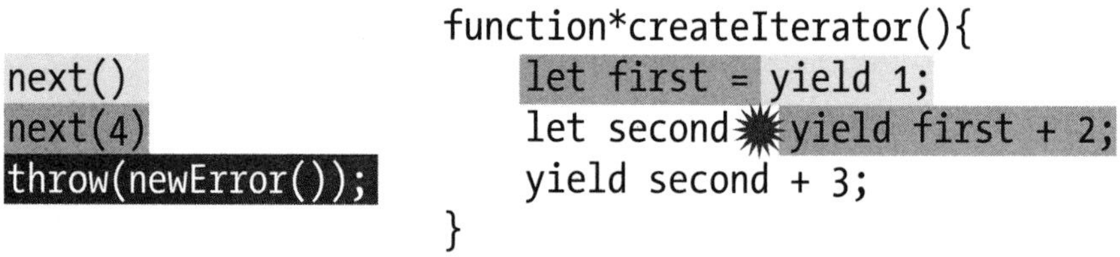

Figure 8-2: Throwing an error inside a generator

As in Figure 8-1, light and medium gray show which next() and yield calls happen together. The throw() call is highlighted in dark gray, and the dark gray star shows approximately when the error is thrown inside the generator. The first two yield statements are executed, and when throw() is called, an error is thrown before any other code executes. Knowing this, you can catch such errors inside the generator using a try-catch block:

```
function *createIterator() {
    let first = yield 1;
    let second;

    try {
        second = yield first + 2;       // yield 4 + 2, then throw
    } catch (ex) {
        second = 6;                     // on error, assign a different value
    }
    yield second + 3;
}

let iterator = createIterator();

console.log(iterator.next());                        // "{ value: 1, done: false }"
console.log(iterator.next(4));                       // "{ value: 6, done: false }"
console.log(iterator.throw(new Error("Boom")));      // "{ value: 9, done: false }"
console.log(iterator.next());                        // "{ value: undefined, done: true }"
```

In this example, a try-catch block is wrapped around the second yield statement. Although this yield executes without error, the error is thrown before any value can be assigned to second, so the catch block assigns it a value of 6. Execution then flows to the next yield and returns 9.

Notice that something interesting happened: the throw() method returned a result object just like the next() method. Because the error was caught inside the generator, code execution continued to the next yield and returned the next value, 9.

It helps to think of next() and throw() as being instructions to the iterator. The next() method instructs the iterator to continue executing (possibly with a given value), and throw() instructs the iterator to continue executing by throwing an error. What happens after that point depends on the code inside the generator.

The next() and throw() methods control execution inside an iterator when you're using yield, but you can also use the return statement. But return works a bit differently than it does in regular functions, as you'll see in the next section.

Generator Return Statements

Because generators are functions, you can use the return statement to exit early and specify a return value for the last call to the next() method. In most examples in this chapter, the last call to next() on an iterator returns undefined, but you can specify an alternate value by using return as you would in any other function. In a generator, return indicates that all processing is done, so the done property is set to true and the value, if provided, becomes the value field. Here's an example that simply exits early using return:

```
function *createIterator() {
    yield 1;
    return;
    yield 2;
    yield 3;
}

let iterator = createIterator();

console.log(iterator.next());        // "{ value: 1, done: false }"
console.log(iterator.next());        // "{ value: undefined, done: true }"
```

In this code, the generator has a yield statement followed by a return statement. The return indicates that no more values are to come, so the rest of the yield statements will not execute (they are unreachable).

You can also specify a return value that will end up in the value field of the returned object. For example:

```
function *createIterator() {
    yield 1;
    return 42;
}

let iterator = createIterator();

console.log(iterator.next());        // "{ value: 1, done: false }"
console.log(iterator.next());        // "{ value: 42, done: true }"
console.log(iterator.next());        // "{ value: undefined, done: true }"
```

Here, the value 42 is returned in the value field on the second call to the next() method (which is the first time that done is true). The third call to next() returns an object whose value property is once again undefined. Any value you specify with return is only available on the returned object one time before the value field is reset to undefined.

NOTE *The spread operator and for-of ignore any value specified by a return statement. As soon as they see done is true, they stop without reading the value. However, iterator return values are helpful when delegating generators.*

Delegating Generators

In some cases, combining the values from two iterators into one is useful. Generators can delegate to other generators using a special form of yield with an asterisk (*). As with generator definitions, where the asterisk appears doesn't matter, as long as the asterisk falls between the yield keyword and the generator function name. Here's an example:

```
function *createNumberIterator() {
    yield 1;
    yield 2;
}

function *createColorIterator() {
    yield "red";
    yield "green";
}

function *createCombinedIterator() {
    yield *createNumberIterator();
    yield *createColorIterator();
    yield true;
}

var iterator = createCombinedIterator();

console.log(iterator.next());        // "{ value: 1, done: false }"
console.log(iterator.next());        // "{ value: 2, done: false }"
console.log(iterator.next());        // "{ value: "red", done: false }"
console.log(iterator.next());        // "{ value: "green", done: false }"
console.log(iterator.next());        // "{ value: true, done: false }"
console.log(iterator.next());        // "{ value: undefined, done: true }"
```

In this example, the createCombinedIterator() generator delegates first to createNumberIterator() and then to createColorIterator(). The returned iterator appears, from the outside, to be one consistent iterator that has produced all of the values. Each call to next() is delegated to the appropriate iterator until the iterators created by createNumberIterator() and createColorIterator() are empty. Then the final yield is executed to return true.

Generator delegation also lets you make further use of generator return values. It's the easiest way to access such returned values and can be quite useful when performing complex tasks. For example:

```
function *createNumberIterator() {
    yield 1;
    yield 2;
    return 3;
}

function *createRepeatingIterator(count) {
    for (let i=0; i < count; i++) {
        yield "repeat";
    }
}
```

```
function *createCombinedIterator() {
    let result = yield *createNumberIterator();
    yield *createRepeatingIterator(result);
}

var iterator = createCombinedIterator();

console.log(iterator.next());          // "{ value: 1, done: false }"
console.log(iterator.next());          // "{ value: 2, done: false }"
console.log(iterator.next());          // "{ value: "repeat", done: false }"
console.log(iterator.next());          // "{ value: "repeat", done: false }"
console.log(iterator.next());          // "{ value: "repeat", done: false }"
console.log(iterator.next());          // "{ value: undefined, done: true }"
```

In this example, the createCombinedIterator() generator delegates to createNumberIterator() and assigns the return value to result. Because createNumberIterator() contains return 3, the returned value is 3. The result variable is then passed to createRepeatingIterator() as an argument indicating how many times to yield the same string (in this case, three times).

Notice that the value 3 was never output from any call to the next() method. Right now, it exists solely inside the createCombinedIterator() generator. But you can output that value as well by adding another yield statement, such as:

```
function *createNumberIterator() {
    yield 1;
    yield 2;
    return 3;
}

function *createRepeatingIterator(count) {
    for (let i=0; i < count; i++) {
        yield "repeat";
    }
}

function *createCombinedIterator() {
    let result = yield *createNumberIterator();
    yield result;
    yield *createRepeatingIterator(result);
}

var iterator = createCombinedIterator();

console.log(iterator.next());          // "{ value: 1, done: false }"
console.log(iterator.next());          // "{ value: 2, done: false }"
console.log(iterator.next());          // "{ value: 3, done: false }"
console.log(iterator.next());          // "{ value: "repeat", done: false }"
console.log(iterator.next());          // "{ value: "repeat", done: false }"
console.log(iterator.next());          // "{ value: "repeat", done: false }"
console.log(iterator.next());          // "{ value: undefined, done: true }"
```

In this code, the extra yield statement explicitly outputs the returned value from the createNumberIterator() generator.

NOTE *You can use yield * directly on strings (as in yield * "hello"), and the string's default iterator will be used.*

Asynchronous Task Running

Much of the excitement around generators is directly related to asynchronous programming. Asynchronous programming in JavaScript is a double-edged sword: simple tasks are easy to do asynchronously, but complex tasks become an adventure in code organization. Because generators allow you to effectively pause code in the middle of execution, they open many possibilities related to asynchronous processing.

The traditional way to perform asynchronous operations is to call a function that has a callback. For example, consider reading a file from the disk in Node.js:

```
let fs = require("fs");

fs.readFile("config.json", function(err, contents) {
    if (err) {
        throw err;
    }

    doSomethingWith(contents);
    console.log("Done");
});
```

The fs.readFile() method is called with the filename to read and a callback function. When the operation is finished, the callback function is called. The callback checks whether an error exists, and if not, processes the returned contents. This works well when you have a small, finite number of asynchronous tasks to complete but gets complicated when you need to nest callbacks or otherwise sequence a series of asynchronous tasks. In those situations, generators and yield are helpful.

A Simple Task Runner

Because yield stops execution and waits for the next() method to be called before starting again, you can implement asynchronous calls without managing callbacks. To start, you need a function that can call a generator and start the iterator, such as this:

```
function run(taskDef) {

    // create the iterator, make available elsewhere
    let task = taskDef();
```

```
    // start the task
    let result = task.next();

    // recursive function to keep calling next()
    function step() {

        // if there's more to do
        if (!result.done) {
            result = task.next();
            step();
        }
    }

    // start the process
    step();

}
```

The run() function accepts a task definition (a generator function) as an argument. It calls the generator to create an iterator and stores the iterator in task. The first call to next() begins the iterator and the result is stored for later use. The step() function checks whether result.done is false and, if so, calls next() before recursively calling itself. Each call to next() stores the return value in result, which is always overwritten to contain the latest information. The initial call to step() starts the process of looking at the result.done variable to see whether there's more to do.

With this implementation of run(), you can run a generator containing multiple yield statements, such as:

```
run(function*() {
    console.log(1);
    yield;
    console.log(2);
    yield;
    console.log(3);
});
```

This example just outputs three numbers to the console, which simply shows that all calls to next() are being made. However, just yielding a couple of times isn't very useful. The next step is to pass values into and out of the iterator.

Task Running with Data

The easiest way to pass data through the task runner is to pass the value specified by yield into the next call to the next() method. To do so, you need only pass result.value, as in this code:

```
function run(taskDef) {

    // create the iterator, make available elsewhere
    let task = taskDef();
```

```
    // start the task
    let result = task.next();

    // recursive function to keep calling next()
    function step() {

        // if there's more to do
        if (!result.done) {
            result = task.next(result.value);
            step();
        }
    }

    // start the process
    step();

}
```

Now that `result.value` is passed to `next()` as an argument, it's possible to pass data between yield calls, like this:

```
run(function*() {
    let value = yield 1;
    console.log(value);        // 1

    value = yield value + 3;
    console.log(value);        // 4
});
```

This example outputs two values to the console: 1 and 4. The value 1 comes from yield 1, because the 1 is passed right back into the value variable. The 4 is calculated by adding 3 to value and passing that result back to value. Now that data is flowing between calls to yield, you just need one small change to allow asynchronous calls.

An Asynchronous Task Runner

The previous example passed static data back and forth between yield calls, but waiting for an asynchronous process is slightly different. The task runner needs to know about callbacks and how to use them. Because yield expressions pass their values into the task runner, any function call must return a value that somehow indicates the call is an asynchronous operation that the task runner should wait for.

Here is one way you might signal that a value is an asynchronous operation:

```
function fetchData() {
    return function(callback) {
        callback(null, "Hi!");
    };
}
```

For the purposes of this example, any function meant to be called by the task runner will return a function that executes a callback. The fetchData() function returns a function that accepts a callback function as an argument. When the returned function is called, it executes the callback function with a single piece of data (the "Hi!" string). The callback argument needs to come from the task runner to ensure executing the callback correctly interacts with the underlying iterator. Although the fetchData() function is synchronous, you can easily extend it to be asynchronous by calling the callback with a slight delay, such as:

```
function fetchData() {
    return function(callback) {
        setTimeout(function() {
            callback(null, "Hi!");
        }, 50);
    };
}
```

This version of fetchData() introduces a 50 ms delay before calling the callback, demonstrating that this pattern works equally well for synchronous and asynchronous code. You just have to make sure each function that wants to be called using yield follows the same pattern.

With a good understanding of how a function can signal that it's an asynchronous process, you can modify the task runner to take that fact into account. Anytime result.value is a function, the task runner will execute it instead of just passing that value to the next() method. Here's the updated code:

```
function run(taskDef) {

    // create the iterator, make available elsewhere
    let task = taskDef();

    // start the task
    let result = task.next();

    // recursive function to keep calling next()
    function step() {

        // if there's more to do
        if (!result.done) {
            if (typeof result.value === "function") {
                result.value(function(err, data) {
                    if (err) {
                        result = task.throw(err);
                        return;
                    }

                    result = task.next(data);
                    step();
                });
```

```
        } else {
            result = task.next(result.value);
            step();
        }

        }
    }

    // start the process
    step();

}
```

When result.value is a function (checked with the === operator), it's called with a callback function. That callback function follows the Node.js convention of passing any possible error as the first argument (err) and the result as the second argument. If err is present, that means an error occurred and task.throw() is called with the error object instead of task.next() so an error is thrown at the correct location. If there is no error, data is passed into task.next() and the result is stored. Then, step() is called to continue the process. When result.value is not a function, it's directly passed to the next() method.

This new version of the task runner is ready for all asynchronous tasks. To read data from a file in Node.js, you need to create a wrapper around fs.readFile() that returns a function similar to the fetchData() function from the beginning of this section. For example:

```
let fs = require("fs");

function readFile(filename) {
    return function(callback) {
        fs.readFile(filename, callback);
    };
}
```

The readFile() method accepts a single argument, the filename, and returns a function that calls a callback. The callback is passed directly to the fs.readFile() method, which will execute the callback upon completion. You can then run this task using yield as follows:

```
run(function*() {
    let contents = yield readFile("config.json");
    doSomethingWith(contents);
    console.log("Done");
});
```

This example performs the asynchronous readFile() operation without making any callbacks visible in the main code. Aside from yield, the code looks the same as synchronous code. As long as the functions performing asynchronous operations all conform to the same interface, you can write logic that reads like synchronous code.

Of course, there are downsides to the pattern used in these examples; namely, you can't always be sure a function that returns a function is asynchronous. But for now, it's only important that you understand the theory behind the task running. Another new feature in ECMAScript 6, promises, offers more flexible ways of scheduling asynchronous tasks, and Chapter 11 covers this topic in more depth.

Summary

Iterators are an important part of ECMAScript 6 and are at the root of several key language elements. On the surface, iterators provide a simple way to return a sequence of values using a simple API. However, there are far more complex ways to use iterators in ECMAScript 6.

The Symbol.iterator symbol is used to define default iterators for objects. Both built-in objects and developer-defined objects can use this symbol to provide a method that returns an iterator. When Symbol.iterator is provided on an object, the object is considered an iterable.

The for-of loop uses iterables to return a series of values in a loop. Using for-of is easier than iterating with a traditional for loop because you no longer need to track values and control when the loop ends. The for-of loop automatically reads all values from the iterator until there are no more, and then it exits.

To make for-of simpler to use, many values in ECMAScript 6 have default iterators. All the collection types—that is, arrays, maps, and sets—have iterators designed to make their contents easy to access. Strings also have a default iterator, which makes iterating over the characters of the string (rather than the code units) easy.

The spread operator works with any iterable and makes converting iterables into arrays easy, too. The conversion works by reading values from an iterator and inserting them individually into an array.

A generator is a special function that automatically creates an iterator when called. Generator definitions are indicated by an asterisk (*) and use of the yield keyword to indicate which value to return for each successive call to the next() method.

Generator delegation encourages good encapsulation of iterator behavior by letting you reuse existing generators in new generators. You can use an existing generator inside another generator by calling yield * instead of yield. This process allows you to create an iterator that returns values from multiple iterators.

Perhaps the most interesting and exciting aspect of generators and iterators is the possibility of creating cleaner-looking asynchronous code. Instead of needing to use callbacks everywhere, you can set up code that looks synchronous but in fact uses yield to wait for asynchronous operations to complete.

9

INTRODUCING JAVASCRIPT CLASSES

Unlike most formal object-oriented programming languages, JavaScript didn't support classes and classical inheritance as the primary way of defining similar and related objects when it was created. This left many developers confused, and from pre–ECMAScript 1 through ECMAScript 5, many libraries created utilities to make JavaScript look like it supported classes. Although some JavaScript developers feel strongly that the language doesn't need classes, the number of libraries created specifically for this purpose led to the inclusion of classes in ECMAScript 6.

When you're exploring ECMAScript 6 classes, it's helpful to understand the underlying mechanisms that classes use, so this chapter starts by discussing how ECMAScript 5 developers achieved class-like behavior. However, as you'll see, ECMAScript 6 classes aren't the same as classes in other languages. They have a uniqueness that embraces the dynamic nature of JavaScript.

Class-Like Structures in ECMAScript 5

As mentioned, in ECMAScript 5 and earlier, JavaScript had no classes. The closest equivalent to a class was creating a constructor and then assigning methods to the constructor's prototype, an approach typically called creating a custom type. For example:

```
function PersonType(name) {
    this.name = name;
}

PersonType.prototype.sayName = function() {
    console.log(this.name);
};

var person = new PersonType("Nicholas");
person.sayName();   // outputs "Nicholas"

console.log(person instanceof PersonType);  // true
console.log(person instanceof Object);      // true
```

In this code, `PersonType` is a constructor function that creates a single property called `name`. The `sayName()` method is assigned to the prototype so the same function is shared by all instances of the `PersonType` object. Then, a new instance of `PersonType` is created via the `new` operator. The resulting `person` object is considered an instance of `PersonType` and of `Object` through prototypal inheritance.

This basic pattern underlies many of the class-mimicking JavaScript libraries, and that's where ECMAScript 6 classes start.

Class Declarations

The simplest class form in ECMAScript 6 is the class declaration, which looks similar to classes in other languages.

A Basic Class Declaration

Class declarations begin with the `class` keyword followed by the name of the class. The rest of the syntax looks similar to concise methods in object literals but doesn't require commas between the elements of the class. Here's a simple class declaration:

```
class PersonClass {

    // equivalent of the PersonType constructor
    constructor(name) {
        this.name = name;
    }

    // equivalent of PersonType.prototype.sayName
    sayName() {
```

```
            console.log(this.name);
    }
}

let person = new PersonClass("Nicholas");
person.sayName();   // outputs "Nicholas"

console.log(person instanceof PersonClass);        // true
console.log(person instanceof Object);             // true

console.log(typeof PersonClass);                   // "function"
console.log(typeof PersonClass.prototype.sayName); // "function"
```

The class declaration for PersonClass behaves similarly to PersonType in the previous example. But instead of defining a function as the constructor, class declarations allow you to define the constructor directly inside the class using the special constructor method name. Because class methods use the concise syntax, there's no need to use the function keyword. All other method names have no special meaning, so you can add as many methods as you want.

Own properties, properties that occur on the instance rather than the prototype, can only be created inside a class constructor or method. In this example, name is an own property. I recommend creating all possible own properties inside the constructor function so a single place in the class is responsible for all of them.

Interestingly, class declarations are just syntactic sugar on top of the existing custom type declarations. The PersonClass declaration actually creates a function that has the behavior of the constructor method, which is why typeof PersonClass gives "function" as the result. The sayName() method also ends up as a method on PersonClass.prototype in this example, similar to the relationship between sayName() and PersonType.prototype in the previous example. These similarities allow you to mix custom types and classes without worrying too much about which you're using.

NOTE   *Class prototypes, such as PersonClass.prototype in the preceding example, are read-only. That means you cannot assign a new value to the prototype like you can with functions.*

Why Use the Class Syntax?

Despite the similarities between classes and custom types, you need to keep some important differences in mind:

- Class declarations, unlike function declarations, are not hoisted. Class declarations act like let declarations, so they exist in the temporal dead zone until execution reaches the declaration.

- All code inside class declarations runs in strict mode automatically. There's no way to opt out of strict mode inside classes.

- All methods are nonenumerable. This is a significant change from custom types, where you need to use Object.defineProperty() to make a method nonenumerable.

- All methods lack an internal [[Construct]] method and will throw an error if you try to call them with new.
- Calling the class constructor without new throws an error.
- Attempting to overwrite the class name within a class method throws an error.

With all of these differences in mind, the PersonClass declaration in the previous example is directly equivalent to the following code, which doesn't use the class syntax:

```
// direct equivalent of PersonClass
let PersonType2 = (function() {

    "use strict";

    const PersonType2 = function(name) {

        // make sure the function was called with new
        if (typeof new.target === "undefined") {
            throw new Error("Constructor must be called with new.");
        }

        this.name = name;
    }

    Object.defineProperty(PersonType2.prototype, "sayName", {
        value: function() {

            // make sure the method wasn't called with new
            if (typeof new.target !== "undefined") {
                throw new Error("Method cannot be called with new.");
            }

            console.log(this.name);
        },
        enumerable: false,
        writable: true,
        configurable: true
    });

    return PersonType2;
}());
```

First, notice that there are two PersonType2 declarations: a let declaration in the outer scope and a const declaration inside the immediately invoked function expression (IIFE)—this is how class methods are forbidden from overwriting the class name while code outside the class is allowed to do so. The constructor function checks new.target to ensure that it's being called with new; if not, an error is thrown. Next, the sayName() method is defined as nonenumerable, and the method checks new.target to ensure that it wasn't called with new. The final step returns the constructor function.

This example shows that although it's possible to do everything classes do without using the new syntax, the class syntax simplifies the functionality significantly.

CONSTANT CLASS NAMES

The class name is only constant inside the class itself. That means you can overwrite the class name outside the class but not inside a class method. For example:

```
class Foo {
    constructor() {
        Foo = "bar";    // throws an error when executed...
    }
}

// but this is okay after the class declaration
Foo = "baz";
```

In this code, the Foo inside the class constructor is a separate binding from the Foo outside the class. The internal Foo is defined as if it's a const and cannot be overwritten. An error is thrown when the constructor attempts to overwrite Foo with any value. But because the external Foo is defined as if it's a let declaration, you can overwrite its value at any time.

Class Expressions

Classes and functions are similar in that they have two forms: declarations and expressions. Function and class declarations begin with an appropriate keyword (function or class, respectively) followed by an identifier. Functions have an expression form that doesn't require an identifier after function; similarly, classes have an expression form that doesn't require an identifier after class. These *class expressions* are designed to be used in variable declarations or passed into functions as arguments.

A Basic Class Expression

Here's the class expression equivalent of the previous PersonClass examples, followed by some code that uses it:

```
let PersonClass = class {

    // equivalent of the PersonType constructor
    constructor(name) {
        this.name = name;
    }
```

```
    // equivalent of PersonType.prototype.sayName
    sayName() {
        console.log(this.name);
    }
};

let person = new PersonClass("Nicholas");
person.sayName();    // outputs "Nicholas"

console.log(person instanceof PersonClass);          // true
console.log(person instanceof Object);               // true

console.log(typeof PersonClass);                     // "function"
console.log(typeof PersonClass.prototype.sayName);   // "function"
```

As this example demonstrates, class expressions do not require identifiers after class. Aside from the syntax, class expressions are functionally equivalent to class declarations. In anonymous class expressions, as in the preceding example, PersonClass.name is an empty string. When you're using a class declaration, PersonClass.name would be the "PersonClass" string.

Whether you use class declarations or class expressions is mostly a matter of style. Unlike function declarations and function expressions, class declarations and class expressions are not hoisted, so your choice has little bearing on the code's runtime behavior. The only significant difference is that anonymous class expressions have a name property that is an empty string, whereas class declarations always have a name property equal to the class name (for instance, PersonClass.name is "PersonClass" when you're using a class declaration).

Named Class Expressions

The previous example used an anonymous class expression, but just like function expressions, you can also name class expressions. To do so, include an identifier after the class keyword, like this:

```
let PersonClass = class PersonClass2 {

    // equivalent of the PersonType constructor
    constructor(name) {
        this.name = name;
    }

    // equivalent of PersonType.prototype.sayName
    sayName() {
        console.log(this.name);
    }
};

console.log(typeof PersonClass);     // "function"
console.log(typeof PersonClass2);    // "undefined"
```

In this example, the class expression is named PersonClass2. The PersonClass2 identifier exists only within the class definition so it can be used inside class methods (such as the sayName() method). Outside the class, typeof PersonClass2 is "undefined" because no PersonClass2 binding exists there; to understand why, look at an equivalent declaration that doesn't use classes:

```
// direct equivalent of PersonClass named class expression
let PersonClass = (function() {

    "use strict";

    const PersonClass2 = function(name) {

        // make sure the function was called with new
        if (typeof new.target === "undefined") {
            throw new Error("Constructor must be called with new.");
        }

        this.name = name;
    }

    Object.defineProperty(PersonClass2.prototype, "sayName", {
        value: function() {

            // make sure the method wasn't called with new
            if (typeof new.target !== "undefined") {
                throw new Error("Method cannot be called with new.");
            }

            console.log(this.name);
        },
        enumerable: false,
        writable: true,
        configurable: true
    });

    return PersonClass2;
}());
```

Creating a named class expression slightly changes what's happening in the JavaScript engine. For class declarations, the outer binding (defined with let) has the same name as the inner binding (defined with const). A named class expression uses its name in the const definition, so PersonClass2 is defined for use only inside the class.

Although named class expressions behave differently from named function expressions, there are still many similarities between the two. Both can be used as values, and that opens several possibilities, which I'll cover next.

Classes as First-Class Citizens

In programming, a *first-class citizen* is a value that can be passed into a function, returned from a function, and assigned to a variable. JavaScript functions are first-class citizens (also called *first-class functions*), and they're part of what makes JavaScript unique.

ECMAScript 6 continues this tradition by making classes first-class citizens as well, allowing you to use classes in many different ways. For example, you can pass them into functions as arguments:

```
function createObject(classDef) {
    return new classDef();
}

let obj = createObject(class {

    sayHi() {
        console.log("Hi!");
    }
});

obj.sayHi();        // "Hi!"
```

In this example, the createObject() function is called with an anonymous class expression as an argument, creates an instance of that class with new, and returns the instance. The variable obj then stores the returned instance.

Another use of class expressions is creating singletons by immediately invoking the class constructor. To do so, you must use new with a class expression and include parentheses at the end. For example:

```
let person = new class {

    constructor(name) {
        this.name = name;
    }

    sayName() {
        console.log(this.name);
    }

}("Nicholas");

person.sayName();   // "Nicholas"
```

Here, an anonymous class expression is created and then executed immediately. This pattern allows you to use the class syntax for creating singletons without leaving a class reference available for inspection. The parentheses at the end of the class expression indicate that you're calling a function and also allow you to pass in an argument.

The examples in this chapter so far have focused on classes with methods. But you can also create accessor properties on classes using a syntax similar to object literals.

Accessor Properties

Although you should create own properties inside class constructors, classes allow you to define accessor properties on the prototype. To create a getter, use the keyword get followed by a space, followed by an identifier; to create a setter, do the same using the keyword set, as shown here:

```
class CustomHTMLElement {

    constructor(element) {
        this.element = element;
    }

    get html() {
        return this.element.innerHTML;
    }

    set html(value) {
        this.element.innerHTML = value;
    }
}

var descriptor = Object.getOwnPropertyDescriptor(CustomHTMLElement.prototype, "html");
console.log("get" in descriptor);        // true
console.log("set" in descriptor);        // true
console.log(descriptor.enumerable);      // false
```

In this code, the CustomHTMLElement class is made as a wrapper around an existing DOM element. It has a getter and setter for html that delegates to the innerHTML method on the element. This accessor property is created on the CustomHTMLElement.prototype and, just like any other method would be, is created as nonenumerable. The equivalent nonclass representation looks like this:

```
// direct equivalent to previous example
let CustomHTMLElement = (function() {

    "use strict";

    const CustomHTMLElement = function(element) {

        // make sure the function was called with new
        if (typeof new.target === "undefined") {
            throw new Error("Constructor must be called with new.");
        }

        this.element = element;
    }
```

```
Object.defineProperty(CustomHTMLElement.prototype, "html", {
    enumerable: false,
    configurable: true,
    get: function() {
        return this.element.innerHTML;
    },
    set: function(value) {
        this.element.innerHTML = value;
    }
});

    return CustomHTMLElement;
}());
```

As in previous examples, this one shows just how much code you can omit by using a class instead of the nonclass equivalent. The html accessor property definition alone is almost the size of the equivalent class declaration.

Computed Member Names

Even more similarities exist between object literals and classes. Class methods and accessor properties can also have computed names. Instead of using an identifier, use square brackets around an expression, which is the same syntax you use for object literal computed names. For example:

```
let methodName = "sayName";

class PersonClass {

    constructor(name) {
        this.name = name;
    }

    [methodName]() {
        console.log(this.name);
    }
};

let me = new PersonClass("Nicholas");
me.sayName();            // "Nicholas"
```

This version of PersonClass uses a variable to assign a name to a method inside its definition. The string "sayName" is assigned to the methodName variable, and then methodName is used to declare the method. The sayName() method is later accessed directly.

Accessor properties can use computed names in the same way, like this:

```
let propertyName = "html";

class CustomHTMLElement {

    constructor(element) {
        this.element = element;
    }

    get [propertyName]() {
        return this.element.innerHTML;
    }

    set [propertyName](value) {
        this.element.innerHTML = value;
    }
}
```

Here, the getter and setter for `html` are set using the `propertyName` variable. Accessing the property by using `.html` only affects the definition.

You've seen several similarities between classes and object literals, including methods, accessor properties, and computed names. There's just one more similarity I need to cover, and that is generators.

Generator Methods

Recall from Chapter 8 that you can define a generator on an object literal by prepending an asterisk (*) to the method name. The same syntax works for classes as well, allowing any method to be a generator. Here's an example:

```
class MyClass {

    *createIterator() {
        yield 1;
        yield 2;
        yield 3;
    }

}

let instance = new MyClass();
let iterator = instance.createIterator();
```

This code creates a class called `MyClass` with a `createIterator()` generator method. The method returns an iterator whose values are hardcoded into the generator. Generator methods are useful when you have an object that represents a collection of values and you want to iterate over those values easily. Arrays, sets, and maps all have multiple generator methods to account for the different ways developers need to interact with their items.

Although generator methods are useful, defining a default iterator for your class is much more helpful if the class represents a collection of values. You can define the default iterator for a class by using `Symbol.iterator` to define a generator method:

```
class Collection {

    constructor() {
        this.items = [];
    }

    *[Symbol.iterator]() {
        yield *this.items.values();
    }
}

var collection = new Collection();
collection.items.push(1);
collection.items.push(2);
collection.items.push(3);

for (let x of collection) {
    console.log(x);
}

// Output:
// 1
// 2
// 3
```

This example uses a computed name for a generator method that delegates to the `values()` iterator of the `this.items` array. Any class that manages a collection of values should include a default iterator because some collection-specific operations require collections they operate on to have an iterator. Now you can use any instance of `Collection` directly in a for-of loop or with the spread operator.

Adding methods and accessor properties to a class prototype is useful when you want them to show up on object instances. If, on the other hand, you want methods or accessor properties on the class, you'll need to use static members.

Static Members

Adding methods directly onto constructors to simulate static members is another common pattern in ECMAScript 5 and earlier. For example:

```
function PersonType(name) {
    this.name = name;
}
```

```
// static method
PersonType.create = function(name) {
    return new PersonType(name);
};

// instance method
PersonType.prototype.sayName = function() {
    console.log(this.name);
};

var person = PersonType.create("Nicholas");
```

In other programming languages, the factory method called `PersonType.create()` would be considered a static method, because it doesn't depend on an instance of `PersonType` for its data. ECMAScript 6 classes simplify the creation of static members by using the formal static annotation before the method or accessor property name. For instance, here's the class equivalent of the preceding example:

```
class PersonClass {

    // equivalent of the PersonType constructor
    constructor(name) {
        this.name = name;
    }

    // equivalent of PersonType.prototype.sayName
    sayName() {
        console.log(this.name);
    }

    // equivalent of PersonType.create
    static create(name) {
        return new PersonClass(name);
    }
}

let person = PersonClass.create("Nicholas");
```

The `PersonClass` definition has a single static method called `create()`. The method syntax is the same as the syntax used for `sayName()` except for the static keyword. You can use the static keyword on any method or accessor property definition within a class. The only restriction is that you can't use static with the constructor method definition.

NOTE *Static members are not accessible from instances. You must always access static members from the class directly.*

Inheritance with Derived Classes

Prior to ECMAScript 6, implementing inheritance with custom types was an extensive process. Proper inheritance required multiple steps. For instance, consider this example:

```
function Rectangle(length, width) {
    this.length = length;
    this.width = width;
}

Rectangle.prototype.getArea = function() {
    return this.length * this.width;
};

function Square(length) {
    Rectangle.call(this, length, length);
}

Square.prototype = Object.create(Rectangle.prototype, {
    constructor: {
        value: Square,
        enumerable: true,
        writable: true,
        configurable: true
    }
});

var square = new Square(3);

console.log(square.getArea());              // 9
console.log(square instanceof Square);      // true
console.log(square instanceof Rectangle);   // true
```

Square inherits from Rectangle, and to do so, it must overwrite Square.prototype with a new object created from Rectangle.prototype as well as call the Rectangle.call() method. These steps often confused JavaScript newcomers and were a source of errors for experienced developers.

Classes make inheritance easier to implement by using the familiar extends keyword to specify the function from which the class should inherit. The prototypes are automatically adjusted, and you can access the base class constructor by calling the super() method. Here's the ECMAScript 6 equivalent of the preceding example:

```
class Rectangle {
    constructor(length, width) {
        this.length = length;
        this.width = width;
    }
```

```
    getArea() {
        return this.length * this.width;
    }
}

class Square extends Rectangle {
    constructor(length) {

        // equivalent of Rectangle.call(this, length, length)
        super(length, length);
    }
}

var square = new Square(3);

console.log(square.getArea());              // 9
console.log(square instanceof Square);      // true
console.log(square instanceof Rectangle);   // true
```

This time, the Square class inherits from Rectangle using the extends keyword. The Square constructor uses super() to call the Rectangle constructor with the specified arguments. Note that unlike the ECMAScript 5 version of the code, the identifier Rectangle is only used within the class declaration (after extends).

Classes that inherit from other classes are referred to as *derived classes*. Derived classes require you to use super() if you specify a constructor; if you don't, an error will occur. If you choose not to use a constructor, super() is automatically called for you with all arguments upon creating a new instance of the class. For instance, the following two classes are identical:

```
class Square extends Rectangle {
    // no constructor
}

// is equivalent to

class Square extends Rectangle {
    constructor(...args) {
        super(...args);
    }
}
```

The second class in this example shows the equivalent of the default constructor for all derived classes. All of the arguments are passed, in order, to the base class constructor. In this case, the functionality isn't quite correct because the Square constructor needs only one argument, so it's best to manually define the constructor.

Shadowing Class Methods

The methods on derived classes always shadow methods of the same name on the base class. For instance, you can add getArea() to Square to redefine that functionality:

```
class Square extends Rectangle {
    constructor(length) {
        super(length, length);
    }

    // override and shadow Rectangle.prototype.getArea()
    getArea() {
        return this.length * this.length;
    }
}
```

Because the getArea() method is defined as part of Square, the method Rectangle.prototype.getArea() will no longer be called by any instances of Square. Of course, you can always decide to call the base class version of the method by using the super.getArea() method, like this:

```
class Square extends Rectangle {
    constructor(length) {
        super(length, length);
    }

    // override, shadow, and call Rectangle.prototype.getArea()
    getArea() {
        return super.getArea();
    }
}
```

Using super in this way works the same as the super references discussed in Chapter 4 (see "Easy Prototype Access with Super References"
on page 77). The this value is automatically set correctly so you can
make a simple method call.

Inherited Static Members

If a base class has static members, those static members are also available
on the derived class. Inheritance works like that in other languages, but this
is a new concept in JavaScript. Here's an example:

```
class Rectangle {
    constructor(length, width) {
        this.length = length;
        this.width = width;
    }

    getArea() {
        return this.length * this.width;
    }

    static create(length, width) {
        return new Rectangle(length, width);
    }
}

class Square extends Rectangle {
    constructor(length) {

        // equivalent of Rectangle.call(this, length, length)
        super(length, length);
    }
}

var rect = Square.create(3, 4);

console.log(rect instanceof Rectangle);     // true
console.log(rect.getArea());                // 12
console.log(rect instanceof Square);        // false
```

In this code, a new static create() method is added to the Rectangle
class. Through inheritance, that method is available as Square.create() and
behaves like the Rectangle.create() method.

Derived Classes from Expressions

Perhaps the most powerful aspect of derived classes in ECMAScript 6 is the
ability to derive a class from an expression. You can use extends with any
expression as long as the expression resolves to a function with [[Construct]]
and a prototype. For instance:

```
function Rectangle(length, width) {
    this.length = length;
```

```
        this.width = width;
    }

    Rectangle.prototype.getArea = function() {
        return this.length * this.width;
    };

    class Square extends Rectangle {
        constructor(length) {
            super(length, length);
        }
    }

    var x = new Square(3);
    console.log(x.getArea());              // 9
    console.log(x instanceof Rectangle);   // true
```

Rectangle is defined as an ECMAScript 5–style constructor, and Square is a class. Because Rectangle has [[Construct]] and a prototype, the Square class can still inherit directly from it.

Accepting any type of expression after extends offers powerful possibilities, such as dynamically determining what to inherit from. For example:

```
    function Rectangle(length, width) {
        this.length = length;
        this.width = width;
    }

    Rectangle.prototype.getArea = function() {
        return this.length * this.width;
    };

    function getBase() {
        return Rectangle;
    }

    class Square extends getBase() {
        constructor(length) {
            super(length, length);
        }
    }

    var x = new Square(3);
    console.log(x.getArea());              // 9
    console.log(x instanceof Rectangle);   // true
```

The getBase() function is called directly as part of the class declaration. It returns Rectangle, making this example functionally equivalent to the previous one. And because you can determine the base class dynamically, it's possible to create different inheritance approaches. For instance, you can effectively create mixins, like this:

```
let SerializableMixin = {
    serialize() {
        return JSON.stringify(this);
    }
};

let AreaMixin = {
    getArea() {
        return this.length * this.width;
    }
};

function mixin(...mixins) {
    var base = function() {};
    Object.assign(base.prototype, ...mixins);
    return base;
}

class Square extends mixin(AreaMixin, SerializableMixin) {
    constructor(length) {
        super();
        this.length = length;
        this.width = length;
    }
}

var x = new Square(3);
console.log(x.getArea());            // 9
console.log(x.serialize());          // "{"length":3,"width":3}"
```

This example uses mixins instead of classical inheritance. The mixin() function takes any number of arguments that represent mixin objects. It creates a function called base and assigns the properties of each mixin object to the prototype. The function is then returned so Square can use extends. Keep in mind that because extends is still used, you're required to call super() in the constructor.

The instance of Square has getArea() from AreaMixin and serialize from SerializableMixin. This is accomplished through prototypal inheritance. The mixin() function dynamically populates the prototype of a new function with all of the own properties of each mixin. Keep in mind that if multiple mixins have the same property, only the last property added will remain.

NOTE *You can use any expression after extends, but not all expressions result in a valid class. Specifically, using null or a generator function (covered in Chapter 8) after extends will cause errors. In these cases, attempting to create a new instance of the class will throw an error because there is no [[Construct]] to call.*

Inheriting from Built-Ins

For almost as long as JavaScript arrays have existed, developers have wanted to create their own special array types through inheritance. In ECMAScript 5 and earlier, this wasn't possible. Attempting to use classical inheritance didn't result in functioning code. For example:

```
// built-in array behavior
var colors = [];
colors[0] = "red";
console.log(colors.length);        // 1

colors.length = 0;
console.log(colors[0]);            // undefined

// trying to inherit from array in ES5

function MyArray() {
    Array.apply(this, arguments);
}

MyArray.prototype = Object.create(Array.prototype, {
    constructor: {
        value: MyArray,
        writable: true,
        configurable: true,
        enumerable: true
    }
});

var colors = new MyArray();
colors[0] = "red";
console.log(colors.length);        // 0

colors.length = 0;
console.log(colors[0]);            // "red"
```

The `console.log()` output at the end of this code shows how using the classical form of JavaScript inheritance on an array results in unexpected behavior. The `length` and numeric properties on an instance of `MyArray` don't behave the same way they do for the built-in array because this functionality isn't covered by either `Array.apply()` or assigning the prototype.

One goal of ECMAScript 6 classes is to allow inheritance from all built-ins. To accomplish this, the inheritance model of classes is slightly different than the classical inheritance model found in ECMAScript 5 and earlier, in two significant ways.

In ECMAScript 5 classical inheritance, the value of `this` is first created by the derived type (for example, `MyArray`) and then the base type constructor (like the `Array.apply()` method) is called. That means `this` starts out as an instance of `MyArray` and then is decorated with additional properties from `Array`.

Conversely, in ECMAScript 6 class-based inheritance, the value of this is first created by the base (`Array`) and then modified by the derived class constructor (`MyArray`). The result is that this starts with all the built-in functionality of the base and correctly receives all functionality related to it.

The following example shows a class-based special array in action:

```
class MyArray extends Array {
    // empty
}

var colors = new MyArray();
colors[0] = "red";
console.log(colors.length);         // 1

colors.length = 0;
console.log(colors[0]);             // undefined
```

`MyArray` inherits directly from `Array` and therefore works like `Array`. Interacting with numeric properties updates the `length` property, and manipulating the `length` property updates the numeric properties. That means you can properly inherit from `Array` to create your own derived array classes and inherit from other built-ins as well. With all this added functionality, ECMAScript 6 and derived classes have effectively removed the last special case of inheriting from built-ins, but that case is still worth exploring.

The Symbol.species Property

A convenient aspect of inheriting from built-ins is that any method that returns an instance of the built-in will automatically return a derived class instance instead. So, if you have a derived class called `MyArray` that inherits from `Array`, methods such as `slice()` return an instance of `MyArray`. For example:

```
class MyArray extends Array {
    // empty
}

let items = new MyArray(1, 2, 3, 4),
    subitems = items.slice(1, 3);

console.log(items instanceof MyArray);      // true
console.log(subitems instanceof MyArray);   // true
```

In this code, the `slice()` method returns a `MyArray` instance. The `slice()` method is inherited from `Array` and returns an instance of `Array` normally. Behind the scenes, the `Symbol.species` property is actually making this change.

The `Symbol.species` well-known symbol is used to define a static accessor property that returns a function. That function is a constructor to use whenever an instance of the class must be created inside an instance method (instead of using the constructor). The following built-in types have `Symbol.species` defined:

- `Array`
- `ArrayBuffer` (discussed in Chapter 10)
- `Map`
- `Promise`
- `RegExp`
- `Set`
- Typed arrays (discussed in Chapter 10)

Each type in the list has a default `Symbol.species` property that returns this, meaning the property will always return the constructor function. If you implemented that functionality on a custom class, the code would look like this:

```
// several built-in types use species similar to this
class MyClass {
    static get [Symbol.species]() {
        return this;
    }

    constructor(value) {
        this.value = value;
    }

    clone() {
        return new this.constructor[Symbol.species](this.value);
    }
}
```

In this example, the `Symbol.species` well-known symbol is used to assign a static accessor property to `MyClass`. Note that there's a getter without a setter, because changing the species of a class isn't possible. Any call to `this.constructor[Symbol.species]` returns `MyClass`. The `clone()` method uses that definition to return a new instance rather than directly using `MyClass`, which allows derived classes to override that value. For example:

```
class MyClass {
    static get [Symbol.species]() {
        return this;
    }

    constructor(value) {
        this.value = value;
    }
```

```
        clone() {
            return new this.constructor[Symbol.species](this.value);
        }
    }

    class MyDerivedClass1 extends MyClass {
        // empty
    }

    class MyDerivedClass2 extends MyClass {
        static get [Symbol.species]() {
            return MyClass;
        }
    }

    let instance1 = new MyDerivedClass1("foo"),
        clone1 = instance1.clone(),
        instance2 = new MyDerivedClass2("bar"),
        clone2 = instance2.clone();

    console.log(clone1 instanceof MyClass);             // true
    console.log(clone1 instanceof MyDerivedClass1);     // true
    console.log(clone2 instanceof MyClass);             // true
    console.log(clone2 instanceof MyDerivedClass2);     // false
```

Here, `MyDerivedClass1` inherits from `MyClass` and doesn't change the
`Symbol.species` property. When `clone()` is called, it returns an instance
of `MyDerivedClass1` because `this.constructor[Symbol.species]` returns
`MyDerivedClass1`. The `MyDerivedClass2` class inherits from `MyClass` and
overrides `Symbol.species` to return `MyClass`. When `clone()` is called on an
instance of `MyDerivedClass2`, the return value is an instance of `MyClass`. Using
`Symbol.species`, any derived class can determine what type of value should
be returned when a method returns an instance.

For instance, `Array` uses `Symbol.species` to specify the class to use for
methods that return an array. In a class derived from `Array`, you can determine the type of object returned from the inherited methods, such as:

```
    class MyArray extends Array {
        static get [Symbol.species]() {
            return Array;
        }
    }

    let items = new MyArray(1, 2, 3, 4),
        subitems = items.slice(1, 3);

    console.log(items instanceof MyArray);          // true
    console.log(subitems instanceof Array);         // true
    console.log(subitems instanceof MyArray);       // false
```

This code overrides `Symbol.species` on `MyArray`, which inherits from `Array`. All of the inherited methods that return arrays will now use an instance of `Array` instead of `MyArray`.

In general, you should use the `Symbol.species` property whenever you might want to use `this.constructor` in a class method. Doing so allows derived classes to override the return type easily. Additionally, if you're creating derived classes from a class that has `Symbol.species` defined, be sure to use that value instead of the constructor.

Using new.target in Class Constructors

In Chapter 3, you learned about `new.target` and how its value changes depending on how a function is called. You can also use `new.target` in class constructors to determine how the class is being invoked. In the simple case, `new.target` is equal to the constructor function for the class, as in this example:

```
class Rectangle {
    constructor(length, width) {
        console.log(new.target === Rectangle);
        this.length = length;
        this.width = width;
    }
}

// new.target is Rectangle
var obj = new Rectangle(3, 4);        // outputs true
```

This code shows that `new.target` is equivalent to `Rectangle` when `new Rectangle(3, 4)` is called. Class constructors can't be called without `new`, so the `new.target` property is always defined inside class constructors. But the value may not always be the same. Consider this code:

```
class Rectangle {
    constructor(length, width) {
        console.log(new.target === Rectangle);
        this.length = length;
        this.width = width;
    }
}

class Square extends Rectangle {
    constructor(length) {
        super(length, length)
    }
}

// new.target is Square
var obj = new Square(3);        // outputs false
```

Square is calling the Rectangle constructor, so new.target is equal to Square when the Rectangle constructor is called. This is important because it gives each constructor the ability to alter its behavior based on how it's being called. For instance, you can create an abstract base class (one that can't be instantiated directly) by using new.target as follows:

```
// abstract base class
class Shape {
    constructor() {
        if (new.target === Shape) {
            throw new Error("This class cannot be instantiated directly.")
        }
    }
}

class Rectangle extends Shape {
    constructor(length, width) {
        super();
        this.length = length;
        this.width = width;
    }
}

var x = new Shape();                    // throws an error

var y = new Rectangle(3, 4);            // no error
console.log(y instanceof Shape);        // true
```

In this example, the Shape class constructor throws an error whenever new.target is Shape, meaning that new Shape() always throws an error. However, you can still use Shape as a base class, which is what Rectangle does. The super() call executes the Shape constructor and new.target is equal to Rectangle so the constructor continues without error.

NOTE *Because classes can't be called without new, the new.target property is never undefined inside a class constructor.*

Summary

ECMAScript 6 classes make inheritance in JavaScript easier to use, so you don't need to disregard any existing understanding of inheritance you might have from other languages. ECMAScript 6 classes started as syntactic sugar for the classical inheritance model in ECMAScript 5 but added several features to reduce mistakes.

ECMAScript 6 classes work with prototypal inheritance by defining nonstatic methods on the class prototype, whereas static methods end up on the constructor. All methods are nonenumerable, which better matches the behavior of built-in objects whose methods are typically nonenumerable by default. Additionally, class constructors can't be called without `new`, ensuring that you can't accidentally call a class as a function.

Class-based inheritance allows you to derive a class from another class, function, or expression. This capability means you can call a function to determine the correct base to inherit from, allowing you to use mixins and other different composition patterns to create a new class. Inheritance works in such a way that inheriting from built-in objects like `Array` is now possible and works as expected.

You can use `new.target` in class constructors to behave differently depending on how the class is called. The most common use is to create an abstract base class that throws an error when instantiated directly but still allows inheritance via other classes.

Overall, classes are an important addition to JavaScript. They provide a more concise syntax and better functionality for defining custom object types in a safe, consistent manner.

10

IMPROVED ARRAY CAPABILITIES

The array is a foundational JavaScript object. But while other aspects of JavaScript have evolved over time, arrays remained the same until ECMAScript 5 introduced several methods to make them easier to use. ECMAScript 6 continues to improve arrays by adding a lot more functionality, such as new creation methods, several useful convenience methods, and the ability to make typed arrays. This chapter walks you through those changes in detail.

Creating Arrays

Prior to ECMAScript 6, the two primary ways to create arrays were the `Array` constructor and array literal syntax. Both approaches required listing array items individually and were otherwise fairly limited. Options for converting an array-like object (that is, an object with numeric indexes and a `length` property) into an array were also limited and often required extra code. To make JavaScript arrays easier to create, ECMAScript 6 has the `Array.of()` and `Array.from()` methods.

The Array.of() Method

One reason ECMAScript 6 added new creation methods to JavaScript was to help developers avoid a quirk of creating arrays with the `Array` constructor. The `Array` constructor actually behaves differently based on the type and number of arguments passed to it. For example:

```
let items = new Array(2);
console.log(items.length);        // 2
console.log(items[0]);            // undefined
console.log(items[1]);            // undefined

items = new Array("2");
console.log(items.length);        // 1
console.log(items[0]);            // "2"

items = new Array(1, 2);
console.log(items.length);        // 2
console.log(items[0]);            // 1
console.log(items[1]);            // 2

items = new Array(3, "2");
console.log(items.length);        // 2
console.log(items[0]);            // 3
console.log(items[1]);            // "2"
```

When the `Array` constructor is passed a single numeric value, the array's length property is set to that value. If a single nonnumeric value is passed, that value becomes the one and only item in the array. If multiple values are passed (numeric or not), those values become items in the array. This behavior is confusing and risky, because you might not always be aware of the type of data being passed.

ECMAScript 6 introduces `Array.of()` to solve this problem. The `Array.of()` method works similarly to the `Array` constructor but has no special case regarding a single numeric value. The `Array.of()` method always creates an array containing its arguments regardless of the number of arguments or the argument types. Here are some examples that use the `Array.of()` method:

```
let items = Array.of(1, 2);
console.log(items.length);        // 2
console.log(items[0]);            // 1
console.log(items[1]);            // 2

items = Array.of(2);
console.log(items.length);        // 1
console.log(items[0]);            // 2
```

```
items = Array.of("2");
console.log(items.length);        // 1
console.log(items[0]);            // "2"
```

To create an array with the `Array.of()` method, just pass it the values you want in your array. This first example creates an array containing two numbers, the second array contains one number, and the last array contains one string. This approach is similar to using an array literal, and you can use an array literal instead of `Array.of()` for native arrays most of the time. But if you ever need to pass the `Array` constructor into a function, you might want to pass `Array.of()` instead to ensure consistent behavior. For example:

```
function createArray(arrayCreator, value) {
    return arrayCreator(value);
}

let items = createArray(Array.of, value);
```

In this code, the `createArray()` function accepts an array creator function and a value to insert into the array. You can pass `Array.of()` as the first argument to `createArray()` to create a new array. It would be dangerous to pass `Array` directly if you cannot guarantee that value won't be a number.

NOTE   *The `Array.of()` method does not use the `Symbol.species` property (see page 185) to determine the type of return value. Instead, it uses the current constructor (`this` inside the `of()` method) to determine the correct data type to return.*

The Array.from() Method

Converting nonarray objects into actual arrays has always been cumbersome in JavaScript. For instance, if you have an `arguments` object (which is array-like) and want to use it like an array, you'd need to convert it first. To convert an array-like object to an array in ECMAScript 5, you'd write a function like the one in this example:

```
function makeArray(arrayLike) {
    var result = [];

    for (var i = 0, len = arrayLike.length; i < len; i++) {
        result.push(arrayLike[i]);
    }

    return result;
}

function doSomething() {
    var args = makeArray(arguments);

    // use args
}
```

This approach manually creates a result array and copies each item from arguments into the new array. Although this approach works, it takes a decent amount of code to perform a relatively simple operation. Eventually, developers discovered they could reduce the amount of code they used by calling the native slice() method for arrays on array-like objects, like this:

```
function makeArray(arrayLike) {
    return Array.prototype.slice.call(arrayLike);
}

function doSomething() {
    var args = makeArray(arguments);

    // use args
}
```

This code is functionally equivalent to the previous example, and it works because it sets the this value for slice() to the array-like object. Because slice() needs only numeric indexes and a length property to function correctly, any array-like object will work.

Even though you don't have to type as much when using this technique, calling Array.prototype.slice.call(arrayLike) doesn't obviously translate to "Convert arrayLike to an array." Fortunately, ECMAScript 6 added the Array.from() method as an obvious, yet clean, way to convert objects into arrays.

Given either an iterable or an array-like object as the first argument, the Array.from() method returns an array. Here's a simple example:

```
function doSomething() {
    var args = Array.from(arguments);

    // use args
}
```

The Array.from() call creates a new array based on the items in arguments. So args is an instance of Array that contains the same values in the same positions as arguments.

NOTE   *The Array.from() method also uses this to determine the type of array to return.*

Mapping Conversion

If you want to take array conversion a step further, you can provide Array.from() with a mapping function as a second argument. That function operates on each value from the array-like object and converts it to some final form before storing the result at the appropriate index in the final array. Consider the following example.

```
function translate() {
    return Array.from(arguments, (value) => value + 1);
}

let numbers = translate(1, 2, 3);

console.log(numbers);              // 2,3,4
```

Here, `Array.from()` is passed `(value) => value + 1` as a mapping function, so it adds 1 to each item in the array before storing the item. If the mapping function is on an object, you can also optionally pass a third argument to `Array.from()` that represents the this value for the mapping function:

```
let helper = {
    diff: 1,

    add(value) {
        return value + this.diff;
    }
};

function translate() {
    return Array.from(arguments, helper.add, helper);
}

let numbers = translate(1, 2, 3);

console.log(numbers);              // 2,3,4
```

This example passes `helper.add()` as the mapping function for the conversion. Because `helper.add()` uses the `this.diff` property, you need to provide the third argument to `Array.from()` specifying the value of this. Thanks to the third argument, `Array.from()` can easily convert data without calling `bind()` or specifying the this value in some other way.

Use on Iterables

The `Array.from()` method works on array-like objects and iterables. That means the method can convert any object with a `Symbol.iterator` property into an array. For example:

```
let numbers = {
    *[Symbol.iterator]() {
        yield 1;
        yield 2;
        yield 3;
    }
};

let numbers2 = Array.from(numbers, (value) => value + 1);

console.log(numbers2);              // 2,3,4
```

Because the `numbers` object is an iterable, you can pass `numbers` directly to `Array.from()` to convert its values into an array. The mapping function adds 1 to each number, so the resulting array contains 2, 3, and 4 instead of 1, 2, and 3.

NOTE *If an object is array-like and an iterable, the iterator is used by `Array.from()` to determine the values to convert.*

New Methods on All Arrays

Continuing the trend from ECMAScript 5, ECMAScript 6 adds several new methods to arrays. The `find()` and `findIndex()` methods are meant to aid developers using arrays with any values, whereas `fill()` and `copyWithin()` are inspired by use cases for *typed arrays*, a form of array introduced in ECMAScript 6 that uses only numbers.

The find() and findIndex() Methods

Prior to ECMAScript 5, searching through arrays was cumbersome because there were no built-in methods for doing so. ECMAScript 5 added the `indexOf()` and `lastIndexOf()` methods, which finally allowed developers to search for specific values inside an array. These two methods were a big improvement, yet they were still fairly limited because you could search for only one value at a time. For example, if you wanted to find the first even number in a series of numbers, you'd need to write your own code to do so. ECMAScript 6 solved that problem by introducing the `find()` and `findIndex()` methods.

Both `find()` and `findIndex()` accept two arguments: a callback function and an optional value to use for this inside the callback function. The callback function is passed an array element, the index of that element in the array, and the actual array—the same arguments passed to methods like `map()` and `forEach()`. The callback should return true if the given value matches some criteria you define. Both `find()` and `findIndex()` also stop searching the array the first time the callback function returns true.

The only difference between these methods is that `find()` returns the value, whereas `findIndex()` returns the index at which the value was found. Here's an example to demonstrate:

```
let numbers = [25, 30, 35, 40, 45];

console.log(numbers.find(n => n > 33));        // 35
console.log(numbers.findIndex(n => n > 33));   // 2
```

This code calls `find()` and `findIndex()` to locate the first value in the `numbers` array that is greater than 33. The call to `find()` returns 35 and `findIndex()` returns 2, the location of 35 in the `numbers` array.

Both `find()` and `findIndex()` are useful to find an array element that matches a condition rather than a value. If you only want to find a value, `indexOf()` and `lastIndexOf()` are better choices.

The fill() Method

The `fill()` method fills one or more array elements with a specific value. When passed a value, `fill()` overwrites all the values in an array with that value. For example:

```
let numbers = [1, 2, 3, 4];

numbers.fill(1);

console.log(numbers.toString());    // 1,1,1,1
```

Here, the call to `numbers.fill(1)` changes all elements in `numbers` to 1. If you want to change only some of the elements rather than all of them, you can optionally include a start index and an exclusive end index, like this:

```
let numbers = [1, 2, 3, 4];

numbers.fill(1, 2);

console.log(numbers.toString());    // 1,2,1,1

numbers.fill(0, 1, 3);

console.log(numbers.toString());    // 1,0,0,1
```

In the `numbers.fill(1, 2)` call, the 2 argument starts filling elements at index 2. The exclusive end index isn't specified with a third argument, so `numbers.length` is used as the end index, meaning the last two elements in `numbers` are filled with 1. The `numbers.fill(0, 1, 3)` operation fills array elements at indexes 1 and 2 with 0. Calling `fill()` with the second and third arguments allows you to fill multiple array elements at once without overwriting the entire array.

NOTE   *If either the start or end index is negative, those values are added to the array's length to determine the final location. For instance, a start location of `-1` gives `array.length - 1` as the index, where `array` is the array on which `fill()` is called.*

The copyWithin() Method

The `copyWithin()` method is similar to `fill()` in that it changes multiple array elements at the same time. However, instead of specifying a single value to assign to array elements, `copyWithin()` lets you copy array element values from the array. To accomplish that, you need to pass two arguments to the `copyWithin()` method: the index where the method should start filling values and the index where the values to be copied begin.

For instance, to copy the values from the first two elements in an array to the last two items in the array, you can do the following:

```
let numbers = [1, 2, 3, 4];

// paste values into array starting at index 2
// copy values from array starting at index 0
numbers.copyWithin(2, 0);

console.log(numbers.toString());    // 1,2,1,2
```

This code pastes values into numbers beginning from index 2, so indexes 2 and 3 will be overwritten. Passing 0 as the second argument to copyWithin() starts copying values from index 0 and continues until there are no more elements to copy into.

By default, copyWithin() always copies values up to the end of the array, but you can provide an optional third argument to limit how many elements will be overwritten. That third argument is an exclusive end index at which copying of values stops. Here's how that looks in code:

```
let numbers = [1, 2, 3, 4];

// paste values into array starting at index 2
// copy values from array starting at index 0
// stop copying values when you hit index 1
numbers.copyWithin(2, 0, 1);

console.log(numbers.toString());    // 1,2,1,4
```

In this example, only the value in index 0 is copied because the optional end index is set to 1. The last element in the array remains unchanged.

NOTE   *As with the fill() method, if you pass a negative number for any argument to the copyWithin() method, the array's length is automatically added to that value to determine the index to use.*

The use cases for fill() and copyWithin() may not be obvious to you at this point. The reason is that these methods originated on typed arrays and were added to regular arrays for consistency. However, as you'll learn in the next section, if you use typed arrays for manipulating the bits of a number, these methods become a lot more useful.

Typed Arrays

Typed arrays are special-purpose arrays designed to work with numeric types (not all types, as the name might imply). The origin of typed arrays can be traced to WebGL, a port of OpenGL ES 2.0 designed for use in web pages with the <canvas> element. Typed arrays were created as part of the port to provide fast bitwise arithmetic in JavaScript.

Arithmetic on native JavaScript numbers was too slow for WebGL because the numbers were stored in a 64-bit floating-point format and converted to 32-bit integers as needed. Typed arrays were introduced to circumvent this limitation and provide better performance for arithmetic operations. The concept is that any single number can be treated like an array of bits and thus can use the familiar methods available on JavaScript arrays.

ECMAScript 6 adopted typed arrays as a formal part of the language to ensure better compatibility across JavaScript engines and interoperability with JavaScript arrays. Although the ECMAScript 6 version of typed arrays is not the same as the WebGL version, enough similarities exist to make the ECMAScript 6 version an evolution of the WebGL version rather than a different approach.

Numeric Data Types

JavaScript numbers are stored in IEEE 754 format, which uses 64 bits to store a floating-point representation of the number. This format represents integers and floats in JavaScript, and the conversion between the two formats happens frequently as numbers change. Typed arrays allow for the storage and manipulation of eight different numeric types:

- Signed 8-bit integer (int8)
- Unsigned 8-bit integer (uint8)
- Signed 16-bit integer (int16)
- Unsigned 16-bit integer (uint16)
- Signed 32-bit integer (int32)
- Unsigned 32-bit integer (uint32)
- 32-bit float (float32)
- 64-bit float (float64)

If you represent a number that fits in an int8 as a normal JavaScript number, you'll waste 56 bits. Those bits might better be used to store additional int8 values or any other number that requires less than 56 bits. Using bits more efficiently is one of the use cases typed arrays address.

All the operations and objects related to typed arrays are centered on these eight data types. But to use them, you'll need to create an array buffer to store the data.

NOTE   *In this book, I refer to the eight data types using the abbreviations I showed in parentheses. Those abbreviations don't appear in actual JavaScript code; they're just shorthand for the much longer descriptions.*

Array Buffers

The foundation for all typed arrays is an *array buffer*, which is a memory location that can contain a specified number of bytes. Creating an array buffer is akin to calling `malloc()` in C to allocate memory without specifying what the memory block contains. You can create an array buffer by using the `ArrayBuffer` constructor as follows:

```
let buffer = new ArrayBuffer(10);    // allocate 10 bytes
```

Just pass the number of bytes the array buffer should contain when you call the constructor. This `let` statement creates an array buffer 10 bytes long. After an array buffer is created, you can retrieve the number of bytes in it by checking the `byteLength` property:

```
let buffer = new ArrayBuffer(10);    // allocate 10 bytes
console.log(buffer.byteLength);      // 10
```

You can also use the `slice()` method to create a new array buffer that contains part of an existing array buffer. The `slice()` method works like the `slice()` method on arrays: you pass it the start index and end index as arguments, and it returns a new `ArrayBuffer` instance composed of those elements from the original. For example:

```
let buffer = new ArrayBuffer(10);    // allocate 10 bytes
let buffer2 = buffer.slice(4, 6);
console.log(buffer2.byteLength);     // 2
```

In this code, `buffer2` is created by extracting the bytes at indexes 4 and 5. Similar to when you call the array version of this method, the second argument to `slice()` is exclusive.

Of course, creating a storage location isn't very helpful without being able to write data into that location. To do so, you'll need to create a view.

NOTE *An array buffer always represents the exact number of bytes specified when it was created. You can change the data contained within an array buffer but never the size of the array buffer.*

Manipulating Array Buffers with Views

Array buffers represent memory locations, and *views* are the interfaces you'll use to manipulate that memory. A view operates on an array buffer or a subset of an array buffer's bytes, reading and writing data in one of the numeric data types. The `DataView` type is a generic view on an array buffer that allows you to operate on all eight numeric data types.

To use a `DataView`, you first create an instance of `ArrayBuffer` and use it to create a new `DataView`. Here's an example:

```
let buffer = new ArrayBuffer(10),
    view = new DataView(buffer);
```

The view object in this example has access to all 10 bytes in buffer. You can also create a view over a portion of a buffer. Just provide a byte offset and, optionally, the number of bytes to include from that offset. When a number of bytes isn't included, the DataView will go from the offset to the end of the buffer by default. For example:

```
let buffer = new ArrayBuffer(10),
    view = new DataView(buffer, 5, 2);       // cover bytes 5 and 6
```

Here, view operates only on the bytes at indexes 5 and 6. This approach allows you to create several views over the same array buffer, which can be useful if you want to use a single memory location for an entire application rather than dynamically allocating space as needed.

Retrieving View Information

You can retrieve information about a view by fetching the following read-only properties:

buffer   The array buffer that the view is tied to

byteOffset   The second argument to the DataView constructor, if provided (0 by default)

byteLength   The third argument to the DataView constructor, if provided (the buffer's byteLength by default)

Using these properties, you can inspect exactly where a view is operating, like this:

```
let buffer = new ArrayBuffer(10),
    view1 = new DataView(buffer),            // cover all bytes
    view2 = new DataView(buffer, 5, 2);      // cover bytes 5 and 6

console.log(view1.buffer === buffer);        // true
console.log(view2.buffer === buffer);        // true
console.log(view1.byteOffset);               // 0
console.log(view2.byteOffset);               // 5
console.log(view1.byteLength);               // 10
console.log(view2.byteLength);               // 2
```

This code creates view1, a view over the entire array buffer, and view2, which operates on a small section of the array buffer. These views have equivalent buffer properties because both work on the same array buffer. However, the byteOffset and byteLength are different for each view. They reflect the portion of the array buffer where each view operates.

Of course, reading information about memory isn't very useful on its own. You need to write data into and read data out of that memory to get any benefit.

Reading and Writing Data

For each of JavaScript's eight numeric data types, the `DataView` prototype has a method to write data and a method to read data from an array buffer. The method names all begin with either *set* or *get* and are followed by the data type abbreviation. For instance, here's a list of the read and write methods that can operate on int8 and uint8 values:

getInt8(*byteOffset, littleEndian*)   Read an int8 starting at *byteOffset*

setInt8(*byteOffset, value, littleEndian*)   Write an int8 starting at *byteOffset*

getUint8(*byteOffset, littleEndian*)   Read a uint8 starting at *byteOffset*

setUint8(*byteOffset, value, littleEndian*)   Write a uint8 starting at *byteOffset*

The get methods accept two arguments: the byte offset to read from and an optional Boolean indicating whether the value should be read as little-endian. (*Little-endian* means the least significant byte is at byte 0 instead of in the last byte.) The set methods accept three arguments: the byte offset to write at, the value to write, and an optional Boolean indicating whether the value should be stored in little-endian format.

Although I've only shown the methods you can use with 8-bit values, the same methods exist for operating on 16- and 32-bit values. Just replace the 8 in each name with 16 or 32. In addition to all those integer methods, `DataView` also has the following read and write methods for floating-point numbers:

getFloat32(*byteOffset, littleEndian*)   Read a float32 starting at *byteOffset*

setFloat32(*byteOffset, value, littleEndian*)   Write a float32 starting at *byteOffset*

getFloat64(*byteOffset, littleEndian*)   Read a float64 starting at *byteOffset*

setFloat64(*byteOffset, value, littleEndian*)   Write a float64 starting at *byteOffset*

The following example shows a set and a get method in action:

```
let buffer = new ArrayBuffer(2),
    view = new DataView(buffer);

view.setInt8(0, 5);
view.setInt8(1, -1);

console.log(view.getInt8(0));       // 5
console.log(view.getInt8(1));       // -1
```

This code uses a two-byte array buffer to store two int8 values. The first value is set at offset 0, and the second is at offset 1, reflecting that each value spans a full byte (8 bits). Those values are later retrieved from their positions with the getInt8() method. Although this example uses int8 values, you can use any of the eight numeric types with their corresponding methods.

Views are unique because they allow you to read and write in any format at any point in time regardless of how data was previously stored. For instance, writing two int8 values and reading the buffer with an int16 method works just fine, as in this example:

```
let buffer = new ArrayBuffer(2),
    view = new DataView(buffer);

view.setInt8(0, 5);
view.setInt8(1, -1);

console.log(view.getInt16(0));      // 1535
console.log(view.getInt8(0));       // 5
console.log(view.getInt8(1));       // -1
```

The call to view.getInt16(0) reads all bytes in the view and interprets those bytes as the number 1535. To understand why this happens, look at Figure 10-1, which shows what each setInt8() line does to the array buffer.

Figure 10-1: The array buffer after two method calls

The array buffer starts with 16 bits that are all 0. Writing 5 to the first byte with setInt8() introduces a couple of 1s (in 8-bit representation, 5 is 00000101). Writing −1 to the second byte sets all bits in that byte to 1, which is the two's complement representation of −1. After the second setInt8() call, the array buffer contains 16 bits, and getInt16() reads those bits as a single 16-bit integer, which is 1535 in decimal.

The DataView object is perfect for use cases that mix different data types in this way. However, if you're only using one specific data type, the type-specific views are a better choice.

Typed Arrays Are Views

ECMAScript 6 typed arrays are actually type-specific views for array buffers. Instead of using a generic DataView object to operate on an array buffer, you can use objects that enforce specific data types. Eight type-specific views correspond to the eight numeric data types, plus an additional option for uint8 values. Table 10-1 shows an abbreviated version of the complete list of type-specific views in section 22.2 of the ECMAScript 6 specification.

Table 10-1: Some Type-Specific Views in ECMAScript 6

Constructor name	Element size (in bytes)	Description	Equivalent C type
Int8Array	1	8-bit two's complement signed integer	signed char
Uint8Array	1	8-bit unsigned integer	unsigned char
Uint8ClampedArray	1	8-bit unsigned integer (clamped conversion)	unsigned char
Int16Array	2	16-bit two's complement signed integer	short
Uint16Array	2	16-bit unsigned integer	unsigned short
Int32Array	4	32-bit two's complement signed integer	int
Uint32Array	4	32-bit unsigned integer	int
Float32Array	4	32-bit IEEE floating point	float
Float64Array	8	64-bit IEEE floating point	double

The Constructor name column lists the typed array constructors, and the other columns describe the data each typed array can contain. A Uint8ClampedArray is the same as a Uint8Array unless values in the array buffer are less than 0 or greater than 255. A Uint8ClampedArray converts values less than 0 to 0 (–1 becomes 0, for instance) and converts values greater than 255 to 255 (so 300 becomes 255).

Typed array operations only work on a particular type of data. For example, all operations on Int8Array use int8 values. The size of an element in a typed array also depends on the type of array. Although an element in an Int8Array is a single byte long, Float64Array uses eight bytes per element. Fortunately, the elements are accessed using numeric indexes just like regular arrays, allowing you to avoid the somewhat awkward calls to the set and get methods of DataView.

Creating Type-Specific Views

Typed array constructors accept multiple types of arguments, so you can create typed arrays in a few ways. First, you can create a new typed array by passing the same arguments DataView takes (an array buffer, an optional byte offset, and an optional byte length). For example:

```
let buffer = new ArrayBuffer(10),
    view1 = new Int8Array(buffer),
    view2 = new Int8Array(buffer, 5, 2);

console.log(view1.buffer === buffer);    // true
console.log(view2.buffer === buffer);    // true
console.log(view1.byteOffset);           // 0
console.log(view2.byteOffset);           // 5
```

```
console.log(view1.byteLength);              // 10
console.log(view2.byteLength);              // 2
```

In this code, the two views are Int8Array instances that use buffer. Both view1 and view2 have the same buffer, byteOffset, and byteLength properties that exist on DataView instances. It's easy to switch to using a typed array wherever you use a DataView as long as you only work with one numeric type.

The second way to create a typed array is to pass a single number to the constructor. That number represents the number of elements (not bytes) to allocate to the array. The constructor will create a new buffer with the correct number of bytes to represent that number of array elements, and you can access the number of elements in the array by using the length property. Here's an example:

```
let ints = new Int16Array(2),
    floats = new Float32Array(5);

console.log(ints.byteLength);       // 4
console.log(ints.length);           // 2

console.log(floats.byteLength);     // 20
console.log(floats.length);         // 5
```

The ints array is created with space for two elements. Each 16-bit integer requires two bytes per value, so the array is allocated four bytes. The floats array is created to hold five elements, so the number of bytes required is 20 (four bytes per element). In both cases, a new buffer is created and can be accessed using the buffer property if necessary.

NOTE *If no argument is passed to a typed array constructor, the constructor acts as if 0 was passed. This creates a typed array that cannot hold data because zero bytes are allocated to the buffer.*

The third way to create a typed array is to pass an object as the only argument to the constructor. The object can be any of the following:

A typed array   Each element is copied into a new element on the new typed array. For example, if you pass an int8 to the Int16Array constructor, the int8 values would be copied into an int16 array. The new typed array has a different array buffer than the one that was passed in.

An iterable   The object's iterator is called to retrieve the items to insert into the typed array. The constructor will throw an error if any elements are invalid for the view type.

An array   The elements of the array are copied into a new typed array. The constructor will throw an error if any elements are invalid for the type.

An array-like object   The object behaves the same as an array.

In each of these cases, a new typed array is created with the data from the source object. This can be especially useful when you want to initialize a typed array with some values, like this:

```
let ints1 = new Int16Array([25, 50]),
    ints2 = new Int32Array(ints1);

console.log(ints1.buffer === ints2.buffer);      // false

console.log(ints1.byteLength);      // 4
console.log(ints1.length);          // 2
console.log(ints1[0]);              // 25
console.log(ints1[1]);              // 50

console.log(ints2.byteLength);      // 8
console.log(ints2.length);          // 2
console.log(ints2[0]);              // 25
console.log(ints2[1]);              // 50
```

This example creates an Int16Array and initializes it with an array of two values. Then, an Int32Array is created and passed the Int16Array. The values 25 and 50 are copied from ints1 into ints2 because the two typed arrays have completely separate buffers. The same numbers are represented in both typed arrays, but ints2 has eight bytes to represent the data and ints1 has only four.

ELEMENT SIZE

Each typed array is made up of a number of elements, and the element size is the number of bytes each element represents. This value is stored on a BYTES_PER_ELEMENT property on each constructor and each instance, so you can easily query the element size:

```
console.log(UInt8Array.BYTES_PER_ELEMENT);      // 1
console.log(UInt16Array.BYTES_PER_ELEMENT);     // 2

let ints = new Int8Array(5);
console.log(ints.BYTES_PER_ELEMENT);            // 1
```

As this code shows, you can check BYTES_PER_ELEMENT on the different typed array classes, and you can also check it on instances of those classes.

Similarities Between Typed and Regular Arrays

Typed arrays and regular arrays are similar in several ways, and as you've seen in this chapter, you can use typed arrays like regular arrays in many situations. For instance, you can check how many elements are in a typed array using the `length` property, and you can access a typed array's elements directly using numeric indexes. For example:

```
let ints = new Int16Array([25, 50]);

console.log(ints.length);       // 2
console.log(ints[0]);           // 25
console.log(ints[1]);           // 50

ints[0] = 1;
ints[1] = 2;

console.log(ints[0]);           // 1
console.log(ints[1]);           // 2
```

In this code, a new `Int16Array` with two items is created. The items are read from and written to using their numeric indexes, and those values are automatically stored and converted into int16 values as part of the operation. But the similarities don't end there.

NOTE   *Unlike regular arrays, you cannot change the size of a typed array using the* `length` *property. The* `length` *property is not writable, so any attempt to change it is ignored in non-strict mode and throws an error in strict mode.*

Common Methods

Typed arrays also include many methods that are functionally equivalent to regular array methods. You can use the following array methods on typed arrays:

copyWithin()	findIndex()	lastIndexOf()	slice()
entries()	forEach()	map()	some()
fill()	indexOf()	reduce()	sort()
filter()	join()	reduceRight()	values()
find()	keys()	reverse()	

Keep in mind that although these methods act like their counterparts on `Array.prototype`, they're not exactly the same. The typed array methods have additional checks for numeric type safety and, when an array is returned, it is a typed array instead of a regular array (due to `Symbol.species`). Here's a simple example to demonstrate the difference:

```
let ints = new Int16Array([25, 50]),
    mapped = ints.map(v => v * 2);

console.log(mapped.length);            // 2
console.log(mapped[0]);                // 50
console.log(mapped[1]);                // 100

console.log(mapped instanceof Int16Array);  // true
```

This code uses the `map()` method to create a new array based on the values in `ints`. The mapping function doubles each value in the array and returns a new `Int16Array`.

The Same Iterators

Typed arrays have the same three iterators as regular arrays, too. Those are the `entries()` method, the `keys()` method, and the `values()` method. That means you can use the spread operator and `for-of` loops with typed arrays just like you would with regular arrays. For example:

```
let ints = new Int16Array([25, 50]),
    intsArray = [...ints];

console.log(intsArray instanceof Array);   // true
console.log(intsArray[0]);                 // 25
console.log(intsArray[1]);                 // 50
```

This code creates a new array called `intsArray` containing the same data as the typed array `ints`. As with other iterables, the spread operator makes converting typed arrays into regular arrays easy.

The of() and from() Methods

Additionally, all typed arrays have static `of()` and `from()` methods that work like the `Array.of()` and `Array.from()` methods. The difference is that the methods on typed arrays return a typed array instead of a regular array. Here are some examples that use these methods to create typed arrays:

```
let ints = Int16Array.of(25, 50),
    floats = Float32Array.from([1.5, 2.5]);

console.log(ints instanceof Int16Array);        // true
console.log(floats instanceof Float32Array);    // true
```

```
console.log(ints.length);        // 2
console.log(ints[0]);            // 25
console.log(ints[1]);            // 50

console.log(floats.length);      // 2
console.log(floats[0]);          // 1.5
console.log(floats[1]);          // 2.5
```

The of() and from() methods in this example create an Int16Array and a Float32Array, respectively. These methods ensure that typed arrays can be created just as easily as regular arrays.

Differences Between Typed and Regular Arrays

The most importance difference between typed arrays and regular arrays is that typed arrays are not regular arrays. Typed arrays don't inherit from Array and Array.isArray() returns false when passed a typed array. For example:

```
let ints = new Int16Array([25, 50]);

console.log(ints instanceof Array);    // false
console.log(Array.isArray(ints));      // false
```

Because the ints variable is a typed array, it isn't an instance of Array and cannot be identified as an array. This distinction is important because although typed arrays and regular arrays are similar, typed arrays behave differently in many ways.

Behavioral Differences

Regular arrays can grow and shrink as you interact with them, but typed arrays always remain the same size. You cannot assign a value to a non-existent numeric index in a typed array like you can with regular arrays, because typed arrays ignore the operation. Here's an example:

```
let ints = new Int16Array([25, 50]);

console.log(ints.length);        // 2
console.log(ints[0]);            // 25
console.log(ints[1]);            // 50

ints[2] = 5;

console.log(ints.length);        // 2
console.log(ints[2]);            // undefined
```

Despite assigning 5 to the numeric index 2 in this example, the `ints` array does not grow at all. The `length` remains the same, and the value is thrown away.

Typed arrays also have checks to ensure that only valid data types are used. Zero is used in place of any invalid values. For example:

```
let ints = new Int16Array(["hi"]);

console.log(ints.length);       // 1
console.log(ints[0]);           // 0
```

This code attempts to use the string value `"hi"` in an `Int16Array`. Of course, strings are invalid data types in typed arrays, so the value is inserted as 0 instead. The `length` of the array is still 1, and even though the `ints[0]` slot exists, it just contains 0.

All methods that modify values in a typed array enforce the same restriction. For example, if the function passed to `map()` returns an invalid value for the type array, then 0 is used instead:

```
let ints = new Int16Array([25, 50]),
    mapped = ints.map(v => "hi");

console.log(mapped.length);     // 2
console.log(mapped[0]);         // 0
console.log(mapped[1]);         // 0

console.log(mapped instanceof Int16Array);  // true
console.log(mapped instanceof Array);       // false
```

Because the string value `"hi"` isn't a 16-bit integer, it's replaced with 0 in the resulting array. Thanks to this error correction behavior, typed array methods don't have to throw errors when invalid data is present, because invalid data will never be in the array.

Missing Methods

Although typed arrays do have many of the same methods as regular arrays, they also lack several array methods. The following methods are not available on typed arrays:

concat()	shift()
pop()	splice()
push()	unshift()

Except for the `concat()` method, the methods in this list can change the size of an array. Typed arrays can't change size, which is why these methods aren't available for typed arrays. The `concat()` method isn't available because the result of concatenating two typed arrays (especially if they deal with different data types) would be uncertain, and that would contradict the reason for using typed arrays in the first place.

Additional Methods

Finally, typed array methods have two methods not present on regular arrays: the set() and subarray() methods. These two methods are opposites in that set() copies another array into an existing typed array, whereas subarray() extracts part of an existing typed array into a new typed array.

The set() method accepts an array (either typed or regular) and an optional offset at which to insert the data; if you pass nothing, the offset defaults to zero. The data from the array argument is copied into the destination typed array while ensuring only valid data types are used. Here's an example:

```
let ints = new Int16Array(4);

ints.set([25, 50]);
ints.set([75, 100], 2);

console.log(ints.toString());    // 25,50,75,100
```

This code creates an Int16Array with four elements. The first call to set() copies two values to the first and second elements in the array. The second call to set() uses an offset of 2 to indicate that the values should be placed in the array starting at the third element.

The subarray() method accepts an optional start and end index (the end index is exclusive, as in the slice() method) and returns a new typed array. You can also omit both arguments to create a clone of the typed array. For example:

```
let ints = new Int16Array([25, 50, 75, 100]),
    subints1 = ints.subarray(),
    subints2 = ints.subarray(2),
    subints3 = ints.subarray(1, 3);

console.log(subints1.toString());    // 25,50,75,100
console.log(subints2.toString());    // 75,100
console.log(subints3.toString());    // 50,75
```

Three typed arrays are created from the original ints array in this example. The subints1 array is a clone of ints that contains the same information. Because the subints2 array copies data starting from index 2, it only contains the last two elements of the ints array (75 and 100). The subints3 array contains only the middle two elements of the ints array, because subarray() was called with a start and an end index.

Summary

ECMAScript 6 continues the work of ECMAScript 5 by making arrays more useful. New features include two more ways to create arrays: the `Array.of()` and `Array.from()` methods. The `Array.from()` method can also convert iterables and array-like objects into arrays. Both methods are inherited by derived array classes and use the `Symbol.species` property to determine what type of value should be returned (other inherited methods also use `Symbol.species` when returning an array).

Also, several new methods on arrays were introduced. The `fill()` and `copyWithin()` methods allow you to alter array elements in place. The `find()` and `findIndex()` methods are useful for finding the first element in an array that matches some criteria. The former returns the first element that fits the criteria, and the latter returns the element's index.

Typed arrays are not technically arrays, because they don't inherit from `Array`, but they do look and behave a lot like arrays. Typed arrays contain one of eight different numeric data types and are built upon `ArrayBuffer` objects that represent the underlying bits of a number or series of numbers. Typed arrays are a more efficient way of doing bitwise arithmetic because the values are not converted back and forth between formats, as is the case with the JavaScript number type.

11

PROMISES AND ASYNCHRONOUS PROGRAMMING

One of the most powerful aspects of JavaScript is how easily it handles asynchronous programming. As a language created for the web, JavaScript needed to be able to respond to asynchronous user interactions, such as clicks and key presses, from the beginning. Node.js made asynchronous programming in JavaScript more popular by using callbacks as an alternative to events. But as more programs started using asynchronous programming, events and callbacks weren't powerful enough to support everything developers wanted to do. *Promises* are the solution to this problem.

Promises are another option for asynchronous programming, and they work like futures and deferreds do in other languages. Like events and callbacks, a promise specifies some code to be executed later, but promises also explicitly indicate whether the code succeeded or failed. You can chain promises together based on success or failure in ways that make your code easier to understand and debug.

This chapter shows you how promises work. However, for a complete understanding, it's important to understand some of the basic concepts upon which promises are built.

Asynchronous Programming Background

JavaScript engines are built on the concept of a single-threaded event loop. *Single-threaded* means that only one piece of code is executed at a time. Contrast this with languages like Java or C++, where threads can allow multiple different pieces of code to execute at the same time. Maintaining and protecting state when multiple pieces of code can access and change that state is a difficult problem and a frequent source of bugs in thread-based software.

JavaScript engines can execute only one piece of code at a time, so they need to keep track of code that is meant to run. That code is kept in a *job queue*. Whenever a piece of code is ready to be executed, it is added to the job queue. When the JavaScript engine is finished executing code, the event loop executes the next job in the queue. The *event loop* is a process inside the JavaScript engine that monitors code execution and manages the job queue. Keep in mind that as a queue, job execution runs from the first job in the queue to the last.

The Event Model

When a user clicks a button or presses a key on the keyboard, an event like onclick is triggered. That event might respond to the interaction by adding a new job to the back of the job queue. This is JavaScript's most basic form of asynchronous programming. The event handler code doesn't execute until the event fires, and when it does execute, it has the appropriate context. For example:

```
let button = document.getElementById("my-btn");
button.onclick = function(event) {
    console.log("Clicked");
};
```

In this code, console.log("Clicked") will not be executed until button is clicked. When button is clicked, the function assigned to onclick is added to the back of the job queue and will be executed when all other jobs ahead of it are complete.

Events work well for simple interactions, but chaining multiple separate asynchronous calls together is more complicated because you must keep track of the event target (button in this example) for each event. Additionally, you need to ensure that all appropriate event handlers are added before the first time an event occurs. For instance, if button is clicked before onclick is assigned, nothing will happen. So although events are useful for responding to user interactions and similar infrequent functionality, they aren't very flexible for more complex needs.

The Callback Pattern

Node.js advanced the asynchronous programming model by popularizing callbacks. The callback pattern is similar to the event model because the asynchronous code doesn't execute until a later point in time. It's different because the function to call is passed in as an argument, as shown here:

```
readFile("example.txt", function(err, contents) {
    if (err) {
        throw err;
    }

    console.log(contents);
});

console.log("Hi!");
```

This example uses the traditional Node.js *error-first* callback style. The readFile() function is intended to read from a file on disk (specified as the first argument) and then execute the callback (the second argument) when complete. If there's an error, the err argument of the callback is an error object; otherwise, the contents argument contains the file contents as a string.

Using the callback pattern, readFile() begins executing immediately and pauses when it starts reading from the disk. That means console.log("Hi!") is output immediately after readFile() is called, before console.log(contents) prints anything. When readFile() finishes, it adds a new job to the end of the job queue with the callback function and its arguments. That job executes upon completion of all other jobs ahead of it.

The callback pattern is more flexible than events because chaining multiple calls together is easier with callbacks. Here's an example:

```
readFile("example.txt", function(err, contents) {
    if (err) {
        throw err;
    }

    writeFile("example.txt", function(err) {
        if (err) {
            throw err;
        }

        console.log("File was written!");
    });
});
```

In this code, a successful call to readFile() results in another asynchronous call, this time to the writeFile() function. Note that the same basic pattern of checking err is present in both functions. When readFile() is complete, it adds a job to the job queue that calls the writeFile() function if there are no errors. Then, writeFile() adds a job to the job queue when it finishes.

This pattern works fairly well, but you can quickly find yourself in *callback hell*. Callback hell occurs when you nest too many callbacks, like this:

```
method1(function(err, result) {

    if (err) {
        throw err;
    }

    method2(function(err, result) {

        if (err) {
            throw err;
        }

        method3(function(err, result) {

            if (err) {
                throw err;
            }

            method4(function(err, result) {

                if (err) {
                    throw err;
                }

                method5(result);
            });

        });

    });

});
```

Nesting multiple method calls, as this example does, creates a tangled web of code that is difficult to understand and debug. Callbacks also present problems when you want to implement more complex functionality. What if you want two asynchronous operations to run in parallel and notify you when they're both complete? What if you want to start two asynchronous operations at the same time but only take the result of the first one to complete? In these cases, you'd need to track multiple callbacks and cleanup operations, and promises greatly improve such situations.

Promise Basics

A promise is a placeholder for the result of an asynchronous operation. Instead of subscribing to an event or passing a callback to a function, the function can return a promise, as shown here:

```
// readFile promises to complete at some point in the future
let promise = readFile("example.txt");
```

In this code, readFile() doesn't start reading the file immediately: that will happen later. Instead, the function returns a promise object representing the asynchronous read operation so you can work with it in the future. Exactly when you'll be able to work with that result depends entirely on how the promise's life cycle concludes.

The Promise Life Cycle

Each promise goes through a short life cycle starting in the *pending* state, which indicates that the asynchronous operation hasn't completed yet. A pending promise is considered *unsettled*. The promise in the previous example is in the pending state as soon as the readFile() function returns it. Once the asynchronous operation completes, the promise is considered *settled* and enters one of two possible states:

Fulfilled   The promise's asynchronous operation has completed successfully.

Rejected   The promise's asynchronous operation didn't complete successfully due to either an error or some other cause.

An internal [[PromiseState]] property is set to "pending", "fulfilled", or "rejected" to reflect the promise's state. This property isn't exposed on promise objects, so you can't determine which state the promise is in programmatically. But you can take a specific action when a promise changes state by using the then() method.

The then() method is present on all promises and takes two arguments. The first argument is a function to call when the promise is fulfilled. Any additional data related to the asynchronous operation is passed to this fulfillment function. The second argument is a function to call when the promise is rejected. Similar to the fulfillment function, the rejection function is passed any additional data related to the rejection.

NOTE   *Any object that implements the then() method as described in the preceding paragraph is called a thenable. All promises are thenables, but all thenables are not promises.*

Both arguments to then() are optional, so you can listen for any combination of fulfillment and rejection. For example, consider this set of then() calls:

```
let promise = readFile("example.txt");

promise.then(function(contents) {
    // fulfillment
    console.log(contents);
}, function(err) {
    // rejection
    console.error(err.message);
});

promise.then(function(contents) {
    // fulfillment
    console.log(contents);
});

promise.then(null, function(err) {
    // rejection
    console.error(err.message);
});
```

All three then() calls operate on the same promise. The first call listens for fulfillment and rejection. The second only listens for fulfillment; errors won't be reported. The third just listens for rejection and doesn't report success.

Promises also have a catch() method that behaves the same as then() when only a rejection handler is passed. For example, the following catch() and then() calls are functionally equivalent:

```
promise.catch(function(err) {
    // rejection
    console.error(err.message);
});

// is the same as:

promise.then(null, function(err) {
    // rejection
    console.error(err.message);
});
```

The then() and catch() methods are intended to be used in combination to properly handle the result of asynchronous operations. This system is better than using events and callbacks because it clearly indicates whether the operation succeeded or failed completely. (Events tend not to fire when there's an error, and in callbacks you must always remember to check the error argument.) Just know that if you don't attach a rejection handler to a promise, all failures will happen silently. Always attach a rejection handler, even if the handler just logs the failure.

A fulfillment or rejection handler will still be executed even if it is added to the job queue after the promise is already settled. This allows you to add new fulfillment and rejection handlers at any time and guarantee that they will be called. For example:

```
let promise = readFile("example.txt");

// original fulfillment handler
promise.then(function(contents) {
    console.log(contents);

    // now add another
    promise.then(function(contents) {
        console.log(contents);
    });
});
```

In this code, the fulfillment handler adds another fulfillment handler to the same promise. The promise is already fulfilled at this point, so the new fulfillment handler is added to the job queue and called when all other preceding jobs on the queue are complete. Rejection handlers work the same way.

NOTE   *Each call to then() or catch() creates a new job to be executed when the promise is resolved. But these jobs end up in a separate job queue that is reserved strictly for promises. The precise details of this second job queue aren't important for under-standing how to use promises as long as you understand how job queues work in general.*

Creating Unsettled Promises

New promises are created using the Promise constructor. This constructor accepts a single argument: a function called the *executor*, which contains the code to initialize the promise. The executor is passed two functions named resolve() and reject() as arguments. The resolve() function is called when the executor has finished successfully to signal that the promise is ready to be resolved, whereas the reject() function indicates that the executor has failed.

Here's an example that uses a promise in Node.js to implement the readFile() function you saw earlier in this chapter:

```
// Node.js example

let fs = require("fs");

function readFile(filename) {
    return new Promise(function(resolve, reject) {
```

```
            // trigger the asynchronous operation
            fs.readFile(filename, { encoding: "utf8" }, function(err, contents) {

                // check for errors
                if (err) {
                    reject(err);
                    return;
                }

                // the read succeeded
                resolve(contents);

            });
        });
    }

    let promise = readFile("example.txt");

    // listen for both fulfillment and rejection
    promise.then(function(contents) {
        // fulfillment
        console.log(contents);
    }, function(err) {
        // rejection
        console.error(err.message);
    });
```

In this example, the native Node.js fs.readFile() asynchronous call is wrapped in a promise. The executor either passes the error object to the reject() function or passes the file contents to the resolve() function.

Keep in mind that the executor runs immediately when readFile() is called. When either resolve() or reject() is called inside the executor, a job is added to the job queue to resolve the promise. This is called *job scheduling*, and if you've ever used the setTimeout() or setInterval() functions, you're already familiar with it. In job scheduling, you add a new job to the job queue to say, "Don't execute this right now, but execute it later." For instance, the setTimeout() function lets you specify a delay before a job is added to the queue:

```
// add this function to the job queue after 500 ms have passed
setTimeout(function() {
    console.log("Timeout");
}, 500)

console.log("Hi!");
```

This code schedules a job to be added to the job queue after 500 ms. The two console.log() calls produce the following output:

```
Hi!
Timeout
```

Thanks to the 500 ms delay, the output that the function passed to setTimeout() was shown after the output from the console.log("Hi!") call.

Promises work similarly. The promise executor executes immediately, before anything that appears after it in the source code. For instance:

```
let promise = new Promise(function(resolve, reject) {
    console.log("Promise");
    resolve();
});

console.log("Hi!");
```

The output for this code is:

```
Promise
Hi!
```

Calling resolve() triggers an asynchronous operation. Functions passed to then() and catch() are executed asynchronously, because these are also added to the job queue. Here's an example:

```
let promise = new Promise(function(resolve, reject) {
    console.log("Promise");
    resolve();
});

promise.then(function() {
    console.log("Resolved.");
});

console.log("Hi!");
```

The output for this example is:

```
Promise
Hi!
Resolved
```

Note that even though the call to then() appears before the line console.log("Hi!"), it doesn't actually execute until later (unlike the executor). The reason is that fulfillment and rejection handlers are always added to the end of the job queue after the executor has completed.

Creating Settled Promises

The Promise constructor is the best way to create unsettled promises due to the dynamic nature of what the promise executor does. But if you want a promise to represent just a single known value, it doesn't make sense to schedule a job that simply passes a value to the resolve() function. Instead, you can use either of two methods that create settled promises given a specific value.

Using Promise.resolve()

The `Promise.resolve()` method accepts a single argument and returns a promise in the fulfilled state. That means no job scheduling occurs, and you need to add one or more fulfillment handlers to the promise to retrieve the value. For example:

```
let promise = Promise.resolve(42);

promise.then(function(value) {
    console.log(value);         // 42
});
```

This code creates a fulfilled promise so the fulfillment handler receives 42 as value. If a rejection handler were added to this promise, the rejection handler would never be called because the promise will never be in the rejected state.

Using Promise.reject()

You can also create rejected promises by using the `Promise.reject()` method. This works like `Promise.resolve()` except the created promise is in the rejected state, as follows:

```
let promise = Promise.reject(42);

promise.catch(function(value) {
    console.log(value);         // 42
});
```

Any additional rejection handlers added to this promise would be called but not fulfillment handlers.

NOTE   *If you pass a promise to either the `Promise.resolve()` or `Promise.reject()` method, the promise is returned without modification.*

Non-Promise Thenables

Both `Promise.resolve()` and `Promise.reject()` also accept non-promise then-ables as arguments. When passed a non-promise thenable, these methods create a new promise that is called after the then() function.

A non-promise thenable is created when an object has a then() method that accepts a resolve and a reject argument, like this:

```
let thenable = {
    then: function(resolve, reject) {
        resolve(42);
    }
};
```

The thenable object in this example has no characteristics associated with a promise other than the then() method. You can call Promise.resolve() to convert thenable into a fulfilled promise:

```
let thenable = {
    then: function(resolve, reject) {
        resolve(42);
    }
};

let p1 = Promise.resolve(thenable);
p1.then(function(value) {
    console.log(value);      // 42
});
```

In this example, Promise.resolve() calls thenable.then() so a promise state can be determined. The promise state for thenable is fulfilled because resolve(42) is called inside the then() method. A new promise called p1 is created in the fulfilled state with the value passed from thenable (that is, 42), and the fulfillment handler for p1 receives 42 as the value.

You can use the same process with Promise.resolve() to create a rejected promise from a thenable:

```
let thenable = {
    then: function(resolve, reject) {
        reject(42);
    }
};

let p1 = Promise.resolve(thenable);
p1.catch(function(value) {
    console.log(value);      // 42
});
```

This example is similar to the previous example, except thenable is rejected. When thenable.then() executes, a new promise is created in the rejected state with a value of 42. That value is then passed to the rejection handler for p1.

Promise.resolve() and Promise.reject() work like this to allow you to easily work with non-promise thenables. Many libraries used thenables prior to promises being introduced in ECMAScript 6, so the ability to convert thenables into formal promises is important for backward compatibility with previously existing libraries. When you're unsure whether an object is a promise, passing the object through Promise.resolve() or Promise.reject() (depending on your anticipated result) is the best way to find out because promises just pass through unchanged.

Executor Errors

If an error is thrown inside an executor, the promise's rejection handler is called. For example:

```
let promise = new Promise(function(resolve, reject) {
    throw new Error("Explosion!");
});

promise.catch(function(error) {
    console.log(error.message);      // "Explosion!"
});
```

In this code, the executor intentionally throws an error. An implicit try-catch is inside every executor so that the error is caught and then passed to the rejection handler. The previous example is equivalent to this:

```
let promise = new Promise(function(resolve, reject) {
    try {
        throw new Error("Explosion!");
    } catch (ex) {
        reject(ex);
    }
});

promise.catch(function(error) {
    console.log(error.message);      // "Explosion!"
});
```

The executor catches any thrown errors to simplify this common use case, but an error thrown in the executor is only reported when a rejection handler is present. Otherwise, the error is suppressed. This became a problem for developers early on when using promises, and JavaScript environments address it by providing hooks for catching rejected promises.

Global Promise Rejection Handling

One of the most controversial aspects of promises is the silent failure that occurs when a promise is rejected without a rejection handler. Some consider this the biggest flaw in the specification because it's the only part of the JavaScript language that doesn't make errors apparent.

Determining whether a promise rejection was handled isn't straightforward due to the nature of promises. For instance, consider this example:

```
let rejected = Promise.reject(42);

// at this point, rejected is unhandled
```

```
// some time later...
rejected.catch(function(value) {
    // now rejected has been handled
    console.log(value);
});
```

You can call then() or catch() at any point and have them work correctly regardless of whether the promise is settled or not, making it difficult to know precisely when a promise will be handled. In this case, the promise is rejected immediately but isn't handled until later.

Although it's possible that a future version of ECMAScript will address this problem, both Node.js and browsers have implemented changes to address this developer pain point. They aren't part of the ECMAScript 6 specification but are valuable tools when you're using promises.

Node.js Rejection Handling

Node.js emits two events on the process object that are related to promise rejection handling:

unhandledRejection   Emitted when a promise is rejected and no rejection handler is called within one turn of the event loop

rejectionHandled   Emitted when a promise is rejected and a rejection handler is called after one turn of the event loop

These events are designed to work together to help identify promises that are rejected and not handled.

The unhandledRejection event handler is passed the rejection reason (frequently an error object) and the promise that was rejected as arguments. The following code shows unhandledRejection in action:

```
let rejected;

process.on("unhandledRejection", function(reason, promise) {
    console.log(reason.message);            // "Explosion!"
    console.log(rejected === promise);      // true
});

rejected = Promise.reject(new Error("Explosion!"));
```

This example creates a rejected promise with an error object and listens for the unhandledRejection event. The event handler receives the error object as the first argument and the promise as the second.

The rejectionHandled event handler has only one argument, which is the promise that was rejected. For example:

```
let rejected;

process.on("rejectionHandled", function(promise) {
    console.log(rejected === promise);      // true
});
```

```
rejected = Promise.reject(new Error("Explosion!"));

// wait to add the rejection handler
setTimeout(function() {
    rejected.catch(function(value) {
        console.log(value.message);          // "Explosion!"
    });
}, 1000);
```

Here, the rejectionHandled event is emitted when the rejection handler is finally called. If the rejection handler were attached directly to rejected after rejected is created, the event wouldn't be emitted. The rejection handler would instead be called during the same turn of the event loop where rejected was created, which isn't useful.

To properly track potentially unhandled rejections, use the events rejectionHandled and unhandledRejection to store a list of potentially unhandled rejections. Then wait some period of time to inspect the list. For example, look at this simple unhandled rejection tracker:

```
let possiblyUnhandledRejections = new Map();

// when a rejection is unhandled, add it to the map
process.on("unhandledRejection", function(reason, promise) {
    possiblyUnhandledRejections.set(promise, reason);
});

process.on("rejectionHandled", function(promise) {
    possiblyUnhandledRejections.delete(promise);
});

setInterval(function() {

    possiblyUnhandledRejections.forEach(function(reason, promise) {
        console.log(reason.message ? reason.message : reason);

        // do something to handle these rejections
        handleRejection(promise, reason);
    });

    possiblyUnhandledRejections.clear();

}, 60000);
```

This code uses a map to store promises and their rejection reasons. Each promise is a key, and the promise's reason is the associated value. Each time unhandledRejection is emitted, the promise and its rejection reason are added to the map. Each time rejectionHandled is emitted, the handled promise is removed from the map. As a result, possiblyUnhandledRejections grows and shrinks as events are called. The setInterval() call periodically checks the list of possible unhandled rejections and outputs the information to the console (in reality, you'll probably want to do something else to log or otherwise handle the rejection). A map is used in this example instead of a weak map because you need to inspect the map periodically to see which promises are present, and that's not possible with a weak map.

Although this example is specific to Node.js, browsers have implemented a similar mechanism for notifying developers about unhandled rejections.

Browser Rejection Handling

Browsers also emit two events to help identify unhandled rejections. These events are emitted by the `window` object and are effectively the same as their Node.js equivalents:

unhandledrejection   Emitted when a promise is rejected and no rejection handler is called within one turn of the event loop

rejectionhandled   Emitted when a promise is rejected and a rejection handler is called after one turn of the event loop

Although the Node.js implementation passes individual parameters to the event handler, the event handler for these browser events receives an event object with the following properties:

type   The name of the event (`"unhandledrejection"` or `"rejectionhandled"`)

promise   The promise object that was rejected

reason   The rejection value from the promise

The other difference in the browser implementation is that the rejection value (reason) is available for both events. For example:

```
let rejected;

window.onunhandledrejection = function(event) {
    console.log(event.type);                // "unhandledrejection"
    console.log(event.reason.message);      // "Explosion!"
    console.log(rejected === event.promise);   // true
});

window.onrejectionhandled = function(event) {
    console.log(event.type);                // "rejectionhandled"
    console.log(event.reason.message);      // "Explosion!"
    console.log(rejected === event.promise);   // true
});

rejected = Promise.reject(new Error("Explosion!"));
```

This code assigns both event handlers using the DOM Level 0 notation of `onunhandledrejection` and `onrejectionhandled`. (You can also use `addEventListener("unhandledrejection")` and `addEventListener("rejectionhandled")` if you prefer.) Each event handler receives an event object containing information about the rejected promise. The `type`, `promise`, and `reason` properties are all available in both event handlers.

The code to keep track of unhandled rejections in the browser is very similar to the code for Node.js, too:

```
let possiblyUnhandledRejections = new Map();

// when a rejection is unhandled, add it to the map
window.onunhandledrejection = function(event) {
    possiblyUnhandledRejections.set(event.promise, event.reason);
};

window.onrejectionhandled = function(event) {
    possiblyUnhandledRejections.delete(event.promise);
};

setInterval(function() {

    possiblyUnhandledRejections.forEach(function(reason, promise) {
        console.log(reason.message ? reason.message : reason);

        // do something to handle these rejections
        handleRejection(promise, reason);
    });

    possiblyUnhandledRejections.clear();

}, 60000);
```

This implementation is almost exactly the same as the Node.js implementation. It uses the same approach of storing promises and their rejection values in a map and then inspecting them later. The only real difference is where the information is retrieved from in the event handlers.

Handling promise rejections can be tricky, but you've just begun to see how powerful promises can really be. It's time to take the next step and chain several promises together.

Chaining Promises

At this point, promises may seem like little more than an incremental improvement over using some combination of a callback and the setTimeout() function, but there is much more to promises than meets the eye. Specifically, a number of ways are available to chain promises together to accomplish more complex asynchronous behavior.

Each call to then() or catch() actually creates and returns another promise. This second promise is resolved only when the first has been fulfilled or rejected. Consider this example:

```
let p1 = new Promise(function(resolve, reject) {
    resolve(42);
});
```

```
p1.then(function(value) {
    console.log(value);
}).then(function() {
    console.log("Finished");
});
```

This code outputs the following:

```
42
Finished
```

The call to p1.then() returns a second promise on which then() is called. The second then() fulfillment handler is only called after the first promise has been resolved. If you unchain this example, it looks like this:

```
let p1 = new Promise(function(resolve, reject) {
    resolve(42);
});

let p2 = p1.then(function(value) {
    console.log(value);
})

p2.then(function() {
    console.log("Finished");
});
```

In this unchained version of the code, the result of p1.then() is stored in p2, and then p2.then() is called to add the final fulfillment handler. As you might have guessed, the call to p2.then() also returns a promise, but this example just doesn't use that promise.

Catching Errors

Promise chaining allows you to catch errors that may occur in a fulfillment or rejection handler from a previous promise. For example:

```
let p1 = new Promise(function(resolve, reject) {
    resolve(42);
});

p1.then(function(value) {
    throw new Error("Boom!");
}).catch(function(error) {
    console.log(error.message);      // "Boom!"
});
```

In this code, the fulfillment handler for p1 throws an error. The chained call to the catch() method, which is on a second promise, is able to receive that error through its rejection handler. The same is true if a rejection handler throws an error:

```
let p1 = new Promise(function(resolve, reject) {
    throw new Error("Explosion!");
});

p1.catch(function(error) {
    console.log(error.message);    // "Explosion!"
    throw new Error("Boom!");
}).catch(function(error) {
    console.log(error.message);    // "Boom!"
});
```

Here, the executor throws an error and triggers the p1 promise's rejection handler. That handler then throws another error that is caught by the second promise's rejection handler. The chained promise calls are aware of errors in other promises in the chain.

NOTE   *Always have a rejection handler at the end of a promise chain to ensure that you can properly handle any errors that may occur.*

Returning Values in Promise Chains

Another important aspect of promise chains is the ability to pass data from one promise to the next. I've shown how a value passed to the resolve() handler inside an executor is passed to the fulfillment handler for that promise, but you can continue passing data along a chain by specifying a return value from the fulfillment handler. For example:

```
let p1 = new Promise(function(resolve, reject) {
    resolve(42);
});

p1.then(function(value) {
    console.log(value);        // "42"
    return value + 1;
}).then(function(value) {
    console.log(value);        // "43"
});
```

The fulfillment handler for p1 returns value + 1 when executed. Because value is 42 (from the executor), the fulfillment handler returns 43. That value is then passed to the fulfillment handler of the second promise, which outputs it to the console.

You could do the same thing with the rejection handler. When a rejection handler is called, it may return a value. If it does, that value is used to fulfill the next promise in the chain, as in the next example.

```
let p1 = new Promise(function(resolve, reject) {
    reject(42);
});

p1.catch(function(value) {
    // first fulfillment handler
    console.log(value);        // "42"
    return value + 1;
}).then(function(value) {
    // second fulfillment handler
    console.log(value);        // "43"
});
```

Here, the executor calls reject() with 42. That value is passed into the rejection handler for the promise, where value + 1 is returned. Even though this return value is coming from a rejection handler, it is still used in the fulfillment handler of the next promise in the chain. The failure of one promise can allow the recovery of the entire chain if necessary.

Returning Promises in Promise Chains

Returning primitive values from fulfillment and rejection handlers allows for the passing of data between promises, but what if you return an object? If the object is a promise, there's an extra step that's taken to determine how to proceed. Consider the following example:

```
let p1 = new Promise(function(resolve, reject) {
    resolve(42);
});

let p2 = new Promise(function(resolve, reject) {
    resolve(43);
});

p1.then(function(value) {
    // first fulfillment handler
    console.log(value);     // 42
    return p2;
}).then(function(value) {
    // second fulfillment handler
    console.log(value);     // 43
});
```

In this code, p1 schedules a job that resolves to 42. The fulfillment handler for p1 returns p2, a promise already in the resolved state. The second fulfillment handler is called because p2 has been fulfilled. If p2 were rejected, a rejection handler (if present) would be called instead of the second fulfillment handler.

The important thing to recognize about this pattern is that the second fulfillment handler is not added to p2 but rather to a third promise. The second fulfillment handler is therefore attached to that third promise, making the previous example equivalent to this:

```
let p1 = new Promise(function(resolve, reject) {
    resolve(42);
});

let p2 = new Promise(function(resolve, reject) {
    resolve(43);
});

let p3 = p1.then(function(value) {
    // first fulfillment handler
    console.log(value);     // 42
    return p2;
});

p3.then(function(value) {
    // second fulfillment handler
    console.log(value);     // 43
});
```

Here, it's clear that the second fulfillment handler is attached to p3 rather than p2. This is a subtle but important distinction, because the second fulfillment handler will not be called if p2 is rejected. For instance:

```
let p1 = new Promise(function(resolve, reject) {
    resolve(42);
});

let p2 = new Promise(function(resolve, reject) {
    reject(43);
});

p1.then(function(value) {
    // first fulfillment handler
    console.log(value);     // 42
    return p2;
}).then(function(value) {
    // second fulfillment handler
    console.log(value);     // never called
});
```

In this example, the second fulfillment handler is never called because p2 is rejected. However, you could attach a rejection handler instead:

```
let p1 = new Promise(function(resolve, reject) {
    resolve(42);
});
```

```
let p2 = new Promise(function(resolve, reject) {
    reject(43);
});

p1.then(function(value) {
    // first fulfillment handler
    console.log(value);      // 42
    return p2;
}).catch(function(value) {
    // rejection handler
    console.log(value);      // 43
});
```

Now the rejection handler is called as a result of p2 being rejected. The rejected value 43 from p2 is passed into that rejection handler.

Returning thenables from fulfillment or rejection handlers doesn't change when the promise executors are executed. The first defined promise will run its executor first, then the second promise executor will run, and so on. Returning thenables simply allows you to define additional responses to the promise results. You defer the execution of fulfillment handlers by creating a new promise within a fulfillment handler. For example:

```
let p1 = new Promise(function(resolve, reject) {
    resolve(42);
});

p1.then(function(value) {
    console.log(value);      // 42

    // create a new promise
    let p2 = new Promise(function(resolve, reject) {
        resolve(43);
    });

    return p2
}).then(function(value) {
    console.log(value);      // 43
});
```

In this example, a new promise is created within the fulfillment handler for p1. That means the second fulfillment handler won't execute until after p2 is fulfilled. This pattern is useful when you want to wait until a previous promise has been settled before triggering another promise.

Responding to Multiple Promises

Each example in this chapter so far has dealt with responding to one promise at a time. But sometimes you'll want to monitor the progress of multiple promises to determine the next action. ECMAScript 6 provides two methods that monitor multiple promises: Promise.all() and Promise.race().

The Promise.all() Method

The `Promise.all()` method accepts a single argument, which is an iterable (such as an array) of promises to monitor, and returns a promise that is resolved only when every promise in the iterable is resolved. The returned promise is fulfilled when every promise in the iterable is fulfilled, as in this example:

```
let p1 = new Promise(function(resolve, reject) {
    resolve(42);
});

let p2 = new Promise(function(resolve, reject) {
    resolve(43);
});

let p3 = new Promise(function(resolve, reject) {
    resolve(44);
});

let p4 = Promise.all([p1, p2, p3]);

p4.then(function(value) {
    console.log(Array.isArray(value));   // true
    console.log(value[0]);               // 42
    console.log(value[1]);               // 43
    console.log(value[2]);               // 44
});
```

Each promise here resolves with a number. The call to `Promise.all()` creates promise p4, which is ultimately fulfilled when promises p1, p2, and p3 are fulfilled. The result passed to the fulfillment handler for p4 is an array containing each resolved value: 42, 43, and 44. The values are stored in the order in which the promises resolved, so you can match promise results to the promises that resolved to them.

If any promise passed to `Promise.all()` is rejected, the returned promise is immediately rejected without waiting for the other promises to complete:

```
let p1 = new Promise(function(resolve, reject) {
    resolve(42);
});

let p2 = new Promise(function(resolve, reject) {
    reject(43);
});

let p3 = new Promise(function(resolve, reject) {
    resolve(44);
});

let p4 = Promise.all([p1, p2, p3]);
```

```
p4.catch(function(value) {
    console.log(Array.isArray(value))    // false
    console.log(value);                  // 43
});
```

In this example, p2 is rejected with a value of 43. The rejection handler for p4 is called immediately without waiting for p1 or p3 to finish executing. (They do finish executing; p4 just doesn't wait.)

The rejection handler always receives a single value rather than an array, and the value is the rejection value from the promise that was rejected. In this case, the rejection handler is passed 43 to reflect the rejection from p2.

The Promise.race() Method

The Promise.race() method provides a slightly different take on monitoring multiple promises. This method also accepts an iterable of promises to monitor and returns a promise, but the returned promise is settled as soon as the first promise is settled. Instead of waiting for all promises to be fulfilled, like the Promise.all() method, the Promise.race() method returns an appropriate promise as soon as any promise in the array is fulfilled. For example:

```
let p1 = Promise.resolve(42);

let p2 = new Promise(function(resolve, reject) {
    resolve(43);
});

let p3 = new Promise(function(resolve, reject) {
    resolve(44);
});

let p4 = Promise.race([p1, p2, p3]);

p4.then(function(value) {
    console.log(value);      // 42
});
```

In this code, p1 is created as a fulfilled promise while the others schedule jobs. The fulfillment handler for p4 is then called with the value of 42 and ignores the other promises. The promises passed to Promise.race() are truly in a race to see which is settled first. If the first promise to settle is fulfilled, the returned promise is fulfilled; if the first promise to settle is rejected, the returned promise is rejected. Here's an example with a rejection:

```
let p1 = new Promise(function(resolve, reject) {
    resolve(42);
});

let p2 = Promise.reject(43);
```

```
let p3 = new Promise(function(resolve, reject) {
    resolve(44);
});

let p4 = Promise.race([p1, p2, p3]);

p4.catch(function(value) {
    console.log(value);     // 43
});
```

Here, p4 is rejected because p2 is already in the rejected state when Promise.race() is called. Even though p1 and p3 are fulfilled, those results are ignored because they occur after p2 is rejected.

Inheriting from Promises

Just like other built-in types, you can use a promise as the base for a derived class. This allows you to define your own variation of promises to extend what built-in promises can do. For instance, suppose you want to create a promise that can use methods named success() and failure() in addition to the usual then() and catch() methods. You could create that promise type as follows:

```
class MyPromise extends Promise {

    // use default constructor

    success(resolve, reject) {
        return this.then(resolve, reject);
    }

    failure(reject) {
        return this.catch(reject);
    }

}

let promise = new MyPromise(function(resolve, reject) {
    resolve(42);
});

promise.success(function(value) {
    console.log(value);         // 42
}).failure(function(value) {
    console.log(value);
});
```

In this example, MyPromise is derived from Promise and has two additional methods. The success() method mimics resolve() and failure() mimics the reject() method.

Each added method uses this to call the method it mimics. The derived promise functions the same as a built-in promise except now you can call success() and failure() if you want.

Because static methods are inherited, the `MyPromise.resolve()` method, the `MyPromise.reject()` method, the `MyPromise.race()` method, and the `MyPromise.all()` method are also present on derived promises. The last two methods behave the same as the built-in methods, but the first two are slightly different.

Both `MyPromise.resolve()` and `MyPromise.reject()` will return an instance of `MyPromise` regardless of the value passed because those methods use the `Symbol.species` property (see page 185) to determine the type of promise to return. If a built-in promise is passed to either method, the promise will be resolved or rejected, and the method will return a new `MyPromise` so you can assign fulfillment and rejection handlers. For example:

```
let p1 = new Promise(function(resolve, reject) {
    resolve(42);
});

let p2 = MyPromise.resolve(p1);
p2.success(function(value) {
    console.log(value);                // 42
});

console.log(p2 instanceof MyPromise);    // true
```

Here, `p1` is a built-in promise that is passed to the `MyPromise.resolve()` method. The result, `p2`, is an instance of `MyPromise` where the resolved value from `p1` is passed into the fulfillment handler.

If an instance of `MyPromise` is passed to the `MyPromise.resolve()` or `MyPromise.reject()` methods, it will just be returned directly without being resolved. In all other ways, these two methods behave like `Promise.resolve()` and `Promise.reject()`.

Promise-Based Asynchronous Task Running

In Chapter 8, I introduced generators and showed you how to use them for asynchronous task running, like this:

```
let fs = require("fs");

function run(taskDef) {

    // create the iterator, make available elsewhere
    let task = taskDef();

    // start the task
    let result = task.next();

    // recursive function to keep calling next()
    function step() {

        // if there's more to do
        if (!result.done) {
            if (typeof result.value === "function") {
```

```
                    result.value(function(err, data) {
                        if (err) {
                            result = task.throw(err);
                            return;
                        }

                        result = task.next(data);
                        step();
                    });
                } else {
                    result = task.next(result.value);
                    step();
                }

            }
        }

        // start the process
        step();

    }

    // define a function to use with the task runner

    function readFile(filename) {
        return function(callback) {
            fs.readFile(filename, callback);
        };
    }

    // run a task

    run(function*() {
        let contents = yield readFile("config.json");
        doSomethingWith(contents);
        console.log("Done");
    });
```

This implementation results in some pain points. First, wrapping every function in a function that returns a function is a bit confusing (even this sentence is confusing). Second, there is no way to distinguish between a function return value intended as a callback for the task runner and a return value that isn't a callback.

You can greatly simplify and generalize this process by ensuring that each asynchronous operation returns a promise. Here's one way you could simplify that task runner by using promises as a common interface for all asynchronous code:

```
let fs = require("fs");

function run(taskDef) {
```

```
        // create the iterator
        let task = taskDef();

        // start the task
        let result = task.next();

        // recursive function to iterate through
        (function step() {

            // if there's more to do
            if (!result.done) {

                // resolve to a promise to make it easy
                let promise = Promise.resolve(result.value);
                promise.then(function(value) {
                    result = task.next(value);
                    step();
                }).catch(function(error) {
                    result = task.throw(error);
                    step();
                });
            }
        }());
}

// define a function to use with the task runner

function readFile(filename) {
    return new Promise(function(resolve, reject) {
        fs.readFile(filename, function(err, contents) {
            if (err) {
                reject(err);
            } else {
                resolve(contents);
            }
        });
    });
}

// run a task

run(function*() {
    let contents = yield readFile("config.json");
    doSomethingWith(contents);
    console.log("Done");
});
```

In this version of the code, a generic run() function executes a generator to create an iterator. It calls task.next() to start the task and recursively
calls step() until the iterator is complete.

Inside the step() function, if there's more work to do, then result.done is
false. At that point, result.value should be a promise, but Promise.resolve()
is called just in case the function in question didn't return a promise.

(Remember, `Promise.resolve()` just passes through any promise passed in and wraps any non-promise in a promise.) Next, a fulfillment handler is added that retrieves the promise value and passes the value back to the iterator. Then, `result` is assigned to the next yield result before the `step()` function calls itself.

A rejection handler stores any rejection results in an error object. The `task.throw()` method passes that error object back into the iterator, and if an error is caught in the task, `result` is assigned to the next yield result. Finally, `step()` is called inside `catch()` to continue.

This `run()` function can run any generator that uses `yield` to achieve asynchronous code without exposing promises (or callbacks) to the developer. In fact, because the return value of the function call is always converted to a promise, the function can even return something other than a promise. That means both synchronous and asynchronous methods work correctly when called using `yield`, and you never have to check that the return value is a promise.

The only concern is ensuring that asynchronous functions like `readFile()` return a promise that correctly identifies its state. For Node.js built-in methods, that means you'll have to convert those methods to return promises instead of using callbacks.

FUTURE ASYNCHRONOUS TASK RUNNING

Bringing a simpler syntax to asynchronous task running in JavaScript is under way. For instance, an `await` syntax is in progress that would closely mirror the promise-based example in the preceding section. The basic idea is to use a function marked with `async` instead of a generator and use `await` instead of `yield` when calling a function, such as:

```
(async function() {
    let contents = await readFile("config.json");
    doSomethingWith(contents);
    console.log("Done");
});
```

The `async` keyword before `function` indicates that the function is meant to run in an asynchronous manner. The `await` keyword signals that the function call to `readFile("config.json")` should return a promise, and if it doesn't, the response should be wrapped in a promise. Just like the implementation of `run()` in the preceding section, `await` will throw an error if the promise is rejected and otherwise return the value from the promise. The end result is that you can write asynchronous code as if it were synchronous without the overhead of managing an iterator-based state machine.

The `await` syntax is expected to be finalized in ECMAScript 2017 (ECMAScript 8).

Summary

Promises are designed to improve asynchronous programming in JavaScript by giving you more control and composability over asynchronous operations than events and callbacks can. Promises schedule jobs to be added to the JavaScript engine's job queue for future execution, and a second job queue tracks promise fulfillment and rejection handlers to ensure proper execution.

Promises have three states: pending, fulfilled, and rejected. A promise starts in a pending state and becomes fulfilled on a successful execution or rejected on a failure. In either case, you can add handlers to indicate when a promise is settled. The then() method allows you to assign a fulfillment and rejection handler, and the catch() method allows you to assign only a rejection handler.

You can chain promises together in a variety of ways and pass information between them. Each call to then() creates and returns a new promise that is resolved when the previous one is resolved. Such chains can be used to trigger responses to a series of asynchronous events. You can also use Promise.race() and Promise.all() to monitor the progress of multiple promises and respond accordingly.

Asynchronous task running is easier when you combine generators and promises, because promises provide a common interface that asynchronous operations can return. You can then use generators and the yield operator to wait for asynchronous responses and respond appropriately.

Most new web APIs are being built on top of promises, and you can expect many more to follow suit in the future.

12

PROXIES AND THE REFLECTION API

ECMAScript 5 and ECMAScript 6 were both developed with demystifying JavaScript functionality in mind. For example, JavaScript environments contained nonenumerable and nonwritable object properties prior to ECMAScript 5, but developers couldn't define their own nonenumerable or nonwritable properties. ECMAScript 5 included the `Object.defineProperty()` method, which allowed developers to do what JavaScript engines could do already.

ECMAScript 6 gives developers further access to JavaScript engine capabilities by adding built-in objects. To allow developers to create built-in objects, the language exposes the inner workings of objects through *proxies*, which are wrappers that can intercept and alter low-level JavaScript engine operations. This chapter starts by describing the problem that proxies are meant to address in detail, and then discusses how you can create and use proxies effectively.

The Array Problem

The JavaScript array object behaves in ways that developers couldn't mimic in their own objects prior to ECMAScript 6. An array's length property is affected when you assign values to specific array items, and you can modify array items by modifying the length property. For example:

```
let colors = ["red", "green", "blue"];

console.log(colors.length);        // 3

colors[3] = "black";

console.log(colors.length);        // 4
console.log(colors[3]);            // "black"

colors.length = 2;

console.log(colors.length);        // 2
console.log(colors[3]);            // undefined
console.log(colors[2]);            // undefined
console.log(colors[1]);            // "green"
```

The colors array starts with three items. Assigning "black" to colors[3] automatically increments the length property to 4. Setting the length property to 2 removes the last two items in the array, leaving only the first two items. Nothing in ECMAScript 5 allows developers to achieve this behavior, but proxies change that.

NOTE   *This nonstandard behavior of numeric properties and the length property is why arrays are considered exotic objects in ECMAScript 6.*

Introducing Proxies and Reflection

Calling new Proxy() creates a proxy to use in place of another object (called the *target*). The proxy *virtualizes* the target so the proxy and the target appear to be functionally the same.

Proxies allow you to intercept low-level object operations on the target that are otherwise internal to the JavaScript engine. These low-level operations are intercepted using a *trap*, which is a function that responds to a specific operation.

The reflection API, represented by the Reflect object, is a collection of methods that provide the default behavior for the same low-level operations that proxies can override. There is a Reflect method for every proxy trap. Those methods have the same name and are passed the same arguments as their respective proxy traps. Table 12-1 summarizes the proxy trap behavior.

Table 12-1: Proxy Traps in JavaScript

Proxy trap	Overrides the behavior of	Default behavior
get	Reading a property value	Reflect.get()
set	Writing to a property	Reflect.set()
has	The in operator	Reflect.has()
deleteProperty	The delete operator	Reflect.deleteProperty()
getPrototypeOf	Object.getPrototypeOf()	Reflect.getPrototypeOf()
setPrototypeOf	Object.setPrototypeOf()	Reflect.setPrototypeOf()
isExtensible	Object.isExtensible()	Reflect.isExtensible()
preventExtensions	Object.preventExtensions()	Reflect.preventExtensions()
getOwnPropertyDescriptor	Object.getOwnPropertyDescriptor()	Reflect.getOwnPropertyDescriptor()
defineProperty	Object.defineProperty()	Reflect.defineProperty
ownKeys	Object.keys(), Object.getOwnPropertyNames(), and Object.getOwnPropertySymbols()	Reflect.ownKeys()
apply	Calling a function	Reflect.apply()
construct	Calling a function with new	Reflect.construct()

Each trap overrides some built-in behavior of JavaScript objects, allowing you to intercept and modify the behavior. If you still need to use the built-in behavior, you can use the corresponding reflection API method. The relationship between proxies and the reflection API becomes clear when you start creating proxies, so it's best to dive in and look at some examples.

NOTE *The original ECMAScript 6 specification had an additional trap called* enumerate *that was designed to alter how* for-in *and* Object.keys() *enumerated properties on an object. However, the* enumerate *trap was removed in ECMAScript 7 (also called ECMAScript 2016) because difficulties were discovered during implementation. The* enumerate *trap no longer exists in any JavaScript environment and is therefore not covered in this chapter.*

Creating a Simple Proxy

When you use the Proxy constructor to make a proxy, you'll pass it two arguments: the target and a handler. A *handler* is an object that defines one or more traps. The proxy uses the default behavior for all operations except when traps are defined for that operation. To create a simple forwarding proxy, you can use a handler with no traps, like this:

```
let target = {};

let proxy = new Proxy(target, {});

proxy.name = "proxy";
```

```
console.log(proxy.name);        // "proxy"
console.log(target.name);       // "proxy"

target.name = "target";
console.log(proxy.name);        // "target"
console.log(target.name);       // "target"
```

In this example, proxy forwards all operations directly to target. When "proxy" is assigned to the proxy.name property, name is created on target. The proxy is not storing this property; it's simply forwarding the operation to target. Similarly, the values of proxy.name and target.name are the same because they are both references to target.name. That also means setting target.name to a new value causes proxy.name to reflect the same change. Of course, proxies without traps aren't very interesting, so what happens when you define a trap?

Validating Properties Using the set Trap

Suppose you want to create an object whose property values must be numbers. That means every new property added to the object must be validated, and an error must be thrown if the value isn't a number. To accomplish this task, you could define a set trap that overrides the default behavior of setting a value. The set trap receives four arguments:

trapTarget   The object that will receive the property (the proxy's target)

key   The property key (string or symbol) to write to

value   The value being written to the property

receiver   The object on which the operation took place (usually the proxy)

Reflect.set() is the set trap's corresponding reflection method, and it's the default behavior for this operation. The Reflect.set() method accepts the same four arguments as the set proxy trap, making the method easy to use inside the trap. The trap should return true if the property was set or false if not. (The Reflect.set() method returns the correct value based on whether the operation succeeded.)

To validate the values of properties, you would use the set trap and inspect the value that is passed in. Here's an example:

```
let target = {
    name: "target"
};

let proxy = new Proxy(target, {
    set(trapTarget, key, value, receiver) {

        // ignore existing properties so as not to affect them
        if (!trapTarget.hasOwnProperty(key)) {
            if (isNaN(value)) {
                throw new TypeError("Property must be a number.");
```

```
            }
        }

        // add the property
        return Reflect.set(trapTarget, key, value, receiver);
    }
});

// adding a new property
proxy.count = 1;
console.log(proxy.count);      // 1
console.log(target.count);     // 1

// you can assign to name because it exists on target already
proxy.name = "proxy";
console.log(proxy.name);       // "proxy"
console.log(target.name);      // "proxy"

// throws an error
proxy.anotherName = "proxy";
```

This code defines a proxy trap that validates the value of any new property added to target. When `proxy.count = 1` is executed, the set trap is called. The `trapTarget` value is equal to target, key is `"count"`, value is 1, and receiver (not used in this example) is proxy. There is no existing property named count in target, so the proxy validates value by passing it to `isNaN()`. If the result is NaN, the property value is not numeric and an error is thrown. Because this code sets count to 1, the proxy calls `Reflect.set()` with the same four arguments that were passed to the trap to add the new property.

When `proxy.name` is assigned a string, the operation completes successfully. Because target already has a name property, that property is omitted from the validation check by calling the `trapTarget.hasOwnProperty()` method. This ensures that previously existing nonnumeric property values are still supported.

However, when `proxy.anotherName` is assigned a string, an error is thrown. The `anotherName` property doesn't exist on the target, so its value needs to be validated. During validation, the error is thrown because `"proxy"` isn't a numeric value.

The set proxy trap lets you intercept when properties are being written to, and the get proxy trap lets you intercept when properties are being read.

Object Shape Validation Using the get Trap

One of the peculiar, and sometimes confusing, aspects of JavaScript is that reading nonexistent properties doesn't throw an error. Instead, the value undefined is used for the property value, as in this example:

```
let target = {};

console.log(target.name);      // undefined
```

In most other languages, attempting to read `target.name` throws an error because the property doesn't exist. But JavaScript just uses `undefined` for the value of the `target.name` property. If you've ever worked on a large code base, you've probably seen how this behavior can cause significant problems, especially when there's a typo in the property name. Proxies help you avoid this problem by having object shape validation.

An *object shape* is the collection of properties and methods available on the object. JavaScript engines use object shapes to optimize code, often creating classes to represent the objects. If you can safely assume an object will always have the same properties and methods it began with (a behavior you can enforce with the `Object.preventExtensions()` method, the `Object.seal()` method, or the `Object.freeze()` method), then throwing an error on attempts to access nonexistent properties can be helpful. Proxies make object shape validation easy.

Because property validation only has to happen when a property is read, you would use the get trap. The get trap is called when a property is read, even if that property doesn't exist on the object, and it takes three arguments:

trapTarget   The object from which the property is read (the proxy's target)

key   The property key (a string or symbol) to read

receiver   The object on which the operation took place (usually the proxy)

These arguments mirror the set trap's arguments but with one noticeable difference. There's no value argument because get traps don't write values. The `Reflect.get()` method accepts the same three arguments as the get trap and returns the property's default value.

You can use the get trap and `Reflect.get()` to throw an error when a property doesn't exist on the target, as follows:

```
let proxy = new Proxy({}, {
    get(trapTarget, key, receiver) {
        if (!(key in receiver)) {
            throw new TypeError("Property " + key + " doesn't exist.");
        }

        return Reflect.get(trapTarget, key, receiver);
    }
});

// adding a property still works
proxy.name = "proxy";
console.log(proxy.name);            // "proxy"

// nonexistent properties throw an error
console.log(proxy.nme);             // throws an error
```

In this example, the get trap intercepts property read operations. The in operator determines whether the property already exists on the receiver. The receiver is used with in instead of trapTarget in case receiver is a proxy with a has trap, a type I'll cover in the next section. Using trapTarget in this case would sidestep the has trap and potentially give you the wrong result. An error is thrown if the property doesn't exist; otherwise, the default behavior is used.

This code allows new properties like proxy.name to be added, written to, and read from without problems. The last line contains a typo: proxy.nme should probably be proxy.name. This throws an error because nme doesn't exist as a property.

Hiding Property Existence Using the has Trap

The in operator determines whether a property exists on a given object and returns true if an own property or a prototype property matches the name or symbol. For example:

```
let target = {
    value: 42;
}

console.log("value" in target);     // true
console.log("toString" in target);  // true
```

Both value and toString exist on object, so in both cases the in operator returns true. The value property is an own property, whereas toString is a prototype property (inherited from Object). Proxies allow you to intercept this operation and return a different value for in with the has trap.

The has trap is called whenever the in operator is used. When called, two arguments are passed to the has trap:

trapTarget The object the property is read from (the proxy's target)

key The property key (string or symbol) to check

The Reflect.has() method accepts these same arguments and returns the default response for the in operator. Using the has trap and Reflect.has() allows you to alter the behavior of in for some properties while reverting to the default behavior for others. For instance, you could hide the value property from the previous example like this:

```
let target = {
    name: "target",
    value: 42
};
```

```
let proxy = new Proxy(target, {
    has(trapTarget, key) {

        if (key === "value") {
            return false;
        } else {
            return Reflect.has(trapTarget, key);
        }
    }
});

console.log("value" in proxy);     // false
console.log("name" in proxy);      // true
console.log("toString" in proxy);  // true
```

The has trap for proxy checks whether key is "value" and returns false if so. Otherwise, the default behavior is used via a call to the Reflect.has() method. As a result, the in operator returns false for the value property, even though value actually exists on the target. The other properties, name and toString, correctly return true when used with the in operator.

Preventing Property Deletion with the deleteProperty Trap

The delete operator removes a property from an object and returns true when it's successful and false when it's unsuccessful. In strict mode, delete throws an error when you attempt to delete a nonconfigurable property; in non-strict mode, delete simply returns false. Here's an example:

```
let target = {
    name: "target",
    value: 42
};

Object.defineProperty(target, "name", { configurable: false });

console.log("value" in target);     // true

let result1 = delete target.value;
console.log(result1);               // true

console.log("value" in target);     // false

// note: the following line throws an error in strict mode
let result2 = delete target.name;
console.log(result2);               // false

console.log("name" in target);      // true
```

The value property is deleted using the delete operator and, as a result, the in operator returns false in the third console.log() call. The nonconfigurable name property can't be deleted, so the delete operator simply returns `false` (if you run this code in strict mode, an error is thrown instead). You can alter this behavior by using the `deleteProperty` trap in a proxy.

The `deleteProperty` trap is called whenever the `delete` operator is used on an object property. The trap is passed two arguments:

trapTarget   The object from which the property should be deleted (the proxy's target)

key   The property key (string or symbol) to delete

The `Reflect.deleteProperty()` method provides the default implementation of the `deleteProperty` trap and accepts the same two arguments. You can combine `Reflect.deleteProperty()` and the `deleteProperty` trap to change how the `delete` operator behaves. For instance, you could ensure that the `value` property can't be deleted, like so:

```
let target = {
    name: "target",
    value: 42
};

let proxy = new Proxy(target, {
    deleteProperty(trapTarget, key) {

        if (key === "value") {
            return false;
        } else {
            return Reflect.deleteProperty(trapTarget, key);
        }
    }
});

// attempt to delete proxy.value

console.log("value" in proxy);      // true

let result1 = delete proxy.value;
console.log(result1);               // false

console.log("value" in proxy);      // true

// attempt to delete proxy.name

console.log("name" in proxy);       // true

let result2 = delete proxy.name;
console.log(result2);               // true

console.log("name" in proxy);       // false
```

This code is very similar to the `has` trap example in that the `deleteProperty` trap checks whether the key is `"value"` and returns `false` if so. Otherwise, the default behavior is used by calling the `Reflect.deleteProperty()` method.

The `value` property can't be deleted through `proxy` because the operation is trapped, but the `name` property is deleted as expected. This approach is especially useful when you want to protect properties from deletion without throwing an error in strict mode.

Prototype Proxy Traps

Chapter 4 introduced the `Object.setPrototypeOf()` method that ECMAScript 6 added to complement the ECMAScript 5 `Object.getPrototypeOf()` method. Proxies allow you to intercept the execution of both methods through the `setPrototypeOf` and `getPrototypeOf` traps. In both cases, the method on `Object` calls the trap of the corresponding name on the proxy, allowing you to alter the methods' behavior.

Because two traps are associated with prototype proxies, a set of methods is associated with each type of trap. The `setPrototypeOf` trap receives these arguments:

trapTarget   The object for which the prototype should be set (the proxy's target)

proto   The object to use as the prototype

These are the same arguments passed to the `Object.setPrototypeOf()` and `Reflect.setPrototypeOf()` methods. The `getPrototypeOf` trap, on the other hand, only receives the `trapTarget` argument, which is the argument passed to the `Object.getPrototypeOf()` and `Reflect.getPrototypeOf()` methods.

How Prototype Proxy Traps Work

Prototype proxy traps have some restrictions. First, the `getPrototypeOf` trap must return an object or `null`, and any other return value results in a runtime error. The return value check ensures that `Object.getPrototypeOf()` will always return an expected value. Second, the return value of the `setPrototypeOf` trap must be `false` if the operation doesn't succeed. When `setPrototypeOf` returns `false`, `Object.setPrototypeOf()` throws an error. If `setPrototypeOf` returns any value other than `false`, `Object.setPrototypeOf()` assumes the operation succeeded.

The following example hides the prototype of the proxy by always returning `null` and also doesn't allow the prototype to be changed:

```
let target = {};
let proxy = new Proxy(target, {
    getPrototypeOf(trapTarget) {
        return null;
    },
    setPrototypeOf(trapTarget, proto) {
        return false;
    }
});
```

```
let targetProto = Object.getPrototypeOf(target);
let proxyProto = Object.getPrototypeOf(proxy);

console.log(targetProto === Object.prototype);       // true
console.log(proxyProto === Object.prototype);        // false
console.log(proxyProto);                             // null

// succeeds
Object.setPrototypeOf(target, {});

// throws an error
Object.setPrototypeOf(proxy, {});
```

This code emphasizes the difference between the behavior of target and proxy. Although Object.getPrototypeOf() returns a value for target, it returns null for proxy because the getPrototypeOf trap is called. Similarly, Object.setPrototypeOf() succeeds when it's used on target but throws an error when it's used on proxy due to the setPrototypeOf trap.

If you want to use the default behavior for these two traps, you can use the corresponding methods on Reflect. For instance, the following code implements the default behavior for the getPrototypeOf and setPrototypeOf traps:

```
let target = {};
let proxy = new Proxy(target, {
    getPrototypeOf(trapTarget) {
        return Reflect.getPrototypeOf(trapTarget);
    },
    setPrototypeOf(trapTarget, proto) {
        return Reflect.setPrototypeOf(trapTarget, proto);
    }
});

let targetProto = Object.getPrototypeOf(target);
let proxyProto = Object.getPrototypeOf(proxy);

console.log(targetProto === Object.prototype);       // true
console.log(proxyProto === Object.prototype);        // true

// succeeds
Object.setPrototypeOf(target, {});

// also succeeds
Object.setPrototypeOf(proxy, {});
```

In this example, you can use target and proxy interchangeably and get the same results, because the getPrototypeOf and setPrototypeOf traps are just passing through to use the default implementation. It's important that this example use the Reflect.getPrototypeOf() and Reflect.setPrototypeOf() methods rather than the methods of the same name on Object due to some important differences.

Why Two Sets of Methods?

The confusing aspect of `Reflect.getPrototypeOf()` and `Reflect.setPrototypeOf()` is that they look suspiciously similar to the `Object.getPrototypeOf()` and `Object.setPrototypeOf()` methods. Although both sets of methods perform similar operations, there are some distinct differences between the two.

`Object.getPrototypeOf()` and `Object.setPrototypeOf()` are higher-level operations that were created for developer use from the start. The `Reflect.getPrototypeOf()` and `Reflect.setPrototypeOf()` methods are lower-level operations that give developers access to the previously internal-only `[[GetPrototypeOf]]` and `[[SetPrototypeOf]]` operations. The `Reflect.getPrototypeOf()` method is the wrapper for the internal `[[GetPrototypeOf]]` operation (with some input validation). The `Reflect.setPrototypeOf()` method and `[[SetPrototypeOf]]` have the same relationship. The corresponding methods on `Object` also call `[[GetPrototypeOf]]` and `[[SetPrototypeOf]]` but perform a few steps before the call and inspect the return value to determine how to behave.

The `Reflect.getPrototypeOf()` method throws an error if its argument is not an object, whereas `Object.getPrototypeOf()` first coerces the value into an object before performing the operation. If you passed a number into each method, you'd get a different result:

```
let result1 = Object.getPrototypeOf(1);
console.log(result1 === Number.prototype);  // true

// throws an error
Reflect.getPrototypeOf(1);
```

The `Object.getPrototypeOf()` method allows you retrieve a prototype for the number 1 because it first coerces the value into a `Number` object and then returns `Number.prototype`. The `Reflect.getPrototypeOf()` method doesn't coerce the value, and because 1 isn't an object, it throws an error.

The `Reflect.setPrototypeOf()` method is also different from the `Object.setPrototypeOf()` method. Specifically, `Reflect.setPrototypeOf()` returns a Boolean value indicating whether the operation was successful. A true value is returned for success, and `false` is returned for failure. If `Object.setPrototypeOf()` fails, it throws an error.

As the first example in "How Prototype Proxy Traps Work" on page 252 showed, when the `setPrototypeOf` proxy trap returns false, it causes `Object.setPrototypeOf()` to throw an error. The `Object.setPrototypeOf()` method returns the first argument as its value and therefore isn't suitable for implementing the default behavior of the `setPrototypeOf` proxy trap. The following code demonstrates these differences:

```
let target1 = {};
let result1 = Object.setPrototypeOf(target1, {});
console.log(result1 === target1);            // true

let target2 = {};
let result2 = Reflect.setPrototypeOf(target2, {});
```

```
console.log(result2 === target2);          // false
console.log(result2);                       // true
```

In this example, Object.setPrototypeOf() returns target1 as its value, but Reflect.setPrototypeOf() returns true. This subtle difference is very important. You'll see more seemingly duplicate methods on Object and Reflect, but always be sure to use the method on Reflect inside any proxy traps.

NOTE   *Reflect.getPrototypeOf()/Object.getPrototypeOf() and Reflect.setPrototypeOf()/ Object.setPrototypeOf() will call the getPrototypeOf and setPrototypeOf proxy traps, respectively, when they're used on a proxy.*

Object Extensibility Traps

ECMAScript 5 added object extensibility modification through the Object.preventExtensions() and Object.isExtensible() methods, and ECMAScript 6 allows proxies to intercept those method calls to the underlying objects through the preventExtensions and isExtensible traps. Both traps receive a single argument called trapTarget that is the object on which the method was called. The isExtensible trap must return a Boolean value indicating whether the object is extensible, and the preventExtensions trap must return a Boolean value indicating whether the operation succeeded.

The Reflect.preventExtensions() and Reflect.isExtensible() methods implement the default behavior. Both return Boolean values, so you can use them directly in their corresponding traps.

Two Basic Examples

To see object extensibility traps in action, consider the following code, which implements the default behavior for the isExtensible and preventExtensions traps:

```
let target = {};
let proxy = new Proxy(target, {
    isExtensible(trapTarget) {
        return Reflect.isExtensible(trapTarget);
    },
    preventExtensions(trapTarget) {
        return Reflect.preventExtensions(trapTarget);
    }
});


console.log(Object.isExtensible(target));   // true
console.log(Object.isExtensible(proxy));    // true

Object.preventExtensions(proxy);

console.log(Object.isExtensible(target));   // false
console.log(Object.isExtensible(proxy));    // false
```

This example shows that the methods `Object.preventExtensions()` and `Object.isExtensible()` correctly pass through from proxy to target. You can, of course, change the behavior. For example, if you don't want to allow `Object.preventExtensions()` to succeed on your proxy, you could return `false` from the `preventExtensions` trap:

```
let target = {};
let proxy = new Proxy(target, {
    isExtensible(trapTarget) {
        return Reflect.isExtensible(trapTarget);
    },
    preventExtensions(trapTarget) {
        return false
    }
});


console.log(Object.isExtensible(target));       // true
console.log(Object.isExtensible(proxy));        // true

Object.preventExtensions(proxy);

console.log(Object.isExtensible(target));       // true
console.log(Object.isExtensible(proxy));        // true
```

Here, the call to `Object.preventExtensions(proxy)` is effectively ignored because the `preventExtensions` trap returns false. The operation isn't forwarded to the underlying target, so `Object.isExtensible()` returns true.

Duplicate Extensibility Methods

You may have noticed that, once again, there are seemingly duplicate methods on `Object` and `Reflect`. In this case, they're more similar than not. The methods `Object.isExtensible()` and `Reflect.isExtensible()` are similar except when passed a nonobject value. In that case, `Object.isExtensible()` always returns false and `Reflect.isExtensible()` throws an error. Here's an example of that behavior:

```
let result1 = Object.isExtensible(2);
console.log(result1);                   // false

// throws an error
let result2 = Reflect.isExtensible(2);
```

This restriction is similar to the difference between the methods `Object.getPrototypeOf()` and `Reflect.getPrototypeOf()`, because the method with lower-level functionality has stricter error checks than its higher-level counterpart.

The `Object.preventExtensions()` and `Reflect.preventExtensions()` methods are also very similar. The `Object.preventExtensions()` method always returns the value that was passed to it as an argument, even if the value isn't an object. The `Reflect.preventExtensions()` method, on the other hand, throws an error if the argument isn't an object; if the argument is an object, `Reflect.preventExtensions()` returns true when the operation succeeds or false if not. For example:

```
let result1 = Object.preventExtensions(2);
console.log(result1);                        // 2

let target = {};
let result2 = Reflect.preventExtensions(target);
console.log(result2);                        // true

// throws an error
let result3 = Reflect.preventExtensions(2);
```

Here, `Object.preventExtensions()` passes through the value 2 as its return value, even though 2 isn't an object. The `Reflect.preventExtensions()` method returns true when an object is passed to it and throws an error when 2 is passed to it.

Property Descriptor Traps

One of the most important features of ECMAScript 5 was the ability to define property attributes using the `Object.defineProperty()` method. In earlier versions of JavaScript, there was no way to define an accessor property, make a property read-only, or make a property nonenumerable. All of these are possible with the `Object.defineProperty()` method, and you can retrieve those attributes with the `Object.getOwnPropertyDescriptor()` method.

Proxies let you intercept calls to the `Object.defineProperty()` method and the `Object.getOwnPropertyDescriptor()` method using the `defineProperty` and `getOwnPropertyDescriptor` traps, respectively. The `defineProperty` trap receives the following arguments:

trapTarget   The object on which the property should be defined (the proxy's target)

key   The string or symbol for the property

descriptor   The descriptor object for the property

The `defineProperty` trap requires you to return true if the operation is successful and false if not. The `getOwnPropertyDescriptor` trap receives only trapTarget and key, and you are expected to return the descriptor. The corresponding `Reflect.defineProperty()` and `Reflect.getOwnPropertyDescriptor()` methods accept the same arguments as their proxy trap counterparts. Here's an example that implements the default behavior for each trap:

```
let proxy = new Proxy({}, {
    defineProperty(trapTarget, key, descriptor) {
        return Reflect.defineProperty(trapTarget, key, descriptor);
    },
```

```
        getOwnPropertyDescriptor(trapTarget, key) {
            return Reflect.getOwnPropertyDescriptor(trapTarget, key);
        }
});


Object.defineProperty(proxy, "name", {
    value: "proxy"
});

console.log(proxy.name);            // "proxy"

let descriptor = Object.getOwnPropertyDescriptor(proxy, "name");

console.log(descriptor.value);      // "proxy"
```

This code defines a property called "name" on the proxy using the
Object.defineProperty() method. The property descriptor for that property
is then retrieved by the Object.getOwnPropertyDescriptor() method.

Blocking Object.defineProperty()

The defineProperty trap requires you to return a Boolean value to indicate whether the operation was successful. When true is returned,
the Object.defineProperty() method succeeds as usual; when false is
returned, the Object.defineProperty() method throws an error. You
can use this functionality to restrict the kinds of properties that the
Object.defineProperty() method can define. For instance, if you want to
prevent symbol properties from being defined, you could check that the
key is a string and return false if not, like this:

```
let proxy = new Proxy({}, {
    defineProperty(trapTarget, key, descriptor) {

        if (typeof key === "symbol") {
            return false;
        }

        return Reflect.defineProperty(trapTarget, key, descriptor);
    }
});


Object.defineProperty(proxy, "name", {
    value: "proxy"
});

console.log(proxy.name);                    // "proxy"

let nameSymbol = Symbol("name");
```

```
// throws an error
Object.defineProperty(proxy, nameSymbol, {
    value: "proxy"
});
```

The defineProperty proxy trap returns false when key is a symbol and otherwise proceeds with the default behavior. When Object.defineProperty() is called with "name" as the key, the method succeeds because the key is a string. When Object.defineProperty() is called with nameSymbol, it throws an error because the defineProperty trap returns false.

You can also have Object.defineProperty() silently fail by returning true and not calling the Reflect.defineProperty() method. That will suppress the error while not actually defining the property.

Descriptor Object Restrictions

To ensure consistent behavior when you're using the Object.defineProperty() and Object.getOwnPropertyDescriptor() methods, descriptor objects passed to the defineProperty trap are normalized. Objects returned from the getOwnPropertyDescriptor trap are always validated for the same reason.

No matter what object is passed as the third argument to the method Object.defineProperty(), only the properties enumerable, configurable, value, writable, get, and set will be on the descriptor object passed to the defineProperty trap. For example:

```
let proxy = new Proxy({}, {
    defineProperty(trapTarget, key, descriptor) {
        console.log(descriptor.value);          // "proxy"
        console.log(descriptor.name);           // undefined

        return Reflect.defineProperty(trapTarget, key, descriptor);
    }
});

Object.defineProperty(proxy, "name", {
    value: "proxy",
    name: "custom"
});
```

Here, Object.defineProperty() is called with a nonstandard name property on the third argument. When the defineProperty trap is called, the descriptor object doesn't have a name property but does have a value property. The reason is that descriptor isn't a reference to the actual third argument passed to the Object.defineProperty() method, but rather a new object that contains only the allowable properties. The Reflect.defineProperty() method also ignores any nonstandard properties on the descriptor.

The getOwnPropertyDescriptor trap has a slightly different restriction that requires the return value to be null, undefined, or an object. If an object is returned, only enumerable, configurable, value, writable, get, and set are allowed as own properties of the object. An error is thrown if you return an object with an own property that isn't allowed, as this code shows:

```
let proxy = new Proxy({}, {
    getOwnPropertyDescriptor(trapTarget, key) {
        return {
            name: "proxy";
        };
    }
});

// throws an error
let descriptor = Object.getOwnPropertyDescriptor(proxy, "name");
```

The property name isn't allowable on property descriptors, so when Object.getOwnPropertyDescriptor() is called, the getOwnPropertyDescriptor return value triggers an error. This restriction ensures that the value returned by Object.getOwnPropertyDescriptor() always has a reliable structure regardless of the method's use on proxies.

Duplicate Descriptor Methods

Once again, ECMAScript 6 has some confusingly similar methods: the Object.defineProperty() and Object.getOwnPropertyDescriptor() methods appear to do the same thing as the Reflect.defineProperty() and Reflect.getOwnPropertyDescriptor() methods, respectively. Like other method pairs discussed earlier in this chapter, these four methods have some subtle but important differences.

defineProperty() Methods

The Object.defineProperty() and Reflect.defineProperty() methods are the same except for their return values. The Object.defineProperty() method returns the first argument, whereas Reflect.defineProperty() returns true if the operation succeeded and false if not. For example:

```
let target = {};

let result1 = Object.defineProperty(target, "name", { value: "target "});

console.log(target === result1);        // true

let result2 = Reflect.defineProperty(target, "name", { value: "reflect" });

console.log(result2);                    // true
```

When `Object.defineProperty()` is called on target, the return value is target. When `Reflect.defineProperty()` is called on target, the return value is true, indicating that the operation succeeded. Because the defineProperty proxy trap requires a Boolean value to be returned, it's best to use `Reflect.defineProperty()` to implement the default behavior when necessary.

getOwnPropertyDescriptor() Methods

The `Object.getOwnPropertyDescriptor()` method coerces its first argument into an object when a primitive value is passed and then continues the operation. On the other hand, the `Reflect.getOwnPropertyDescriptor()` method throws an error if the first argument is a primitive value. Here's an example that shows both:

```
let descriptor1 = Object.getOwnPropertyDescriptor(2, "name");
console.log(descriptor1);        // undefined

// throws an error
let descriptor2 = Reflect.getOwnPropertyDescriptor(2, "name");
```

The `Object.getOwnPropertyDescriptor()` method returns undefined because it coerces 2 into an object, and that object has no name property. This is the method's standard behavior when a property with the given name isn't found on an object. However, when `Reflect.getOwnPropertyDescriptor()` is called, an error is thrown immediately because that method doesn't accept primitive values for the first argument.

The ownKeys Trap

The ownKeys proxy trap intercepts the internal method [[OwnPropertyKeys]] and allows you to override that behavior by returning an array of values. This array is used in four methods: the `Object.keys()` method, the `Object.getOwnPropertyNames()` method, the `Object.getOwnPropertySymbols()` method, and the `Object.assign()` method. (The `Object.assign()` method uses the array to determine which properties to copy.)

The default behavior for the ownKeys trap is implemented by the `Reflect.ownKeys()` method and returns an array of all own property keys, including strings and symbols. The `Object.getOwnPropertyNames()` method and the `Object.keys()` method filter symbols out of the array and return the result, whereas `Object.getOwnPropertySymbols()` filters the strings out of the array and returns the result. The `Object.assign()` method uses the array with both strings and symbols.

The ownKeys trap receives a single argument, the target, and must always return an array or array-like object; otherwise, an error is thrown. You can use the ownKeys trap to, for example, filter out certain property keys that you don't want used when the `Object.keys()` method, the `Object.getOwnPropertyNames()` method, the `Object.getOwnPropertySymbols()`

method, or the `Object.assign()` method is used. Suppose you don't want to include any property names that begin with an underscore character—a common notation in JavaScript indicating that a field is private. You can use the `ownKeys` trap to filter out those keys as follows:

```
let proxy = new Proxy({}, {
    ownKeys(trapTarget) {
        return Reflect.ownKeys(trapTarget).filter(key => {
            return typeof key !== "string" || key[0] !== "_";
        });
    }
});

let nameSymbol = Symbol("name");

proxy.name = "proxy";
proxy._name = "private";
proxy[nameSymbol] = "symbol";

let names = Object.getOwnPropertyNames(proxy),
    keys = Object.keys(proxy),
    symbols = Object.getOwnPropertySymbols(proxy);

console.log(names.length);      // 1
console.log(names[0]);          // "proxy"

console.log(keys.length);       // 1
console.log(keys[0]);           // "proxy"

console.log(symbols.length);    // 1
console.log(symbols[0]);        // "Symbol(name)"
```

This example uses an `ownKeys` trap that first calls `Reflect.ownKeys()` to get the default list of keys for the target. Next, the `filter()` method is used to filter out keys that are strings and begin with an underscore character. Then, three properties are added to the proxy object: `name`, `_name`, and `nameSymbol`. When `Object.getOwnPropertyNames()` and `Object.keys()` are called on proxy, only the `name` property is returned. Similarly, only `nameSymbol` is returned when `Object.getOwnPropertySymbols()` is called on proxy. The `_name` property doesn't appear in either result because it is filtered out.

Although the `ownKeys` proxy trap allows you to alter the keys returned from a small set of operations, it doesn't affect more commonly used operations, such as the `for-of` loop and the `Object.keys()` method. Those can't be altered using proxies. The `ownKeys` trap also affects the `for-in` loop, which calls the trap to determine which keys to use inside of the loop.

Function Proxies with the apply and construct Traps

Of all the proxy traps, only `apply` and `construct` require the proxy target to be a function. Recall from Chapter 3 that functions have two internal methods called `[[Call]]` and `[[Construct]]` that are executed when a function is called without and with the new operator, respectively. The apply and construct traps correspond to and let you override those internal methods. When a function is called without new, the apply trap receives, and Reflect.apply() expects, the following arguments:

trapTarget The function being executed (the proxy's target)

thisArg The value of this inside the function during the call

argumentsList An array of arguments passed to the function

The construct trap, which is called when the function is executed using new, receives the following arguments:

trapTarget The function being executed (the proxy's target)

argumentsList An array of arguments passed to the function

The Reflect.construct() method also accepts these two arguments and has an optional third argument called newTarget. When given, the newTarget argument specifies the value of new.target inside the function.

Together, the apply and construct traps completely control the behavior of any proxy target function. To mimic the default behavior of a function, you can do this:

```
let target = function() { return 42 },
    proxy = new Proxy(target, {
        apply: function(trapTarget, thisArg, argumentList) {
            return Reflect.apply(trapTarget, thisArg, argumentList);
        },
        construct: function(trapTarget, argumentList) {
            return Reflect.construct(trapTarget, argumentList);
        }
    });

// a proxy with a function as its target looks like a function
console.log(typeof proxy);              // "function"

console.log(proxy());                   // 42

var instance = new proxy();
console.log(instance instanceof proxy);   // true
console.log(instance instanceof target);  // true
```

Here, you have a function that returns the number 42. The proxy for that function uses the apply and construct traps to delegate those behaviors to the Reflect.apply() and Reflect.construct() methods, respectively. The end result is that the proxy function works exactly like the target function, including identifying itself as a function when typeof is used. The proxy is called without new to return 42 and then is called with new to create an object called instance. The instance object is considered an instance of both proxy and target because instanceof uses the prototype chain to determine this information. Prototype chain lookup is not affected by this proxy, which is why proxy and target appear to have the same prototype.

Validating Function Parameters

The apply and construct traps open several possibilities for altering the way a function is executed. For instance, suppose you want to validate that all arguments are of a specific type. You can check the arguments in the apply trap:

```
// adds together all arguments
function sum(...values) {
    return values.reduce((previous, current) => previous + current, 0);
}

let sumProxy = new Proxy(sum, {
    apply: function(trapTarget, thisArg, argumentList) {

        argumentList.forEach((arg) => {
            if (typeof arg !== "number") {
                throw new TypeError("All arguments must be numbers.");
            }
        });

        return Reflect.apply(trapTarget, thisArg, argumentList);
    },
    construct: function(trapTarget, argumentList) {
        throw new TypeError("This function can't be called with new.");
    }
});

console.log(sumProxy(1, 2, 3, 4));          // 10

// throws an error
console.log(sumProxy(1, "2", 3, 4));

// also throws an error
let result = new sumProxy();
```

This example uses the apply trap to ensure that all arguments are numbers. The sum() function adds all the arguments that are passed. If a nonnumber value is passed, the function will still attempt the operation, which can cause unexpected results. By wrapping sum() inside the sumProxy() proxy, this code intercepts function calls and ensures that each argument is a number before allowing the call to proceed. To be safe, the code also uses the construct trap to ensure that the function can't be called with new.

You can also do the opposite, ensuring that a function must be called with new and validating its arguments as numbers:

```
function Numbers(...values) {
    this.values = values;
}
```

```
let NumbersProxy = new Proxy(Numbers, {
    apply: function(trapTarget, thisArg, argumentList) {
        throw new TypeError("This function must be called with new.");
    },

    construct: function(trapTarget, argumentList) {
        argumentList.forEach((arg) => {
            if (typeof arg !== "number") {
                throw new TypeError("All arguments must be numbers.");
            }
        });

        return Reflect.construct(trapTarget, argumentList);
    }
});

let instance = new NumbersProxy(1, 2, 3, 4);
console.log(instance.values);           // [1,2,3,4]

// throws an error
NumbersProxy(1, 2, 3, 4);
```

Here, the apply trap throws an error, and the construct trap uses the Reflect.construct() method to validate input and return a new instance. Of course, you can accomplish the same thing without proxies using new.target instead.

Calling Constructors Without new

Chapter 3 introduced the new.target metaproperty. To review, new.target is a reference to the function on which new is called, meaning that you can determine whether a function was called using new or not by checking the value of new.target, like this:

```
function Numbers(...values) {

    if (typeof new.target === "undefined") {
        throw new TypeError("This function must be called with new.");
    }

    this.values = values;
}

let instance = new Numbers(1, 2, 3, 4);
console.log(instance.values);           // [1,2,3,4]

// throws an error
Numbers(1, 2, 3, 4);
```

This code throws an error when Numbers() is called without using new, which is similar to the second example in "Validating Function Parameters" on page 264 but doesn't use a proxy. Writing code like this is much simpler than using a proxy and is preferable if your only goal is to prevent calling the function without new. But sometimes you're not in control of the function whose behavior needs to be modified. In that case, using a proxy makes sense.

Suppose the Numbers() function is defined in code you can't modify. You know that the code relies on new.target and want to avoid that check while still calling the function. The behavior when using new is already set, so you can just use the apply trap:

```
function Numbers(...values) {

    if (typeof new.target === "undefined") {
        throw new TypeError("This function must be called with new.");
    }

    this.values = values;
}


let NumbersProxy = new Proxy(Numbers, {
    apply: function(trapTarget, thisArg, argumentsList) {
        return Reflect.construct(trapTarget, argumentsList);
    }
});


let instance = NumbersProxy(1, 2, 3, 4);
console.log(instance.values);           // [1,2,3,4]
```

The NumbersProxy() function allows you to call Numbers() without using new and have it behave as if new were used. To do so, the apply trap calls Reflect.construct() with the arguments passed into apply. The new.target inside Numbers() is equal to Numbers(), so no error is thrown. Although this is a simple example of modifying new.target, you can also do so more directly.

Overriding Abstract Base Class Constructors

You can go one step further to modify new.target by specifying the third argument to Reflect.construct() as the specific value to assign to new.target. This technique is useful when a function is checking new.target against a known value, such as when you're creating an abstract base class constructor (discussed in Chapter 9). In an abstract base class constructor, new.target is expected to be something other than the class constructor, as in this example:

```
class AbstractNumbers {

    constructor(...values) {
        if (new.target === AbstractNumbers) {
            throw new TypeError("This function must be inherited from.");
        }

        this.values = values;
```

```
        }
}

class Numbers extends AbstractNumbers {}

let instance = new Numbers(1, 2, 3, 4);
console.log(instance.values);          // [1,2,3,4]

// throws an error
new AbstractNumbers(1, 2, 3, 4);
```

When new AbstractNumbers() is called, new.target is equal to AbstractNumbers and an error is thrown. Calling new Numbers() still works because new.target is equal to Numbers. You can bypass the constructor restriction by manually assigning new.target with a proxy:

```
class AbstractNumbers {

    constructor(...values) {
        if (new.target === AbstractNumbers) {
            throw new TypeError("This function must be inherited from.");
        }

        this.values = values;
    }
}

let AbstractNumbersProxy = new Proxy(AbstractNumbers, {
    construct: function(trapTarget, argumentList) {
        return Reflect.construct(trapTarget, argumentList, function() {});
    }
});


let instance = new AbstractNumbersProxy(1, 2, 3, 4);
console.log(instance.values);              // [1,2,3,4]
```

The AbstractNumbersProxy uses the construct trap to intercept the call to the new AbstractNumbersProxy() method. Then, the Reflect.construct() method is called with arguments from the trap and adds an empty function as the third argument. That empty function is used as the value of new.target inside the constructor. Because new.target is not equal to AbstractNumbers, no error is thrown and the constructor executes completely.

Callable Class Constructors

Chapter 9 explained that class constructors must always be called with new because the internal [[Call]] method for class constructors is specified to throw an error. But proxies can intercept calls to the [[Call]] method, meaning you can effectively create callable class constructors by using a proxy. For instance, if you want a class constructor to work without using new, you can use the apply trap to create a new instance. Here's some sample code to demonstrate:

```
class Person {
    constructor(name) {
        this.name = name;
    }
}

let PersonProxy = new Proxy(Person, {
    apply: function(trapTarget, thisArg, argumentList) {
        return new trapTarget(...argumentList);
    }
});


let me = PersonProxy("Nicholas");
console.log(me.name);                  // "Nicholas"
console.log(me instanceof Person);     // true
console.log(me instanceof PersonProxy); // true
```

The PersonProxy object is a proxy of the Person class constructor. Class constructors are just functions, so they behave like functions when they're used in proxies. The apply trap overrides the default behavior and instead returns a new instance of trapTarget that's equal to Person. (I used trapTarget in this example to show that you don't need to manually specify the class.) The argumentList is passed to trapTarget using the spread operator to pass each argument separately. Calling PersonProxy() without using new returns an instance of Person; if you attempt to call Person() without new, the constructor will still throw an error. Creating callable class constructors is only possible using proxies.

Revocable Proxies

Normally, a proxy can't be unbound from its target once the proxy has been created. All of the examples to this point in this chapter have used non-revocable proxies. But there may be situations in which you want to revoke a proxy so it can no longer be used. You'll find it most helpful to revoke proxies when you want to provide an object through an API for security purposes and maintain the ability to cut off access to some functionality at any point in time.

You can create revocable proxies using the Proxy.revocable() method, which takes the same arguments as the Proxy constructor—a target object and the proxy handler. The return value is an object with the following properties:

proxy   The proxy object that can be revoked

revoke   The function to call to revoke the proxy

When the revoke() function is called, no further operations can be performed through the proxy. Any attempt to interact with the proxy object in a way that would trigger a proxy trap throws an error. For example:

```
let target = {
    name: "target"
};

let { proxy, revoke } = Proxy.revocable(target, {});

console.log(proxy.name);        // "target"

revoke();

// throws an error
console.log(proxy.name);
```

This example creates a revocable proxy. It uses destructuring to assign the proxy and revoke variables to the properties of the same name on the object returned by the Proxy.revocable() method. After that, the proxy object can be used just like a nonrevocable proxy object, so proxy.name returns "target" because it passes through to target.name. However, once the revoke() function is called, proxy no longer functions. Attempting to access proxy.name throws an error, as will any other operation that would trigger a trap on proxy.

Solving the Array Problem

At the beginning of this chapter, I explained how developers couldn't mimic the behavior of an array accurately in JavaScript prior to ECMAScript 6. Proxies and the reflection API allow you to create an object that behaves in the same manner as the built-in Array type when properties are added and removed. To refresh your memory, here's an example that shows the behavior that proxies help to mimic:

```
let colors = ["red", "green", "blue"];

console.log(colors.length);     // 3

colors[3] = "black";

console.log(colors.length);     // 4
console.log(colors[3]);         // "black"

colors.length = 2;

console.log(colors.length);     // 2
console.log(colors[3]);         // undefined
console.log(colors[2]);         // undefined
console.log(colors[1]);         // "green"
```

Notice two particularly important behaviors in this example:

- The `length` property is increased to 4 when `colors[3]` is assigned a value.
- The last two items in the array are deleted when the `length` property is set to 2.

These two behaviors are the only ones that need to be mimicked to accurately re-create how built-in arrays work. The next few sections describe how to make an object that correctly mimics them.

Detecting Array Indexes

Keep in mind that assigning a value to an integer property key is a special case for arrays, because they're treated differently from non-integer keys. The ECMAScript 6 specification gives the following instructions on how to determine whether a property key is an array index:

> A String property name P is an array index if and only if `ToString(ToUint32(P))` is equal to P and `ToUint32(P)` is not equal to 232-1.

This operation can be implemented in JavaScript as follows:

```
function toUint32(value) {
    return Math.floor(Math.abs(Number(value))) % Math.pow(2, 32);
}

function isArrayIndex(key) {
    let numericKey = toUint32(key);
    return String(numericKey) == key && numericKey < (Math.pow(2, 32) - 1);
}
```

The `toUint32()` function converts a given value into an unsigned 32-bit integer using an algorithm described in the specification. The `isArrayIndex()` function first converts the key into a uint32 and then performs the comparisons to determine whether or not the key is an array index. With these two utility functions available, you can start to implement an object that will mimic a built-in array.

Increasing length When Adding New Elements

Notice that both array behaviors I described previously rely on the assignment of a property. That means you only need to use the set proxy trap to accomplish both behaviors. To get started, look at this example, which implements the first of the two behaviors by incrementing the `length` property when an array index larger than `length - 1` is used:

```
function toUint32(value) {
    return Math.floor(Math.abs(Number(value))) % Math.pow(2, 32);
}
```

```
function isArrayIndex(key) {
    let numericKey = toUint32(key);
    return String(numericKey) == key && numericKey < (Math.pow(2, 32) - 1);
}

function createMyArray(length=0) {
    return new Proxy({ length }, {
        set(trapTarget, key, value) {

            let currentLength = Reflect.get(trapTarget, "length");

            // the special case
            if (isArrayIndex(key)) {
                let numericKey = Number(key);

                if (numericKey >= currentLength) {
                    Reflect.set(trapTarget, "length", numericKey + 1);
                }
            }

            // always do this regardless of key type
            return Reflect.set(trapTarget, key, value);
        }
    });
}

let colors = createMyArray(3);
console.log(colors.length);        // 3

colors[0] = "red";
colors[1] = "green";
colors[2] = "blue";

console.log(colors.length);        // 3

colors[3] = "black";

console.log(colors.length);        // 4
console.log(colors[3]);            // "black"
```

This code uses the set proxy trap to intercept the setting of an array index. If the key is an array index, it is converted into a number because keys are always passed as strings. Next, if that numeric value is greater than or equal to the current length property, the length property is updated to be one more than the numeric key (setting an item in position 3 means the length must be 4). Then, the default behavior for setting a property is used via Reflect.set(), because you want the property to receive the value as specified.

The initial custom array is created by calling createMyArray() with a length of 3, and the values for those three items are added immediately afterward. The length property correctly remains at 3 until the value "black" is assigned to position 3. At that point, length is set to 4.

With the first array behavior working, it's time to move on to the second behavior.

Deleting Elements When Reducing length

The first array behavior to mimic is used only when an array index is greater than or equal to the length property. The second behavior does the opposite and removes array items when the length property is set to a smaller value than it previously contained. That involves not only changing the length property but also deleting all items that might otherwise exist. For instance, if an array with a length of 4 has length set to 2, the items in positions 2 and 3 are deleted. You can accomplish this inside the set proxy trap alongside the first behavior. Here's the previous example again but with an updated createMyArray method:

```
function toUint32(value) {
    return Math.floor(Math.abs(Number(value))) % Math.pow(2, 32);
}

function isArrayIndex(key) {
    let numericKey = toUint32(key);
    return String(numericKey) == key && numericKey < (Math.pow(2, 32) - 1);
}

function createMyArray(length=0) {
    return new Proxy({ length }, {
        set(trapTarget, key, value) {

            let currentLength = Reflect.get(trapTarget, "length");

            // the special case
            if (isArrayIndex(key)) {
                let numericKey = Number(key);

                if (numericKey >= currentLength) {
                    Reflect.set(trapTarget, "length", numericKey + 1);
                }
            } else if (key === "length") {

                if (value < currentLength) {
                    for (let index = currentLength - 1; index >= value;
                            index--) {
                        Reflect.deleteProperty(trapTarget, index);
                    }
                }

            }

            // always do this regardless of key type
            return Reflect.set(trapTarget, key, value);
        }
    });
}

let colors = createMyArray(3);
console.log(colors.length);        // 3
```

```
colors[0] = "red";
colors[1] = "green";
colors[2] = "blue";
colors[3] = "black";

console.log(colors.length);         // 4

colors.length = 2;

console.log(colors.length);         // 2
console.log(colors[3]);             // undefined
console.log(colors[2]);             // undefined
console.log(colors[1]);             // "green"
console.log(colors[0]);             // "red"
```

The set proxy trap in this code checks whether key is "length" in order to adjust the rest of the object correctly. When that check happens, the current length is first retrieved using Reflect.get() and compared against the new value. If the new value is less than the current length, a for loop deletes all properties on the target that should no longer be available. The for loop goes backward from the current array length (currentLength) and deletes each property until it reaches the new array length (value).

This example adds four colors to colors and then sets the length property to 2. That effectively removes the items in positions 2 and 3, so they now return undefined when you attempt to access them. The length property is correctly set to 2, and the items in positions 0 and 1 are still accessible.

With both behaviors implemented, you can easily create an object that mimics the behavior of built-in arrays. But doing so with a function isn't as desirable as creating a class to encapsulate this behavior, so the next step is to implement this functionality as a class.

Implementing the MyArray Class

The simplest way to create a class that uses a proxy is to define the class as usual and then return a proxy from the constructor. That way, the object returned when a class is instantiated will be the proxy instead of the instance. (The instance is the value of this inside the constructor.) The instance becomes the target of the proxy, and the proxy is returned as if it were the instance. The instance will be completely private, and you won't be able to access it directly, although you'll be able to access it indirectly through the proxy.

Here's a simple example of returning a proxy from a class constructor:

```
class Thing {
    constructor() {
        return new Proxy(this, {});
    }
}

let myThing = new Thing();
console.log(myThing instanceof Thing);    // true
```

In this example, the class Thing returns a proxy from its constructor. The proxy target is this, and the proxy is returned from the constructor. That means myThing is actually a proxy, even though it was created by calling the Thing constructor. Because proxies pass through their behavior to their targets, myThing is still considered an instance of Thing, making the proxy completely transparent to anyone using the Thing class.

With the understanding that you can return a proxy from a constructor in mind, creating a custom array class using a proxy is relatively straightforward. The code is mostly the same as the code in "Deleting Elements When Reducing length" on page 272. You can use the same proxy code, but this time you need to place it inside a class constructor. Here's the complete example:

```
function toUint32(value) {
    return Math.floor(Math.abs(Number(value))) % Math.pow(2, 32);
}

function isArrayIndex(key) {
    let numericKey = toUint32(key);
    return String(numericKey) == key && numericKey < (Math.pow(2, 32) - 1);
}

class MyArray {
    constructor(length=0) {
        this.length = length;

        return new Proxy(this, {
            set(trapTarget, key, value) {

                let currentLength = Reflect.get(trapTarget, "length");

                // the special case
                if (isArrayIndex(key)) {
                    let numericKey = Number(key);

                    if (numericKey >= currentLength) {
                        Reflect.set(trapTarget, "length", numericKey + 1);
                    }
                } else if (key === "length") {

                    if (value < currentLength) {
                        for (let index = currentLength - 1; index >= value;
                                index--) {
                            Reflect.deleteProperty(trapTarget, index);
                        }
                    }
                }

            }
```

```
                    // always do this regardless of key type
                    return Reflect.set(trapTarget, key, value);
                }
            });

        }
    }


    let colors = new MyArray(3);
    console.log(colors instanceof MyArray);      // true

    console.log(colors.length);            // 3

    colors[0] = "red";
    colors[1] = "green";
    colors[2] = "blue";
    colors[3] = "black";

    console.log(colors.length);            // 4

    colors.length = 2;

    console.log(colors.length);            // 2
    console.log(colors[3]);                // undefined
    console.log(colors[2]);                // undefined
    console.log(colors[1]);                // "green"
    console.log(colors[0]);                // "red"
```

This code creates a MyArray class that returns a proxy from its constructor. The length property is added in the constructor (initialized to either the value that is passed in or to a default value of 0) and then a proxy is created and returned. This makes the colors variable appear as though it's just an instance of MyArray and implements both key array behaviors.

Although returning a proxy from a class constructor is easy, it also means that a new proxy is created for every instance. However, there is a way to have all instances share one proxy: you can use the proxy as a prototype.

Using a Proxy as a Prototype

Although you can use proxies as prototypes, doing so is a bit more involved than the previous examples in this chapter. When a proxy is a prototype, the proxy traps are only called when the default operation would normally continue on to the prototype, which limits a proxy's capabilities as a prototype. Consider the following example.

```
let target = {};
let newTarget = Object.create(new Proxy(target, {

    // never called
    defineProperty(trapTarget, name, descriptor) {

        // would cause an error if called
        return false;
    }
}));

Object.defineProperty(newTarget, "name", {
    value: "newTarget"
});

console.log(newTarget.name);                    // "newTarget"
console.log(newTarget.hasOwnProperty("name"));  // true
```

The newTarget object is created with a proxy as the prototype. Making target the proxy target effectively makes target the prototype of newTarget because the proxy is transparent. Now, proxy traps will only be called if an operation on newTarget would pass the operation through to happen on target.

The Object.defineProperty() method is called on newTarget to create an own property called name. Defining a property on an object isn't an operation that normally continues to the object's prototype, so the defineProperty trap on the proxy is never called and the name property is added to newTarget as an own property.

Although proxies are severely limited when they're used as prototypes, a few traps are still useful. I'll cover those in the next few sections.

Using the get Trap on a Prototype

When the internal [[Get]] method is called to read a property, the operation looks for own properties first. If an own property with the given name isn't found, the operation continues to the prototype and looks for a property there. The process continues until there are no further prototypes to check.

Because of that process, if you set up a get proxy trap, the trap will be called on a prototype whenever an own property of the given name doesn't exist. You can use the get trap to prevent unexpected behavior when accessing properties that you can't guarantee will exist. Just create an object that throws an error whenever you try to access a property that doesn't exist:

```
let target = {};
let thing = Object.create(new Proxy(target, {
    get(trapTarget, key, receiver) {
        throw new ReferenceError(`${key} doesn't exist`);
    }
}));

thing.name = "thing";
```

```
console.log(thing.name);        // "thing"

// throws an error
let unknown = thing.unknown;
```

In this code, the thing object is created with a proxy as its prototype. The get trap throws an error when called to indicate that the given key doesn't exist on the thing object. When thing.name is read, the operation never calls the get trap on the prototype because the property exists on thing. The get trap is called only when the thing.unknown property, which doesn't exist, is accessed.

When the last line executes, unknown isn't an own property of thing, so the operation continues to the prototype. The get trap then throws an error. This type of behavior can be very useful in JavaScript where unknown properties silently return undefined instead of throwing an error (which happens in other languages).

It's important to understand that in this example, trapTarget and receiver are different objects. When a proxy is used as a prototype, the trapTarget is the prototype object and the receiver is the instance object. In this case, that means trapTarget is equal to target and receiver is equal to thing. That allows you access to the original target of the proxy and the object on which the operation is meant to take place.

Using the set Trap on a Prototype

The internal [[Set]] method also checks for own properties and then continues to the prototype if needed. When you assign a value to an object property, the value is assigned to the own property with the same name if it exists. If no own property with the given name exists, the operation continues to the prototype. The tricky part is that even though the assignment operation continues to the prototype, assigning a value to that property will create a property on the instance (not the prototype) by default regardless of whether a property of that name exists on the prototype.

To get a better idea of when the set trap will be called on a prototype and when it won't, consider the following example, which shows the default behavior:

```
let target = {};
let thing = Object.create(new Proxy(target, {
    set(trapTarget, key, value, receiver) {
        return Reflect.set(trapTarget, key, value, receiver);
    }
}));

console.log(thing.hasOwnProperty("name"));    // false

// triggers the `set` proxy trap
thing.name = "thing";

console.log(thing.name);                       // "thing"
console.log(thing.hasOwnProperty("name"));    // true
```

```
// does not trigger the `set` proxy trap
thing.name = "boo";

console.log(thing.name);                          // "boo"
```

In this example, target starts with no own properties. The thing object has a proxy as its prototype that defines a set trap to catch the creation of any new properties. When thing.name is assigned "thing" as its value, the set proxy trap is called because thing doesn't have an own property called name. Inside the set trap, trapTarget is equal to target and receiver is equal to thing. The operation should ultimately create a new property on thing, and fortunately, Reflect.set() implements this default behavior for you if you pass in receiver as the fourth argument.

Once the name property is created on thing, setting thing.name to a different value will no longer call the set proxy trap. At that point, name is an own property, so the [[Set]] operation never continues on to the prototype.

Using the has Trap on a Prototype

Recall that the has trap intercepts the use of the in operator on objects. The in operator searches first for an object's own property with the given name. If an own property with that name doesn't exist, the operation continues to the prototype. If there's no own property on the prototype, the search continues through the prototype chain until the own property is found or there are no more prototypes to search.

The has trap is therefore only called when the search reaches the proxy object in the prototype chain. When you're using a proxy as a prototype, the has trap is only called when there's no own property of the given name. For example:

```
let target = {};
let thing = Object.create(new Proxy(target, {
    has(trapTarget, key) {
        return Reflect.has(trapTarget, key);
    }
}));

// triggers the `has` proxy trap
console.log("name" in thing);                     // false

thing.name = "thing";

// does not trigger the `has` proxy trap
console.log("name" in thing);                     // true
```

This code creates a has proxy trap on the prototype of thing. The has trap isn't passed a receiver object like the get and set traps are, because searching the prototype happens automatically when the in operator is used. Instead, the has trap must operate only on trapTarget, which is equal to target. The first time the in operator is used in this example, the has trap is called because the property name doesn't exist as an own property of thing.

When `thing.name` is given a value and the `in` operator is used again, the `has` trap isn't called because the operation stops after finding the own property `name` on `thing`.

The prototype examples to this point have focused on objects created using the `Object.create()` method. But if you want to create a class that has a proxy as a prototype, the process is a bit more involved.

Proxies as Prototypes on Classes

Classes cannot be directly modified to use a proxy as a prototype because their `prototype` property is nonwritable. However, you can use a bit of misdirection to create a class that has a proxy as its prototype by using inheritance. To start, you need to create an ECMAScript 5–style type definition using a constructor function. You can then overwrite the prototype to be a proxy. Here's an example:

```
function NoSuchProperty() {
    // empty
}

NoSuchProperty.prototype = new Proxy({}, {
    get(trapTarget, key, receiver) {
        throw new ReferenceError(`${key} doesn't exist`);
    }
});

let thing = new NoSuchProperty();

// throws an error due to `get` proxy trap
let result = thing.name;
```

The `NoSuchProperty` function represents the base from which the class will inherit. There are no restrictions on the `prototype` property of functions, so you can overwrite it with a proxy. The `get` trap is used to throw an error when the property doesn't exist. The `thing` object is created as an instance of `NoSuchProperty` and throws an error when the nonexistent `name` property is accessed.

The next step is to create a class that inherits from `NoSuchProperty`. You can simply use the `extends` syntax discussed in Chapter 9 to introduce the proxy into the class's prototype chain, like this:

```
function NoSuchProperty() {
    // empty
}

NoSuchProperty.prototype = new Proxy({}, {
    get(trapTarget, key, receiver) {
        throw new ReferenceError(`${key} doesn't exist`);
    }
});
```

```
class Square extends NoSuchProperty {
    constructor(length, width) {
        super();
        this.length = length;
        this.width = width;
    }
}

let shape = new Square(2, 6);

let area1 = shape.length * shape.width;
console.log(area1);                        // 12

// throws an error because "wdth" doesn't exist
let area2 = shape.length * shape.wdth;
```

The Square class inherits from NoSuchProperty, so the proxy is in the Square class's prototype chain. The shape object is then created as a new instance of Square and has two own properties: length and width. Reading the values of those properties succeeds because the get proxy trap is never called. Only when a property that doesn't exist on shape is accessed (shape.wdth, an obvious typo) does the get proxy trap trigger and throw an error, proving that the proxy is in the prototype chain of shape. But it might not be obvious that the proxy is not the direct prototype of shape. In fact, the proxy is a couple of steps up the prototype chain from shape. You can see this more clearly by slightly altering the preceding example:

```
function NoSuchProperty() {
    // empty
}

// store a reference to the proxy that will be the prototype
let proxy = new Proxy({}, {
    get(trapTarget, key, receiver) {
        throw new ReferenceError(`${key} doesn't exist`);
    }
});

NoSuchProperty.prototype = proxy;

class Square extends NoSuchProperty {
    constructor(length, width) {
        super();
        this.length = length;
        this.width = width;
    }
}

let shape = new Square(2, 6);

let shapeProto = Object.getPrototypeOf(shape);
```

```
console.log(shapeProto === proxy);                      // false

let secondLevelProto = Object.getPrototypeOf(shapeProto);

console.log(secondLevelProto === proxy);                // true
```

This version of the code stores the proxy in a variable called proxy, making it easier to identify later. The prototype of shape is Shape.prototype, which is not a proxy. But the prototype of Shape.prototype is the proxy that was inherited from NoSuchProperty.

The inheritance adds another step in the prototype chain, and that matters because operations that might result in calling the get trap on proxy need to go through one extra step before doing so. If there's a property on Shape.prototype, that will prevent the get proxy trap from being called, as in this example:

```
function NoSuchProperty() {
    // empty
}

NoSuchProperty.prototype = new Proxy({}, {
    get(trapTarget, key, receiver) {
        throw new ReferenceError(`${key} doesn't exist`);
    }
});

class Square extends NoSuchProperty {
    constructor(length, width) {
        super();
        this.length = length;
        this.width = width;
    }

    getArea() {
        return this.length * this.width;
    }
}

let shape = new Square(2, 6);

let area1 = shape.length * shape.width;
console.log(area1);                      // 12

let area2 = shape.getArea();
console.log(area2);                      // 12

// throws an error because "wdth" doesn't exist
let area3 = shape.length * shape.wdth;
```

Here, the Square class has a getArea() method. The getArea() method is automatically added to Square.prototype, so when shape.getArea() is called, the search for the method getArea() starts on the shape instance and then proceeds to its prototype. Because getArea() is found on the prototype, the search stops and the proxy is never called. That is actually the behavior you want in this situation, because you wouldn't want to incorrectly throw an error when getArea() is called.

Even though it takes a bit of extra code to create a class with a proxy in its prototype chain, it can be worth the effort if you need such functionality.

Summary

Prior to ECMAScript 6, certain objects (such as arrays) displayed non-standard behavior that developers couldn't replicate. Proxies change that. They let you define your own nonstandard behavior for several low-level JavaScript operations, so you can replicate all behaviors of built-in JavaScript objects through proxy traps. These traps are called behind the scenes when various operations take place, like the use of the in operator.

A reflection API was also introduced in ECMAScript 6 to allow developers to implement the default behavior for each proxy trap. Each proxy trap has a corresponding method of the same name on the Reflect object, which is another ECMAScript 6 addition. Using a combination of proxy traps and reflection API methods, it's possible to filter some operations to behave differently only in certain conditions while defaulting to the built-in behavior.

Revocable proxies are special proxies that can be effectively disabled by using a revoke() function. The revoke() function terminates all functionality on the proxy, so any attempt to interact with the proxy's properties throws an error after revoke() is called. Revocable proxies are important for application security where third-party developers may need access to certain objects for a specified amount of time.

Although using proxies directly is the most powerful use case, you can also use a proxy as the prototype for another object. In that case, you are severely limited in the number of proxy traps you can effectively use. Only the get, set, and has proxy traps will ever be called on a proxy when it's used as a prototype, resulting in fewer use cases.

13

ENCAPSULATING CODE WITH MODULES

JavaScript's "shared everything" approach to loading code is one of the most error-prone and confusing aspects of the language. Other languages use concepts such as packages to define code scope, but before ECMAScript 6, everything defined in every JavaScript file of an application shared one global scope. As web applications became more complex and started using even more JavaScript code, that approach caused problems, such as naming collisions and security concerns. One goal of ECMAScript 6 was to solve the scope problem and bring some order to JavaScript applications. That's where modules come in.

What Are Modules?

A *module* is JavaScript code that automatically runs in strict mode with no way to opt out. Contrary to a shared-everything architecture, variables created in the top level of a module aren't automatically added to the shared global scope. The variables exist only within the top-level scope of the module, and the module must export any elements, like variables or functions, that should be available to code outside the module. Modules may also import bindings from other modules.

Two other module features relate less to scope but are important nonetheless. First, the value of this in the top level of a module is undefined. Second, modules also don't allow HTML-style comments within code, which is a residual feature from JavaScript's early browser days.

Scripts, which include any JavaScript code that isn't a module, lack these features. The differences between modules and other JavaScript code may seem minor at first glance, but they represent a significant change in how JavaScript code is loaded and evaluated, which I'll discuss throughout this chapter. The real power of modules is the ability to export and import only bindings you need rather than everything in a file. A good understanding of exporting and importing is fundamental to understanding how modules differ from scripts.

Basic Exporting

You can use the export keyword to expose parts of published code to other modules. In the simplest case, you can place export in front of any variable, function, or class declaration to export it from the module, like this:

```
// export data
export var color = "red";
export let name = "Nicholas";
export const magicNumber = 7;

// export function
export function sum(num1, num2) {
    return num1 + num1;
}

// export class
export class Rectangle {
    constructor(length, width) {
        this.length = length;
        this.width = width;
    }
}

// this function is private to the module
function subtract(num1, num2) {
    return num1 - num2;
}

// define a function...
function multiply(num1, num2) {
    return num1 * num2;
}
```

```
// ...and then export it later
export multiply;
```

There are a few details to notice in this example. Apart from the export keyword, every declaration is the same as it would be in a script. Each exported function or class also has a name, because exported function and class declarations require a name. You can't export anonymous functions or classes using this syntax unless you use the default keyword (discussed in detail in "Default Values in Modules" on page 289).

Also, consider the multiply() function, which isn't exported when it's defined. That works because you don't always need to export a declaration: you can also export references. Additionally, notice that this example doesn't export the subtract() function. That function won't be accessible from outside this module because any variables, functions, or classes that are not explicitly exported remain private to the module.

Basic Importing

When you have a module with exports, you can access the functionality in another module by using the import keyword. The two parts of an import statement are the identifiers you're importing and the module from which those identifiers should be imported.

This is the statement's basic form:

```
import { identifier1, identifier2 } from "./example.js";
```

The curly braces after import indicate the bindings to import from a given module. The keyword from indicates the module from which to import the given binding. The module is specified by a string representing the path to the module (called the *module specifier*). Browsers use the same path format you might pass to the <script> element, which means you must include a file extension. Node.js, on the other hand, follows its convention of differentiating between local files and packages based on a filesystem prefix. For instance, example would be a package and *./example.js* would be a local file.

NOTE *The list of bindings to import looks similar to a destructured object, but it isn't one.*

When you're importing a binding from a module, the binding acts as though it was defined using const. As a result, you can't define another variable with the same name (including importing another binding of the same name), use the identifier before the import statement, or change binding's value.

Importing a Single Binding

Suppose that the example in "Basic Exporting" on page 284 is in a module with the filename *example.js*. You can import and use bindings from that module in a number of ways. For instance, you can just import one identifier:

```
// import just one
import { sum } from "./example.js";

console.log(sum(1, 2));      // 3

sum = 1;                     // throws an error
```

Even though *example.js* exports more than just that one function, this example imports only the sum() function. If you try to assign a new value to sum, the result is an error because you can't reassign imported bindings.

NOTE   *Be sure to include /, ./, or ../ at the beginning of the string representing the file you're importing for the best compatibility across browsers and Node.js.*

Importing Multiple Bindings

If you want to import multiple bindings from the example module, you can explicitly list them as follows:

```
// import multiple
import { sum, multiply, magicNumber } from "./example.js";
console.log(sum(1, magicNumber));      // 8
console.log(multiply(1, 2));           // 2
```

Here, three bindings are imported from the example module: sum, multiply, and magicNumber. They are then used as though they were locally defined.

Importing an Entire Module

A special case allows you to import the entire module as a single object. All exports are then available on that object as properties. For example:

```
// import everything
import * as example from "./example.js";
console.log(example.sum(1,
        example.magicNumber));      // 8
console.log(example.multiply(1, 2));   // 2
```

In this code, all exported bindings in *example.js* are loaded into an object called example. The named exports (the sum() function, the multiple() function, and magicNumber) are then accessible as properties on example.

This import format is called a *namespace import* because the example object doesn't exist inside the *example.js* file and is instead created to be used as a namespace object for all the exported members of *example.js*.

However, keep in mind that no matter how many times you use a module in `import` statements, the module will execute only once. After the code to import the module executes, the instantiated module is kept in memory and reused whenever another `import` statement references it. Consider the following:

```
import { sum } from "./example.js";
import { multiply } from "./example.js";
import { magicNumber } from "./example.js";
```

Even though three `import` statements are in this module, *example.js* will execute only once. If other modules in the same application were to import bindings from *example.js*, those modules would use the same module instance this code uses.

MODULE SYNTAX LIMITATIONS

An important limitation of both export and import is that they must be used outside other statements and functions. For instance, this code will give a syntax error:

```
if (flag) {
    export flag;    // syntax error
}
```

The export statement is inside an if statement, which isn't allowed. Exports cannot be conditional or done dynamically in any way. One reason module syntax exists is to let the JavaScript engine statically determine what will be exported. As such, you can only use export at the top level of a module.

Similarly, you can't use import inside a statement; you can only use it at the top-level. That means this code also gives a syntax error:

```
function tryImport() {
    import flag from "./example.js";    // syntax error
}
```

You can't dynamically import bindings for the same reason you can't dynamically export bindings. The export and import keywords are designed to be static so tools like text editors can easily identify what information is available from a module.

A Subtle Quirk of Imported Bindings

ECMAScript 6's `import` statements create read-only bindings to variables, functions, and classes rather than simply referencing the original bindings like normal variables. Even though the module that imports the binding can't change the binding's value, the module that exports that identifier can. For example, suppose you want to use this module:

```
export var name = "Nicholas";
export function setName(newName) {
    name = newName;
}
```

When you import these two bindings, the `setName()` function can change the value of `name`:

```
import { name, setName } from "./example.js";

console.log(name);       // "Nicholas"
setName("Greg");
console.log(name);       // "Greg"

name = "Nicholas";       // throws an error
```

The call to `setName("Greg")` goes back into the module from which `setName()` was exported and executes there, setting `name` to `"Greg"` instead. Note that this change is automatically reflected on the imported `name` binding. The reason is that `name` is the local name for the exported `name` identifier. The `name` used in this code and the `name` used in the module being imported from aren't the same.

Renaming Exports and Imports

Sometimes, you may not want to use the original name of a variable, function, or class you've imported from a module. Fortunately, you can change the name of an export during the export and during the import.

In the first case, suppose you have a function that you want to export with a different name. You can use the as keyword to specify the name that the function should be known as outside of the module:

```
function sum(num1, num2) {
    return num1 + num2;
}

export { sum as add };
```

Here, the function with the *local name* sum() is exported using add() as its exported name. That means when another module wants to import this function, it will have to use the name add:

```
import { add } from "./example.js";
```

If the module importing the function wants to use a different name, it can also use as:

```
import { add as sum } from "./example.js";
console.log(typeof add);        // "undefined"
console.log(sum(1, 2));         // 3
```

This code imports the add() function using an *import name* to rename the function sum() (the local name in this context). Changing the function's local name on import means there is no identifier named add() in this module, even though the module imports the add() function.

Default Values in Modules

The module syntax is optimized for exporting and importing default values from modules, because this pattern was quite common in other module systems, such as CommonJS (another specification for using JavaScript outside the browser). The *default value* for a module is a single variable, function, or class as specified by the default keyword, and you can only set one default export per module. Using the default keyword with multiple exports is a syntax error.

Exporting Default Values

Here's a simple example that uses the default keyword:

```
export default function(num1, num2) {
    return num1 + num2;
}
```

This module exports a function as its default value. The default keyword indicates that this is a default export. The function doesn't require a name because the module represents the function.

You can also specify an identifier as the default export by placing it after export default, like this:

```
function sum(num1, num2) {
    return num1 + num2;
}

export default sum;
```

The sum() function is first defined and later exported as the default value of the module. You might want to use this approach if the default value needs to be calculated.

A third way to specify an identifier as the default export is by using the renaming syntax as follows:

```
function sum(num1, num2) {
    return num1 + num2;
}

export { sum as default };
```

The identifier default has special meaning in a renaming export and indicates a value should be the default for the module. Because default is a keyword in JavaScript, you can't use it for a variable, function, or class name; however, you can use it as a property name. So using default to rename an export is a special case to create consistency with how non-default exports are defined. This syntax is useful if you want to use a single export statement to specify multiple exports, including the default, simultaneously.

Importing Default Values

You can import a default value from a module using the following syntax:

```
// import the default
import sum from "./example.js";

console.log(sum(1, 2));     // 3
```

This import statement imports the default from the module *example.js*. Note that no curly braces are used, unlike what you'd see in a non-default import. The local name sum is used to represent whatever default function the module exports. This syntax is the cleanest, and the creators of ECMAScript 6 expect it to be the dominant form of import on the web, allowing you to use an already existing object.

For modules that export a default and one or more non-default bindings, you can import all exported bindings using one statement. For instance, suppose you have this module:

```
export let color = "red";

export default function(num1, num2) {
    return num1 + num2;
}
```

You can import color and the default function using the following import statement:

```
import sum, { color } from "./example.js";

console.log(sum(1, 2));    // 3
console.log(color);        // "red"
```

The comma separates the default local name from the non-defaults, which are also surrounded by curly braces. Keep in mind that the default must come before the non-defaults in the import statement.

As with exporting defaults, you can import defaults with the renaming syntax, too:

```
import { default as sum, color } from "./example.js";

console.log(sum(1, 2));    // 3
console.log(color);        // "red"
```

In this code, the default export (default) is renamed to sum and the additional color export is also imported. This example is otherwise equivalent to the preceding example.

Re-exporting a Binding

Eventually, you may want to re-export something that your module has imported. For instance, perhaps you're creating a library from several small modules. You can re-export an imported value using the patterns already discussed in this chapter, as follows:

```
import { sum } from "./example.js";
export { sum }
```

Although that works, a single statement can also do the same task:

```
export { sum } from "./example.js";
```

This form of export looks into the specified module for the declaration of sum and then exports it. Of course, you can also export a different name for the same value:

```
export { sum as add } from "./example.js";
```

Here, sum is imported from *example.js* and then exported as add.

If you want to export everything from another module, you can use the * pattern:

```
export * from "./example.js";
```

By exporting everything, you're including the default as well as any named exports, which may affect what you can export from your module. For instance, if *example.js* has a default export, you'd be unable to define a new default export when using this syntax.

Importing Without Bindings

Some modules may not export anything; instead, they might only modify objects in the global scope. Even though top-level variables, functions, and classes inside modules don't automatically end up in the global scope, that doesn't mean modules cannot access the global scope. The shared definitions of built-in objects, such as Array and Object, are accessible inside a module, and changes to those objects will be reflected in other modules.

For instance, if you want to add a pushAll() method to all arrays, you might define a module like this:

```
// module code without exports or imports
Array.prototype.pushAll = function(items) {

    // items must be an array
    if (!Array.isArray(items)) {
        throw new TypeError("Argument must be an array.");
    }

    // use built-in push() and spread operator
    return this.push(...items);
};
```

This is a valid module, even though there are no exports or imports. This code can be used as a module and as a script. Because it doesn't export anything, you can use a simplified import to execute the module code without importing any bindings:

```
import "./example.js";

let colors = ["red", "green", "blue"];
let items = [];

items.pushAll(colors);
```

This code imports and executes the module containing the pushAll() method, so pushAll() is added to the array prototype. That means pushAll() is now available for use on all arrays inside this module.

NOTE   *Imports without bindings are most likely to be used to create polyfills and shims.*

Loading Modules

Although ECMAScript 6 defines the syntax for modules, it doesn't define how to load them. This is part of the complexity of a specification that's supposed to be agnostic to implementation environments. Rather than trying to create a single specification that would work for all JavaScript environments, ECMAScript 6 specifies only the syntax and abstracts out the loading mechanism to an undefined internal operation called `HostResolveImportedModule`. Web browser and Node.js developers are left to decide how to implement `HostResolveImportedModule` in a way that makes sense for their respective environments.

Using Modules in Web Browsers

Even before ECMAScript 6, web browsers had multiple ways of including JavaScript in a web application. Those script loading options are:

- Loading JavaScript code files using the `<script>` element with the `src` attribute specifying a location from which to load the code
- Embedding JavaScript code inline using the `<script>` element without the `src` attribute
- Loading JavaScript code files to execute as workers (such as a web worker or service worker)

To fully support modules, web browsers had to update each of these mechanisms. These details are fully defined in the HTML specification, and I'll summarize them in the following sections.

Using Modules with `<script>`

The default behavior of the `<script>` element is to load JavaScript files as scripts, not modules. This happens when the `type` attribute is missing or when the `type` attribute contains a JavaScript content type (such as `"text/javascript"`). The `<script>` element can then execute inline code or load the file specified in `src`. To support modules, the `"module"` value was added as a type option. Setting `type` to `"module"` tells the browser to load any inline code or code contained in the file specified by `src` as a module instead of a script. Here's a simple example:

```
<!-- load a module JavaScript file -->
<script type="module" src="module.js"></script>

<!-- include a module inline -->
<script type="module">

import { sum } from "./example.js";

let result = sum(1, 2);

</script>
```

The first `<script>` element in this example loads an external module file using the src attribute. The only difference between this and loading a script is that "module" is given as the type. The second `<script>` element contains a module that is embedded directly in the web page. The variable result is not exposed globally because it exists only within the module (as defined by the `<script>` element) and is therefore not added to window as a property.

As you can see, including modules in web pages is fairly simple and similar to including scripts. However, there are some differences in how modules are actually loaded.

NOTE *You may have noticed that "module" is not a content type like the "text/javascript" type. Module JavaScript files are served with the same content type as script JavaScript files, so it's not possible to differentiate between them solely based on content type. Also, browsers ignore `<script>` elements when the type is unrecognized, so browsers that don't support modules will automatically ignore the `<script type="module">` line, providing good backward compatibility.*

Module Loading Sequence in Web Browsers

Modules are unique in that, unlike scripts, they may use import to specify that other files must be loaded to execute correctly. To support that functionality, `<script type="module">` always acts as though the defer attribute is applied.

The defer attribute is optional for loading script files but is always applied for loading module files. The module file begins downloading as soon as the HTML parser encounters `<script type="module">` with a src attribute but doesn't execute until after the document has been completely parsed. Modules are also executed in the order in which they appear in the HTML file. That means the first `<script type="module">` is always guaranteed to execute before the second, even if one module contains inline code instead of specifying src. For example:

```
<!-- this will execute first -->
<script type="module" src="module1.js"></script>

<!-- this will execute second -->
<script type="module">
import { sum } from "./example.js";

let result = sum(1, 2);
</script>

<!-- this will execute third -->
<script type="module" src="module2.js"></script>
```

These three `<script>` elements execute in the order they are specified, so the *module1.js* module is guaranteed to execute before the inline module, and the inline module is guaranteed to execute before the *module2.js* module.

Each module can `import` from one or more other modules, which complicates matters. For that reason, modules are parsed completely first to identify all `import` statements. Each `import` statement then triggers a fetch (either from the network or from the cache), and no module is executed until all `import` resources have been loaded and executed.

All modules, those explicitly included using `<script type="module">` and those implicitly included using `import`, are loaded and executed in order. In this example, the complete loading sequence is as follows:

1. Download and parse *module1.js*.
2. Recursively download and parse `import` resources in *module1.js*.
3. Parse the inline module.
4. Recursively download and parse `import` resources in the inline module.
5. Download and parse *module2.js*.
6. Recursively download and parse `import` resources in *module2.js*.

When loading is complete, nothing is executed until after the document has been completely parsed. After document parsing is completed, the following actions happen:

1. Recursively execute `import` resources for *module1.js*.
2. Execute *module1.js*.
3. Recursively execute `import` resources for the inline module.
4. Execute the inline module.
5. Recursively execute `import` resources for *module2.js*.
6. Execute *module2.js*.

Notice that the inline module acts like the other two modules except the code doesn't have to be downloaded first. Otherwise, the sequence of loading `import` resources and executing modules is the same.

NOTE *The `defer` attribute is ignored on `<script type="module">` because it already behaves as though `defer` is applied.*

Asynchronous Module Loading in Web Browsers

You may already be familiar with the `async` attribute on the `<script>` element. When used with scripts, `async` causes the script file to be executed as soon as the file is completely downloaded and parsed. However, the order of `async` scripts in the document doesn't affect the order in which the scripts are executed. The scripts are always executed as soon as they finish downloading without waiting for the containing document to finish parsing.

The `async` attribute can be applied to modules as well. Using `async` on `<script type="module">` causes the module to execute in a manner similar to a script. The only difference is that all `import` resources for the module are downloaded before the module is executed. That guarantees all resources the module needs to function will be downloaded before the module executes; you just can't guarantee *when* the module will execute. Consider the following code:

```
<!-- no guarantee which one of these will execute first -->
<script type="module" async src="module1.js"></script>
<script type="module" async src="module2.js"></script>
```

In this example, two module files are loaded asynchronously. It's impossible to determine which module will execute first simply by looking at this code. If *module1.js* finishes downloading first (including all of its import resources), it will execute first. If *module2.js* finishes downloading first, it will execute first instead.

Loading Modules as Workers

Workers, such as web workers and service workers, execute JavaScript code outside of the web page context. Creating a new worker involves creating a new instance Worker (or another class) and passing in the location of the JavaScript file. The default loading mechanism is to load files as scripts, like this:

```
// load script.js as a script
let worker = new Worker("script.js");
```

To support loading modules, the developers of the HTML standard added a second argument to these constructors. The second argument is an object with a type property with a default value of "script". You can set type to "module" to load module files:

```
// load module.js as a module
let worker = new Worker("module.js", { type: "module" });
```

This example loads *module.js* as a module instead of a script by passing a second argument with "module" as the type property's value. (The type property is meant to mimic how the type attribute of <script> differentiates modules and scripts.) The second argument is supported for all worker types in the browser.

Worker modules are generally the same as worker scripts, but there are a couple of exceptions. First, worker scripts can only be loaded from the same origin as the web page in which they're referenced, but worker modules aren't quite as limited. Although worker modules have the same default restriction, they can also load files that have appropriate Cross-Origin Resource Sharing (CORS) headers to allow access. Second, although a worker script can use the self.importScripts() method to load additional scripts into the worker, self.importScripts() always fails on worker modules because you should use import instead.

Browser Module Specifier Resolution

All examples to this point in the chapter have used a relative path (as in the string `"./example.js"`) for the module specifier. Browsers require module specifiers to be in one of the following formats:

- Begin with / to resolve from the root directory
- Begin with ./ to resolve from the current directory
- Begin with ../ to resolve from the parent directory
- URL format

For example, suppose you have a module file located at *https://www .example.com/modules/module.js* that contains the following code:

```
// imports from https://www.example.com/modules/example1.js
import { first } from "./example1.js";

// imports from https://www.example.com/example2.js
import { second } from "../example2.js";

// imports from https://www.example.com/example3.js
import { third } from "/example3.js";

// imports from https://www2.example.com/example4.js
import { fourth } from "https://www2.example.com/example4.js";
```

Each module specifier in this example is valid for use in a browser, including the complete URL in the final line. (You'd just need to be sure *www2.example.com* has properly configured its CORS headers to allow cross-domain loading.) These are the only module specifier formats that browsers can resolve by default, though the not-yet-complete module loader specification will provide ways to resolve other formats.

Until then, some normal-looking module specifiers are actually invalid in browsers and will result in an error, such as:

```
// invalid - doesn't begin with /, ./, or ../
import { first } from "example.js";

// invalid - doesn't begin with /, ./, or ../
import { second } from "example/index.js";
```

Each of these module specifiers cannot be loaded by a browser. The two module specifiers are in an invalid format (missing the correct beginning characters), even though both will work when used as the value of src in a `<script>` tag. This is an intentional difference in behavior between `<script>` and `import`.

Summary

ECMAScript 6 adds modules to the language as a way to package and encapsulate functionality. Modules behave differently than scripts in that they don't modify the global scope with their top-level variables, functions, and classes, and `this` is `undefined`. To achieve that behavior, modules are loaded using a different mode.

You must export any functionality you want to make available to consumers of a module. Variables, functions, and classes can all be exported, and there is also one default export allowed per module. After exporting, another module can import all or some of the exported names. These names act as though they were defined by `let` and operate as block bindings that can't be redeclared in the same module.

Modules don't need to export anything if they're manipulating something in the global scope. You can actually import from such a module without introducing any bindings into the module scope.

Because modules must run in a different mode, browsers introduced `<script type="module">` to signal that the source file or inline code should be executed as a module. Module files loaded with `<script type="module">` are loaded as though the `defer` attribute is applied to them. Modules are also executed in the order in which they appear in the containing document after the document is fully parsed.

A

MINOR CHANGES IN ECMASCRIPT 6

In addition to the major changes covered in this book, ECMAScript 6 incorporates several other smaller changes that are helpful in improving JavaScript. Those changes include making integers easier to use, adding new methods for calculations, tweaking Unicode identifiers, and formalizing the __proto__ property, all of which I describe in this appendix.

Working with Integers

JavaScript uses the IEEE 754 encoding system to represent integers and floats, which has caused much confusion over the years. The language takes great pains to ensure that developers don't need to be concerned about the details of number encoding, but problems still occur from time to time. ECMAScript 6 addresses these problems by making integers easier to identify and work with.

Identifying Integers

ECMAScript 6 added the `Number.isInteger()` method, which can determine whether a value represents an integer in JavaScript. Although JavaScript uses IEEE 754 to represent both types of numbers, floats and integers are stored differently. The `Number.isInteger()` method takes advantage of that storage difference, and when the method is called on a value, the JavaScript engine looks at the underlying representation of the value to determine whether that value is an integer. As a result, numbers that look like floats might actually be stored as integers and cause `Number.isInteger()` to return true. For example:

```
console.log(Number.isInteger(25));      // true
console.log(Number.isInteger(25.0));    // true
console.log(Number.isInteger(25.1));    // false
```

In this code, `Number.isInteger()` returns true for both 25 and 25.0, even though the latter looks like a float. Simply adding a decimal point to a number doesn't automatically make it a float in JavaScript. Because 25.0 is really just 25, it is stored as an integer. However, the number 25.1 is stored as a float because there is a fraction value.

Safe Integers

IEEE 754 can only accurately represent integers between -2^{53} and 2^{53}, and outside this "safe" range, binary representations are reused for multiple numeric values. That means JavaScript can only safely represent integers within the IEEE 754 range before problems become apparent. For instance, consider this code:

```
console.log(Math.pow(2, 53));       // 9007199254740992
console.log(Math.pow(2, 53) + 1);   // 9007199254740992
```

This example doesn't contain a typo, yet two different numbers are represented by the same JavaScript integer. The effect becomes more prevalent the further the value is outside the safe range.

ECMAScript 6 introduced the `Number.isSafeInteger()` method to better identify integers that the language can accurately represent. It also added the `Number.MAX_SAFE_INTEGER` and `Number.MIN_SAFE_INTEGER` properties to represent the upper and lower bounds of the integer range, respectively. The `Number.isSafeInteger()` method ensures that a value is an integer and falls within the safe range of integer values, as in this example:

```
var inside = Number.MAX_SAFE_INTEGER,
    outside = inside + 1;
```

```
console.log(Number.isInteger(inside));        // true
console.log(Number.isSafeInteger(inside));    // true

console.log(Number.isInteger(outside));       // true
console.log(Number.isSafeInteger(outside));   // false
```

The number `inside` is the largest safe integer, so it causes the methods `Number.isInteger()` and `Number.isSafeInteger()` to return true. The number `outside` is the first questionable integer value, and it isn't considered safe, even though it's still an integer.

Most of the time, you only want to deal with safe integers when you're doing integer arithmetic or comparisons in JavaScript; therefore, using `Number.isSafeInteger()` as part of input validation is a good idea.

New Math Methods

The new emphasis on gaming and graphics that led ECMAScript 6 to include typed arrays in JavaScript also led to the realization that a JavaScript engine could do many mathematical calculations more efficiently. But optimization strategies like asm.js, which works on a subset of JavaScript to improve performance, need more information to perform calculations in the fastest way possible. For instance, knowing whether the numbers should be treated as 32-bit integers or as 64-bit floats is important for hardware-based operations, which are much faster than software-based operations.

As a result, ECMAScript 6 added several methods to the Math object to improve the speed of common mathematical calculations. Improving the speed of common calculations also improves the overall speed of applications that perform many calculations, such as those in graphics programs. Table A-1 shows the new methods.

Table A-1: Math Object Methods in ECMAScript 6

Method	Returns
Math.acosh(x)	The inverse hyperbolic cosine of x
Math.asinh(x)	The inverse hyperbolic sine of x
Math.atanh(x)	The inverse hyperbolic tangent of x
Math.cbrt(x)	The cubed root of x
Math.clz32(x)	The number of leading zero bits in the 32-bit integer representation of x
Math.cosh(x)	The hyperbolic cosine of x
Math.expm1(x)	The result of subtracting 1 from the exponential function of x
Math.fround(x)	The nearest single-precision float of x
Math.hypot(...$values$)	The square root of the sum of the squares of each argument

(continued)

Table A-1: *(continued)*

Method	Returns
`Math.imul(x, y)`	The result of performing true 32-bit multiplication of the two arguments
`Math.log1p(x)`	The natural logarithm of $1 + x$
`Math.log2(x)`	The base 2 logarithm of x
`Math.log10(x)`	The base 10 logarithm of x
`Math.sign(x)`	-1 if x is negative, 0 if x is $+0$ or -0, or 1 if x is positive
`Math.sinh(x)`	The hyperbolic sine of x
`Math.tanh(x)`	The hyperbolic tangent of x
`Math.trunc(x)`	An integer (removes fraction digits from a float)

Explaining each new method and what it does in detail is beyond the scope of this book. But if your application needs to do a reasonably common calculation, be sure to check the new `Math` methods before implementing it yourself.

Unicode Identifiers

ECMAScript 6 offers better Unicode support than earlier versions of JavaScript, and it also changes which characters you can use as identifiers. In ECMAScript 5, it was possible to use Unicode escape sequences for identifiers. For example:

```
// valid in ECMAScript 5 and 6
var \u0061 = "abc";

console.log(\u0061);     // "abc"

// equivalent to:
console.log(a);          // "abc"
```

After the var statement in this example, you can use either \u0061 or a to access the variable. In ECMAScript 6, you can also use Unicode code point escape sequences as identifiers, like this:

```
// valid in ECMAScript 5 and 6
var \u{61} = "abc";

console.log(\u{61});     // "abc"

// equivalent to:
console.log(a);          // "abc"
```

This example just replaces \u0061 with its code point equivalent. Otherwise, the code does the same thing as the previous example.

Additionally, ECMAScript 6 formally specifies valid identifiers in terms of Unicode Standard Annex #31, "Unicode Identifier and Pattern Syntax" (*http://unicode.org/reports/tr31/*), which includes the following rules:

- The first character must be $, _, or any Unicode symbol with a derived core property of ID_Start.
- Each subsequent character must be $, _, \u200c (a zero-width non-joiner), \u200d (a zero-width joiner), or any Unicode symbol with a derived core property of ID_Continue.

The ID_Start and ID_Continue derived core properties are defined in "Unicode Identifier and Pattern Syntax" as a way to identify symbols that are appropriate for use in identifiers, such as variables and domain names. The specification is not specific to JavaScript.

Formalizing the __proto__ Property

Even before ECMAScript 5 was completed, several JavaScript engines already implemented a custom property called __proto__ that could be used to get and set the [[Prototype]] property. Effectively, __proto__ was an early precursor to the Object.getPrototypeOf() and Object.setPrototypeOf() methods. Expecting all JavaScript engines to remove this property was unrealistic (multiple popular JavaScript libraries used __proto__), so ECMAScript 6 also formalized the __proto__ behavior. But the formalization appears in Appendix B of ECMA-262 along with this warning:

> These features are not considered part of the core ECMAScript language. Programmers should not use or assume the existence of these features and behaviours when writing new ECMAScript code. ECMAScript implementations are discouraged from implementing these features unless the implementation is part of a web browser or is required to run the same legacy ECMAScript code that web browsers encounter.

The ECMAScript specification recommends using Object.getPrototypeOf() and Object.setPrototypeOf() instead because __proto__ has the following characteristics:

- You can only specify __proto__ once in an object literal. If you specify two __proto__ properties, an error is thrown. This is the only object literal property with that restriction.
- The computed form ["__proto__"] acts like a regular property and doesn't set or return the current object's prototype. All rules related to object literal properties apply in this form, as opposed to the non-computed form, which has exceptions.

Although you should avoid using the __proto__ property, the way the specification defines that property is noteworthy. In ECMAScript 6 engines, Object.prototype.__proto__ is defined as an accessor property whose get method calls `Object.getPrototypeOf()` and whose set method calls the `Object.setPrototypeOf()` method. Therefore, the only real difference between using __proto__ and the `Object.getPrototypeOf()` or `Object.setPrototypeOf()` methods is that __proto__ allows you to set the prototype of an object literal directly. Here's how that works:

```
let person = {
    getGreeting() {
        return "Hello";
    }
};

let dog = {
    getGreeting() {
        return "Woof";
    }
};

// prototype is person
let friend = {
    __proto__: person
};
console.log(friend.getGreeting());                      // "Hello"
console.log(Object.getPrototypeOf(friend) === person);  // true
console.log(friend.__proto__ === person);               // true

// set prototype to dog
friend.__proto__ = dog;
console.log(friend.getGreeting());                      // "Woof"
console.log(friend.__proto__ === dog);                  // true
console.log(Object.getPrototypeOf(friend) === dog);     // true
```

Instead of calling `Object.create()` to make the friend object, this example creates a standard object literal that assigns a value to the __proto__ property. On the other hand, when you're creating an object with the `Object.create()` method, you must specify full property descriptors for any additional object properties.

B

UNDERSTANDING ECMASCRIPT 7 (2016)

The development of ECMAScript 6 took about four years, and after that, TC-39 decided that such a long development process was unsustainable. Instead, it moved to a yearly release cycle to ensure new language features would make it into development sooner.

More frequent releases mean that each new edition of ECMAScript should have fewer new features than ECMAScript 6. To signify this change, new versions of the specification no longer prominently feature the edition number and instead refer to the year in which the specification was published. As a result, ECMAScript 6 is also known as ECMAScript 2015, and ECMAScript 7 is formally known as ECMAScript 2016. TC-39 expects to use the year-based naming system for all future ECMAScript editions.

ECMAScript 2016 was finalized in March 2016 and contained only three additions to the language: a new mathematical operator, a new array method, and a new syntax error. All three are covered in this appendix.

The Exponentiation Operator

The only change to JavaScript syntax introduced in ECMAScript 2016 is the *exponentiation operator*, which is a mathematical operation that applies an exponent to a base. JavaScript already had the `Math.pow()` method to perform exponentiation, but JavaScript was also one of the only languages that required a method rather than a formal operator. In addition, some developers argue the operator is easier to read and reason about.

The exponentiation operator is two asterisks (**): the left operand is the base, and the right operand is the exponent. For example:

```
let result = 5 ** 2;

console.log(result);                    // 25
console.log(result === Math.pow(5, 2)); // true
```

This example calculates 5^2, which is equal to 25. You can still use `Math.pow()` to achieve the same result.

Order of Operations

The exponentiation operator has the highest precedence of all binary operators in JavaScript (unary operators have higher precedence than **). That means it is applied first to any compound operation, as in this example:

```
let result = 2 * 5 ** 2;
console.log(result);      // 50
```

The calculation of 5^2 happens first. The resulting value is then multiplied by 2 for a final result of 50.

Operand Restriction

The exponentiation operator does have a somewhat unusual restriction that other operators lack. The left side of an exponentiation operation cannot be a unary expression other than ++ or --. For example, this code uses invalid syntax:

```
// syntax error
let result = -5 ** 2;
```

The -5 in this example is a syntax error because the order of operations is ambiguous. Does the - apply just to 5 or the result of the 5 ** 2 expression? Disallowing unary expressions on the left side of the exponentiation operator eliminates that ambiguity. To clearly specify intent, you need to include parentheses either around -5 or around 5 ** 2 as follows:

```
// okay
let result1 = -(5 ** 2);  // equal to -25
```

```
// also okay
let result2 = (-5) ** 2;     // equal to 25
```

If you put the parentheses around the expression, the - is applied to the entire expression. Surrounding -5 with parentheses makes it clear that you want to raise −5 to the second power.

You don't need parentheses to use ++ and -- on the left side of the exponentiation operator because both operators have clearly defined behavior on their operands. A prefix ++ or -- changes the operand before any other operations take place, and the postfix versions don't apply any changes until after the entire expression has been evaluated. Both use cases are safe on the left side of the operator in the following code:

```
let num1 = 2,
    num2 = 2;

console.log(++num1 ** 2);     // 9
console.log(num1);            // 3

console.log(num2-- ** 2);     // 4
console.log(num2);            // 1
```

In this example, num1 is incremented before the exponentiation operator is applied, so num1 becomes 3 and the result of the operation is 9. For num2, the value remains 2 for the exponentiation operation and then is decremented to 1.

The Array.prototype.includes() Method

You might recall that ECMAScript 6 added String.prototype.includes() to check whether certain substrings exist within a given string. Originally, ECMAScript 6 was also going to introduce an Array.prototype.includes() method to continue the trend of treating strings and arrays similarly. But the specification for Array.prototype.includes() was incomplete by the ECMAScript 6 deadline, so Array.prototype.includes() ended up in ECMAScript 2016 instead.

How to Use Array.prototype.includes()

The Array.prototype.includes() method accepts two arguments: the value to search for and an optional index from which to start the search. When the second argument is provided, includes() starts the match from that index. (The default starting index is 0.) The return value is true if the value is found inside the array and false if not. For example:

```
let values = [1, 2, 3];

console.log(values.includes(1));     // true
console.log(values.includes(0));     // false
```

```
// start the search from index 2
console.log(values.includes(1, 2));      // false
```

Here, calling `values.includes()` returns `true` for the value of `1` and `false` for the value of `0` because `0` isn't in the array. When the second argument is used to start the search at index 2 (which contains the value 3), the `values.includes()` method returns `false` because `1` is not between index 2 and the end of the array.

Value Comparison

The value comparison performed by the `includes()` method uses the `===` operator with one exception: `NaN` is considered equal to `NaN` even though `NaN === NaN` evaluates to `false`. This is different than the behavior of the `indexOf()` method, which strictly uses `===` for comparison. To see the difference, consider this code:

```
let values = [1, NaN, 2];

console.log(values.indexOf(NaN));        // -1
console.log(values.includes(NaN));       // true
```

The `values.indexOf()` method returns -1 for `NaN` even though `NaN` is contained in the `values` array. On the other hand, `values.includes()` returns `true` for `NaN` because it uses a different value comparison operator.

When you just want to check for the existence of a value in an array and don't need to know the index, I recommend using `includes()` because of the difference in how `NaN` is treated by the `includes()` and `indexOf()` methods. If you do need to know where in the array a value exists, you have to use the `indexOf()` method.

Another quirk of this implementation is that +0 and −0 are considered equal. In this case, the behavior of `indexOf()` and `includes()` is the same:

```
let values = [1, +0, 2];

console.log(values.indexOf(-0));         // 1
console.log(values.includes(-0));        // true
```

Here, both `indexOf()` and `includes()` find +0 when −0 is passed because the two values are considered equal. Note that this is different than the behavior of the `Object.is()` method, which considers +0 and −0 to be different values.

A Change to Function-Scoped Strict Mode

When strict mode was introduced in ECMAScript 5, the language was quite a bit simpler than it became in ECMAScript 6, but ECMAScript 6 still allowed you to specify strict mode using the "use strict" directive. When the directive was used in the global scope, all code would run in strict mode; using the directive in a function scope caused the function to run only in strict mode. The latter was a problem in ECMAScript 6 because parameters could be defined in more complex ways—specifically, through destructuring and default parameter values.

To understand the problem, consider the following code:

```
function doSomething(first = this) {
    "use strict";
    return first;
}
```

Here, the named parameter first is assigned a default value of this. You might expect the value of first to be undefined because the ECMAScript 6 specification instructed JavaScript engines to treat the parameters as being run in strict mode in cases like this. But implementing parameters running in strict mode when "use strict" is present inside the function was quite difficult because parameter default values can be functions as well. This difficulty led most JavaScript engines to not implement this feature and instead leave this equal to the global object.

This implementation difficulty is why ECMAScript 2016 makes using a "use strict" directive inside a function whose parameters are either destructured or have default values illegal. Only *simple parameter lists*, those that don't contain destructuring or default values, are allowed when "use strict" is present in the body of a function. For reference, here are some legal and illegal uses of the directive:

```
// okay - uses simple parameter list
function okay(first, second) {
    "use strict";
    return first;
}

// syntax error
function notOkay1(first, second=first) {
    "use strict";
    return first;
}

// syntax error
function notOkay2({ first, second }) {
    "use strict";
    return first;
}
```

You can still use "use strict" with simple parameter lists, which is why okay() works as you would expect (that is, the same way it would in ECMAScript 5). The notOkay1() function is a syntax error because you can no longer use "use strict" in functions with default parameter values in ECMAScript 2016. Similarly, the notOkay2() function is a syntax error because you can't use "use strict" in a function with destructured parameters.

Overall, this change removes a point of confusion for JavaScript developers and an implementation problem for JavaScript engines.

INDEX

static members, 176–177, 181
using proxies as prototypes on,
279–282
class keyword, 166
clear() method
for maps, 130
for sets, 123–124
clone() method, 186–187
codePointAt() method, 15–16
code points, 14–15
code units, 13–14
collection iterators, 145–149
default for collection types, 148–149
entries() iterator, 146
keys() iterator, 147–148
values() iterator, 146–147
colon (:), 69, 88
computed member names, 174–175
computed property names, 70–71
concat() method, 93, 107–108, 210–211
concise method syntax, 69–70
console.log() method, 61, 103
const declarations, 4–5
in global scope, 11
let declarations versus, 5
in loops, 10–11
for objects, 6
temporal dead zone, 6
using by default, 11
[[Construct]] method, 50–51
constructors, 50–52
construct trap, 245, 262–267
copyWithin() method, 197–198, 207
CORS (Cross-Origin Resource
Sharing), 296
count variable, 4
createIterator() function, 139–142
create() method, 181
Crockford, Douglas, 113
Cross-Origin Resource Sharing
(CORS), 296
curly braces ({}), 56–57, 88–89, 285

D

DataView type, 200–201
default keyword, 289–290
default parameter values, 36–43
default parameter expressions,
40–41
for destructured parameters, 96–97

in ECMAScript 5, 36
in ECMAScript 6, 37–38
effect on arguments object, 38–39
object destructuring, 86–87
temporal dead zone, 41–43
defineProperty trap, 245, 257–261
delete() method
for maps, 130
for sets, 123–124
for weak maps, 133–134
for weak sets, 127–128
delete operator, 250
deleteProperty trap, 245, 250–252
derived classes, 178–188
from expressions, 181–183
inherited static members, 181
inheriting from built-ins, 184–185
shadowing class methods, 180–181
Symbol.species property, 185–188
destructuring, 83–97
for arrays, 90–93
default values, 92
destructuring assignment,
90–92
nested array destructuring, 92
rest items, 92–93
for-of loops and, 149
initializers and, 85
mixed, 93–94
for objects, 84–89
assigning to different local
variable names, 87–88
default values, 86–87
destructuring assignment,
85–86
nested object destructuring,
88–89
for parameters, 94–97
default values, 96–97
required, 95–96
usefulness of, 84
domain-specific languages (DSLs), 25

E

ECMAScript 2016 (ECMAScript 7), 305
Array.prototype.includes() method,
307–308
exponentiation operator, 306–307
function-scoped strict mode,
308–309

getFloat64() method, 202
getInt8() method, 202–203
getInt16() method, 203
get() method
    for maps, 129
    for weak maps, 132–134
getOwnPropertyDescriptor trap, 245,
        257–261
getPrototypeOf trap, 245, 252–254
get trap, 245
    object shape validation using,
        247–249
    using on prototypes, 276–277
getUint8() method, 202
getValue() function, 2–3, 40–41
g flag, 22, 24
global block bindings, 11–12

H

handlers, 245
has() method
    for maps, 130
    for sets, 123
    for weak maps, 133–134
    for weak sets, 127–128
has trap, 245
    hiding property existence using,
        249–250
    using on prototypes, 278–279
hoisting, 2–3, 53
[[HomeObject]] property, 80–81
HTML escaping, 25

I

identically equals operator (===), 72
i flag, 24
if statements, 121–122
immediately invoked function
        expressions (IIFEs), 8–9,
        57–58, 135, 168
importing modules, 285–288
    entire module, 286–287
    multiple bindings, 286
    quirk of imported bindings, 288
    renaming imports, 288–289
    single binding, 286
    without bindings, 292
import keyword, 285
includes() method, 19–20, 307–308
indentLevel variable, 21

indexOf() method, 19–20, 196–197, 207
inheritance. *See* derived classes
initializers, destructuring and, 85
init() method, 58–60
in operator, 122
instanceof, 50
Int8Array constructor, 204–205
Int16Array constructor, 204–207
Int32Array constructor, 204, 206
integers, 299–301
isExtensible trap, 245, 255–257
iterables, 142
    creating typed arrays, 205
    for-of loops and, 142–145
        accessing default iterator,
            143–144
        creating iterables, 144–145
        spread operator and nonarray,
            151–152
    using Array.from() method on,
        195–196
iterators, 137–139, 142–155, 159–164
    asynchronous task running,
        159–164
        asynchronous task runner
            example, 161–164
        simple task runner example,
            159–160
        task running with data, 160–161
    built-in, 145–151
        collection iterators, 145–149
        NodeList iterators, 151
        string iterators, 149–150
    for-of loops and iterables, 142–145
        accessing default iterator,
            143–144
        creating iterables, 144–145
    loops and complexity, 138
    passing arguments to, 152–154
    spread operator and nonarray
        iterables, 151–152
    throwing errors in, 154–155
i variable, 7–9

J

job queues, 214
job scheduling, 220
join() method, 207
json2.js, 113
JSON global object, 113
JSON.stringify() method, 76

K

keys() iterator, 145, 147–148, 207–208

L

lastIndexOf() method, 19–20,
    196–197, 207
let declarations
    const declarations versus, 5
    in global scope, 11
    in loops, 9–10
    no redeclaration, 4
    syntax for, 3–4
    temporal dead zone, 6
lexical scopes (block scopes), 3
little-endian, 202
loading modules, 293–297
    asynchronous module loading,
      295–296
    browser module specifier
      resolution, 297
    loading sequence, 294–295
    <script> element, 293–294
    as workers, 296
localName variable, 87–88
localType variable, 87
logical OR operator (||), 36
loops. *See also names of specific loops*
    block bindings in, 7–11
      const declarations in loops,
        10–11
      functions in loops, 8
      let declarations in loops, 9–10
    complexity and, 138

M

makeRequest() method, 37–38
Map constructor, 131
map() method, 207–208
maps, 119–122, 129–136
    array conversion with mapping
      functions, 194–195
    in ECMAScript 5, 120–122
    forEach() method for, 131–132
    initializing, 131
    methods for, 130
    rejection handling, 226–227
    weak, 132–136
      initializing, 133
      limitations of, 136

methods for, 133–134
private object data, 134–135
using, 132–133
match() method, 18, 109
Math.max() method, 47–48
Math object methods, 301–302
MAX_SAFE_INTEGER property, 300
memory leaks, 127
metaproperties, 51
methods. *See also names of specific methods*
    for arrays, 196–198
      copyWithin() method, 197–198
      fill() method, 197
      findIndex() method, 196–197
      find() method, 196–197
      typed versus regular, 207–211
    formal definition, 80–81
    for generators, 142, 175–176
    for identifying substrings, 19–21
    for maps, 130
    math, 301–302
    on Object global, 71–74
      accessor properties, 74
      Object.assign() method, 72–74
      Object.is() method, 72
    for weak maps, 133–134
MIN_SAFE_INTEGER property, 300
mixArgs() function, 38–39
mixin() function, 73, 183
mixins, 72
modules, 283–298
    default values, 289–291
      exporting, 289–290
      importing, 290–291
    exporting, 284–285
      re-exporting bindings, 291–292
      renaming exports and imports,
        288–289
    importing, 285–288
      entire module, 286–287
      multiple bindings, 286
      quirk of imported bindings, 288
      renaming imports, 288–289
      single binding, 286
      without bindings, 292
    loading, 293–297
      asynchronous module loading,
        295–296
      browser module specifier
        resolution, 297
      loading sequence, 294–295

<script> element, 293–294
    as workers, 296
    syntax limitations, 287
module specifiers, 285, 297
multiline strings, 26–28

N

name property, 48–49, 55
    choosing appropriate names, 48
    concise method syntax, 70
    special cases of, 49
nested array destructuring, 92
nested object destructuring, 88–89
new.target metaproperty, 51–52,
        188–189, 265–266
next() method
    for iterators, 138–140, 143
    passing arguments to iterators,
        152–154
    return statements for generators,
        155–156
    simple task runners, 160
    task running with data, 160–161
    throwing errors in iterators,
        154–155
NodeList iterators, 151
normalization forms, 16–17
normalize() method, 16–17
Number.isInteger() method, 300–301
Number.isSafeInteger() method, 300–301
numeric data types, for typed
        arrays, 199

O

Object.assign() method, 72–75, 261–262
Object.create() method, 76, 116, 279
Object.defineProperties() method,
        101–102
Object.defineProperty() method, 101,
        106, 167, 243, 257–261, 275
object extensibility traps, 255–257
    duplicate extensibility methods,
        256–257
    examples of, 255–256
Object.freeze() method, 248
Object.getOwnPropertyDescriptor()
        method, 257–261
Object.getOwnPropertyNames() method,
        75–76, 104, 261–262
Object.getOwnPropertySymbols() method,
        104, 261–262

Object.getPrototypeOf() method, 76,
        78–79, 252–254, 303–304
object literals
    duplicate properties, 75
    syntax extensions, 68–71
        computed property names,
            70–71
        concise method syntax, 69–70
        property initializer shorthand,
            68–69
Object.isExtensible() method, 255–256
Object.is() method, 72, 122
Object.keys() method, 76, 104, 261–262
Object.preventExtensions() method, 248,
        255–257
Object.prototype.toString() method,
        114–115
objects, 67–81
    categories of, 68
    destructuring for, 84–89
        assigning to different local
            variable names, 87–88
        default values, 86–87
        destructuring assignment,
            85–86
        mixed with array destructuring,
            93–94
        nested object destructuring,
            88–89
    duplicate object literal
        properties, 75
    method definition, 80–81
    methods on Object global, 71–74
        accessor properties, 74
        Object.assign() method, 72–74
        Object.is() method, 72
    object literal syntax extensions,
        68–71
        computed property names,
            70–71
        concise method syntax, 69–70
        property initializer shorthand,
            68–69
    own property enumeration order,
        75–76
    prototypes, 76–80
        accessing with super references,
            77–80
        changing, 76–77
Object.seal() method, 248
Object.setPrototypeOf() method, 76–77,
        252, 254, 303–304

T

tagged templates, 29–32
    defining tags, 30–31
    using raw values in template
        literals, 31–32
tail call optimization, 61–64
    in ECMAScript 6, 62–63
    making use of, 63–64
targets, 244–246
TDZ (temporal dead zone), 6–7, 41–43
template literals, 25–32
    multiline strings, 26–28
    substitutions, 28–29
    syntax for, 26
    tagged templates, 29–32
        defining tags, 30–31
        raw values, 31–32
temporal dead zone (TDZ), 6–7, 41–43
test() method, 23
then() method, 217–219, 221–223, 225,
        228–229
this binding, 54, 58–60
throw() method, 154–155
toString() method, 100, 111, 113–114
traps, 244–245
    function proxies with, 262–268
        callable class constructors,
            267–268
        calling constructors without
            new, 265–266
        overriding abstract base class
            constructors, 266–267
        validating function parameters,
            264–265
    hiding property existence using,
        249–250
    object extensibility, 255–257
        duplicate extensibility methods,
            256–257
        examples of, 255–256
    object shape validation using,
        247–249
    ownKeys, 261–262
    preventing property deletion with,
        250–252
    property descriptor, 257–261
        blocking Object.defineProperty(),
            258–259
        defineProperty() methods,
            260–261

descriptor object restrictions,
    259–260
duplicate descriptor
    methods, 260
getOwnPropertyDescriptor()
    methods, 261
prototype proxy, 252–255
    function of, 252–253
    purpose of two sets of methods,
        254–255
validating properties using, 246–247
trim() method, 28
type coercion, 103–104
typed arrays, 198–206
    array buffers, 199–206
        creating, 199–200
        manipulating with views,
            200–206
    element size, 206
    numeric data types, 199
    regular arrays versus, 207
        behavioral differences between,
            209–210
        iterators, 208
        methods in common, 207–208
        methods missing from typed
            arrays, 210–211
        methods present in typed
            arrays, 211
        of() and from() methods,
            208–209
typeof operator, 6–7, 36, 101

U

u flag, 18–19
Uint8Array constructor, 204
Uint8ClampedArray constructor, 204
Uint16Array constructor, 204
Uint32Array constructor, 204
unhandledrejection event, 227–228
unhandledRejection event, 225–226
Unicode support, 13–19
    codePointAt() method, 15–16
    identifiers, 302–303
    normalize() method, 16–17
    String.fromCodePoint() method, 16
    u flag, 18–19
    UTF-16 code points, 14–15, 18
unnamed parameters, 43–46
    in ECMAScript 5, 43–44
    rest parameters, 44–46

The Electronic Frontier Foundation (EFF) is the leading organization defending civil liberties in the digital world. We defend free speech on the Internet, fight illegal surveillance, promote the rights of innovators to develop new digital technologies, and work to ensure that the rights and freedoms we enjoy are enhanced — rather than eroded — as our use of technology grows.

EFF.ORG

ELECTRONIC FRONTIER FOUNDATION

Protecting Rights and Promoting Freedom on the Electronic Frontier

UPDATES

Visit *https://www.nostarch.com/ecmascript6/* for updates, errata, and other information.